OUT-OF-THE-PARK RAVES FOR
IT'S ANYBODY'S BALLGAME

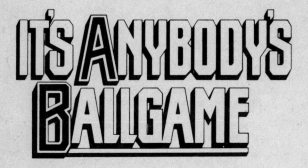

IT'S ANYBODY'S BALLGAME

JOE GARAGIOLA

JOVE BOOKS, NEW YORK

This Jove book contains the complete
text of the original hardcover edition.
It has been completely reset in a typeface
designed for easy reading, and was printed
from new film.

IT'S ANYBODY'S BALLGAME

A Jove Book / published by arrangement with
Contemporary Books, Inc.

PRINTING HISTORY
Contemporary Books, Inc. edition published 1988
Published simultaneously in Canada by Beaverbooks, Ltd.
Jove edition / April 1989

ISBN: 0-515-09979-1

Jove Books are published by The Berkley Publishing Group,
200 Madison Avenue, New York, New York 10016.
The name "JOVE" and the "J" logo
are trademarks belonging to Jove Publications, Inc.

PRINTED IN THE UNITED STATES OF AMERICA

10 9 8 7 6 5 4 3 2

To my wife Audrie,
our three great children,
two great daughters-in-law,
one great son-in-law,
and four sensational grandchildren.
(The preceding is a totally objective view
from an unbiased and impartial husband,
father, and grandfather.)

Contents

○   ○   ○

Contents

A Letter from Joe

IN A QUIET, strong way, Audrie, my wife of thirty-eight years, is the one who makes things happen in my life. That's why I've always said she's the best catch I ever made. I have her to thank for getting me started on this book, and like always, all I can do is say, "Thanks, sweetheart, you're great."

What really made this book happen goes back to an inside joke in our family, a question my daughter, Gina, always used to ask when she was little: "Daddy, could you tell us one of your little boy stories?"

Ever since our children were young, they always found my stories about growing up on The Hill in St. Louis more interesting than Audrie's stories about growing up down by the Carondelet. (In fairness to Audrie, she didn't have Lawdie, River, Poochie, and the rest of the guys to help make her life as "interesting" as mine.)

Gina used this same approach to sell me on the idea of writing this book. "Tell your 'little boy' stories, your baseball stories, and your TV stories, and we'll put them together into a book," she said. But I wasn't convinced it would be that simple, because I'd tried to write a book a couple of times since *Baseball Is a Funny Game* was published in 1960, and it just didn't work out.

But unknown to me, Gina had already taken a chapter I'd written (and thought I'd finished) and completely reworked it. When I read her version, it sounded good, not like the disorganized chapter I'd written. The stories and the ideas were the same, and it sounded just like me, but it was easier to read. It was the same suit but a much better fit.

She also gave me a written proposal outlining exactly how she thought we could work together to write the book. She convinced me we could do it, and we did.

But that's not the important part; that's not what makes this more than a book to me. My job has always taken me away from home a lot, so I missed seeing our kids grow up in many ways. I missed a lot of school plays, picnics, graduations—all the things that make it worthwhile. You just hope the snapshots turn out, and that your family can maintain some of their original excitement when they tell you about it a few days later.

At the same time, a lot of things happened in my life that our kids just didn't understand, like why I left baseball for the uncertainty of a broadcasting career, or why we left our home in St. Louis and moved to New York. They were so young when these things happened. Joe, Jr., our oldest, barely remembers when I was playing major-league baseball. Steve, our second son, barely remembers my start in television, and Gina, our youngest, doesn't remember it at all.

In researching this book, Gina learned a lot about why things happened as they did in our life, and why we made certain choices. She came to know and understand me better, and it brought her a lot closer to me. Any father would welcome that.

Once we got into the actual writing, working together practically every day brought me closer to her. Even the differences we had—and there were many—were good for us. After each disagreement we ended up with a little more respect for each other. She remained as objective as possible, and even in meetings with our editor, Shari Lesser Wenk, it was never "us" against "her," but always what was best for the book. As a researcher, organizer, and writer, Gina did a very good job.

I'd often think how lucky I was to be writing a book with my "little girl." But then I'd remember back to her wedding day, and realize she's Paul's wife now, and not my "little girl" anymore. I'm sure any father of the bride knows that feeling. Yet working together on this book has given us new respect for each other that I don't think could have developed in any other way, even if she could have stayed my "little girl" forever.

I wanted to tell you all this because without Audrie, this book would never have been started. And without my daughter, Gina Bridgeman, it would never have been written.

Now you know why this is more than a book to me.

Joe Garagiola

"How can you hit inside a dome when you grew up listening to your mother tell you not to play ball inside the house?"

O

1

Playing Inside the Goodyear Blimp: The Ballpark You Can Dry-Clean

RIP VAN WINKLE could really sleep—twenty years makes him Hall of Fame material. If he decided to go to a ballgame on the day he woke up, would he recognize the game? The mound is still 60 feet, 6 inches from home plate, and the bases are still 90 feet apart. It's still three outs, three strikes, four balls, and nine men on each side, at least on defense. But I'd like to be sitting next to him when he spotted the artificial turf and the designated hitter. And that would be only the beginning. You can just hear it:

"What's he putting on his bat? Why is he wearing gloves? Why doesn't he take them off when he runs? Why did the other player take off his gloves and put on a different pair to run? Does he just want to look good when he gets to second base? Why is the scoreboard exploding? What happened to dirt? What's the 'League Championship Series'? Four divisions? St. Louis is in the East, but Atlanta is in the West? And what happened in Chicago? The White

Sox are in the *West*, but the Cubs are in the *East*? No wonder they never win. So does the Mississippi River now run east and west?"

Hold on, Rip, ol' boy. To paraphrase an old song, there've been some changes made.

When you talk about changes in baseball, you can begin by realizing it's not so easy to understand the language anymore. You used to hear "split finger" and immediately think of the catcher, but now it's the pitcher with his split-finger fastball. Today, baseball people talk about velocity and projected potential. Pitchers have "good location" instead of control, and arm extension and quality starts. Trainers talk about modalities.

We have statistics for grass and artificial surfaces. We have fully computerized scoreboards. How long until a pennant is decided by a fuse box and a circuit breaker? The clubhouses are plush and comfortable, filled with modern conveniences. But can a player run out for the National Anthem if the hair dryer doesn't work?

Let's start with the ballpark. In Houston, Montreal, Seattle, and Minnesota, who cares if it's raining? The domed stadium guarantees a game. Well, almost; Houston once had flash floods so bad that nobody could get to the park and the game was called off. Another time, it rained so hard during the game that nobody could *leave* the park. As Tony Kubek said, "I've heard of rain-outs, but this is the first time I've ever heard of a rain-in."

Players have always had a hard time adjusting to domed stadiums. "It's like playing inside the Goodyear blimp," said pitcher DeWayne Buice the first time he stepped into Seattle's Kingdome.

And he's not the only one with an opinion. The Cardinals will tell you it's too noisy in the "Decibeldome" in Minnesota, while visitors to Seattle like the privacy and the short fences. Players going to Houston are concerned about size: the size of the park, which reminds them of an airport, and the size of the zippers joining the turf, which cause bad hops. Kurt Bevacqua may have said it best for all players: "How can you hit inside a dome when you grew up listening to your mother tell you not to play ball inside the house?"

When the Astrodome opened, it had real grass and a glass-paneled roof so the grass could get plenty of sunlight. But all that sunlight made it impossible to see balls hit into the air. "Don't get in a slump here," outfielder Al Spangler said, "because they don't force you to take extra batting practice—they make you wash the windows."

Because players were losing fly balls, they finally painted the glass panels to help the outfielders. Of course, all the grass died, so AstroTurf was born. Then everyone had to have it, and not only the domed stadiums. The boom has slowed in the last few years, but 10 ball clubs still use it and love it because it means a faster, more exciting game.

In the "old days," the game was played on grass that needed watering. With artificial turf, you just dry-clean. Groundskeepers are turning in their rakes for vacuum cleaners and spot remover. Soon the clubhouse attendant will be asking the dry cleaner to pick up the dirty uniforms, left field, and some of foul territory and have it back by the home stand on Tuesday.

Rain-outs are rare because the famous Zamboni machine vacuums the water off the surface in a hurry. A wet artificial surface can make a game look like the Marx Brothers against the Keystone Kops. Balls bounce higher and players slide farther. Diving catches end up looking like the Olympic swimming trials.

The artificial surface brought back what Casey Stengel called the "butcher boy" hit. On Sportsman's Park's hard infield in St. Louis, Ol' Case would encourage hitters to "butcher boy," or chop down on the ball, get the big hop, and beat it out for an infield hit.

That strategy is one reason infielders have a love-hate relationship with artificial surfaces. While they can play deeper to cover more ground, the ball gets to them faster. Yet they can play more confidently knowing the ball won't take very many bad hops. When Dave Concepcion was playing shortstop for the Cincinnati Reds, he turned this into an art. He started playing deep in the hole and learned that when he threw to first base on one bounce the ball came off the surface quicker and got to first faster.

Outfielders not only have to be faster on artificial turf; they also have to be careful about how they play the bounce. Let the ball bounce too close to you, and the next thing you know it's over your head for an inside-the-park home run. Missing a shoestring catch can also mean an inside-the-park home run, along with the added bonus of the state-of-the-art injury "carpet burn."

In one word, the artificial surface means speed. The routine ground out on grass is a deadly weapon on the artificial surface. Hit hard enough, it gets through the infield. Hit "butcher boy" style with a high hop, it's beaten out by a fast runner. Some teams, like the St. Louis Cardinals, have perfected this style of play. When the Cardinals are on an artificial surface in a big ballpark, it's run, rabbit, run. In addition to their pitching coach and hitting coach, they ought to add a starter's gun. They can turn a nine-inning game into a track meet.

Unfortunately, one of the casualties of the fast surface is the bunt. If you thought you couldn't bunt on grass, you *know* you can't bunt on an artificial surface. The excuse is "you can't deaden the ball." Tell that to Leo Durocher, who always said, "A good bunter can bunt on ice."

Many people have never liked artificial surfaces, and there have even been experiments testing the possibility of growing grass under a dome. I'm sure former big leaguer Richie Allen spoke for many when he said, "I don't want to play on any grass a horse won't eat."

In many ballparks, the grass is just part of a much bigger show. In Royals Stadium in Kansas City, you see a game *plus* a display of dancing waters between innings. Time was when the only water display at the ballpark was when the groundskeepers hosed down the infield dirt.

The rumor in Kansas City was that the louder the fans cheered, the higher the fountains would rise. Whether or not it was true, it was an idea just a little ahead of its time. Now the Yankees have the Rally Meter: the louder the crowd gets, the higher the needle on the meter goes, with the top score at 100. Now you're told when to clap, when to sing, when to stand, and whether you're loud enough. You get so busy following instructions, you hardly have time to watch the game, much less be a part of The Wave.

The operators of these computerized scoreboards usually work in a room on the press box level, seated in front of a keyboard that looks like the instrument panel of a 747. And why shouldn't it look like that? Today's scoreboards explode, deliver commercials, show "blooper films," replay home runs and great plays, give the words to "Take Me Out to the Ballgame," welcome every group in attendance, salute special people, and play trivia games. And once in a while they even give the score.

I like watching the numbers go up on the manually operated scoreboards in Fenway Park, Wrigley Field, and Oakland Coliseum. We lost a little of the human touch when computerized scoreboards came into the park.

For example, the Cardinals once had a hard-hitting minor leaguer playing in Rochester. He was a terrible outfielder, and the manager routinely replaced him for defense in the late innings. In one particular game, our hero hit a home run in the second inning, and the Red Wings were holding on to that 1–0 lead going into the seventh when his defensive replacement ran onto the field. Our man, tired of being taken out, had his own plan. Instead of running to the bench, he went straight to the scoreboard, took down the 1, and went to the clubhouse saying, "If you take me out of the game, I'm taking my run with me."

The computerized versions also take away the potential of using the scoreboard as an accomplice to steal the catcher's signals. Since the Wrigley Field scoreboard is operated manually, and every once in a while you see a head peek out to watch the game, it's been a spy suspect for 50 years. "Watch that open space—the Cubs might have somebody in there stealing our pitching signs." I heard that in my rookie year in 1946, and I'll bet they're still saying it.

Besides all the other complicated gimmicks on the scoreboard, most ballparks also now have "Tale of the Tape," a "feature" that really started with baseball's first tape measure home run, hit by Mickey Mantle off Chuck Stobbs in Washington. Red Patterson, the Yankees' publicity director, found the ball, paced off the distance, and estimated it was hit 565 feet. It wasn't an exact reading, but baseball had a new statistic. Now each ballpark is surveyed, and a computer estimates the distance of every home run hit. Pitchers just love this information.

Scoreboard lights can tell you all you need to know about a player: his batting average, RBIs, birthday, where he's from—some even show his picture. Progress? Maybe, but only if you're playing well.

A player hitting .330 will walk up to the plate and take his time looking for a sign from the third-base coach, even with nobody on and nothing happening. Then he might back out and have the coach repeat the sign, even though there's nothing to repeat. And after all this, he'll ask the umpire to look at the ball. Why? His .330 average is 30 feet tall and lit up for 40,000 fans to see. You *really* don't want to see your average in lights when you're hitting .206. All the scoreboard does then is make you a first ball hitter. You've got to get up to the plate and somehow put out those lights.

In 1986, Whitey Herzog asked the Cardinals not to put the averages up on the scoreboard because he felt it was hurting the team more than it was helping. "I had four of my regulars hitting under .200, and it can be embarrassing for a player to see those numbers up in lights," Whitey said. But fans don't forget. "They came out with placards, and when a batter'd get up to hit, somebody'd hold up a sign with his average on it."

While the new scoreboards improved the game for the fans, the clubhouse is where you'll find the major improvements for the players. Today's clubhouses look like they were designed by *Architectural Digest* (unlike my day, when they might have been done by *Popular Mechanics*). Locker rooms now have comfortable lounges and big showers. Gone are the days when pitchers sometimes didn't mind getting knocked out early because at least they knew they'd get to the showers while the water was still hot.

Some of the facilities in the old visiting clubhouses were unbelievable. The clubhouse at Brooklyn's Ebbets Field was in need of a good fire. Air-conditioning? Forget it. The window to the street was always open, so maybe we'd get a breeze (along with some viewers) as we made our way to the showers. Many a peeping fan was doused with a bucket of water as he turned around to tell his pals about the great view he was getting through the window.

The visiting clubhouse at Crosley Field in Cincinnati was a classic, always hot and steamy. The bathroom was a one-seater. For the other necessity there was a trough long enough to accommodate the entire starting lineup. At times it looked like the starting gate at the Kentucky Derby. And forget about privacy; whoever designed that clubhouse didn't even know how to spell it. Being on the one-seater was a performance in front of a pack of hecklers. If you were lucky, you used your hotel facility, but for most of us, the morning coffee and the bus ride made a pit stop in the clubhouse necessary. On Sunday mornings, when a lot of players were coming from church and barely making the bus, there'd be a wait for the one-seater as long as the line for the pay toilet at the bus station. It was the only time

Glaviano and Garagiola ever batted ahead of Musial and Slaughter.

Connie Mack Stadium in Philadelphia had a naturally heated steam room—the visiting clubhouse. Two words describe it: narrow and hot. To get to the trainer's room we had to walk up a stairway to a ledge. They should have posted a sign: "Danger. Occupancy by more than two people is unsafe, unhealthy, and unlikely."

The clubhouse at the Polo Grounds, home of the New York Giants, always smelled like a bad wine cellar. Up the steps to get in, down the steps to the lockers, up the steps to the showers. You felt like you were always climbing steps and smelling bad.

Today's clubhouses are well out of the Dark Ages and into the modern era of comfort. They offer all the pleasures of home or, better yet, of somebody else's home, and they're giving a party. Players can eat, read, watch television, play cards, and in some clubhouses, even play pool and Ping-Pong. It's so comfortable, some managers have a tough time getting players out of the clubhouse to sit on the bench and watch the game, even when their team is winning. In the sixth game of the 1986 World Series, Keith Hernandez watched the Mets' winning rally on the TV in the clubhouse. When they tied the game, Hernandez says he considered going back out on the bench, but then figured he was in a "lucky spot" and decided he'd better not move.

Some players claim they like to watch how the pitcher is working, and "you can see better on the clubhouse TV than on the bench." That's probably true. But particularly when it's warmer in the clubhouse (in a place like San Francisco) or cooler (in places like St. Louis or Kansas City), it's no wonder that suddenly everyone wants to watch the opposing pitcher work.

Guys who've been around awhile, like Rocky Bridges, really know how to make the clubhouse feel like home. When Rocky managed the Phoenix team in the Pacific

Coast League, he had his own room in the ballpark. "All I needed was a TV, a bathroom, and a bed. I got them, and now I don't have too far to walk to the park," he said.

Another good place to spend time during a game is the bullpen, if it's properly situated. This means far enough away from the manager that you can't hear him and he can't see you, but close enough to the fans that they can feed you.

The perfect bullpen is on the same side of the field as the dugout. Wrigley Field's bullpens are the best. The visitors' bullpen is on the first-base side, right next to the dugout. If it were on the third-base side, *across* from the dugout, the manager would be looking right at you, watching the fans feed you all those peanuts and hot dogs. So keep those bullpens right where they are for those "spear carriers" who spend their best days there. The last thing I always checked when my pitcher left the bullpen wasn't whether he had his glove, but if he had any mustard on his face.

Players who spend a lot of time in the bullpen like to make it as livable as possible. When Gene Garber was with the Atlanta Braves, he and pitcher Jim Acker cultivated a beautiful garden in their bullpen surrounded by a little white picket fence, complete with rows of begonias, some grass, and even a banana tree. When Joe Pignatano was bullpen coach for the Mets, he had an award-winning Italian garden. I think he was as proud of his tomatoes as he was of his pitchers.

Unfortunately, the once-peaceful life in the bullpen has been interrupted by the telephone. Before teams put phones in the bullpens, the manager had to play charades when he wanted a certain pitcher. If he held his hands high over his head, he wanted the tall pitcher up. If he joined his hands in front of him making a beer belly (which wasn't too hard for some guys), the round man would get up. A submarine motion meant the sinkerballer. Every time I got traded I had to learn new sign language for the bullpen. The telephone took all that away.

One of the most popular places to hang out *after* a game is the trainer's room, a restricted area for players only. No press or unauthorized personnel is allowed, so it's an ideal hiding place after a bad game. Fort Worth writer Bob Lindley says it's become "like a tax shelter—a lot of wealthy people hide out in it."

The biggest change in baseball since I played has to be the money. Don Zimmer couldn't believe it when he got $617 in meal money for a 13-day road trip. "That's only $83 less than I made in my first year in pro ball in 1950." Vern Hoscheit topped that: he says in 1941, his first year in the minors, he could keep his meal money in his watch crystal. Mike Schmidt sums up how much things have changed: "If I really wanted to, I could live off my meal money. You know, my meal money [$47 a day for every day the Phillies are on the road] generally lasts me long enough so that I don't need to cash checks against my allowance."

Yet money isn't the only issue; security is just as important. Years ago, players didn't have security—they had winter jobs. I sold used trucks one year and Christmas trees another. One winter Yogi and I both worked at Sears. They wouldn't let us work in the same department, so Yogi worked in hardware and I worked in sporting goods. Although Sears didn't know it, it had suddenly developed a self-service hardware department: whatever the customer asked for, from a two-penny nail to a ball-peen hammer, the answer from the crackerjack salesman was "It's here, so when you find what you want, bring it here." We managed to keep our jobs only until our "benefactor," the boss who happened to be a baseball fan, retired.

In those days, contracts were for one year, and you got paid only during the season. Your salary was based on how well you did and how the team finished the year before. You don't have to be an accountant to like today's deals a lot better, with guaranteed long-term contracts, deferred payments, and all the other ingredients of the "goodie packages." Birdie Tebbetts once said, "I love baseball. Everything I have I owe to baseball, but I never want to be at the mercy of baseball." And thanks to better advice, better representation, and a strong players' union, most of today's players never will be at the mercy of baseball.

Today's players have security; in fact, security is their principal goal, and the owners have obliged in a big way. According to a 1986 Player Relations Committee report, major-league teams are obligated to pay $56.7 million in long-term contracts to *players no longer on their rosters*. One hundred seventeen players are being paid from 1983 through 2014 by teams that have either traded or released them. Someday they're going to have an Old-Timers Game where every player on the field is still getting paid.

Three of the most spectacular current agreements are the "lifetime contracts" of the Kansas City Royals' George Brett, Dan Quisenberry, and Willie Wilson. According to *The Sporting News*, the three will earn a combined total of more than $93 million through the year 2026. Brett's agreement runs through the year 2000, including a seven-year front office contract at the end of his playing career, at $75,000 per year. His total contract could pay as much as $16.95 million by the year 2000.

Both Quisenberry's and Wilson's contracts involve investments in Royals' owner Avron Fogelman's real estate development business. On an investment of $2.6 million of his $6 million salary (for six seasons), Quisenberry will earn more than $45 million by the year 2026 (I'd like to see him defer payment and then one bright, sunny Sunday afternoon, walk up to the Royals' ticket window and ask for his $45 million). His total contract is worth almost $50 million. Wilson, under a similar agreement, will earn at least $27 million by the year 2025.

Kansas City general manager John Schuerholz called these kinds of contracts "the wave of the future" at the time they were signed, because they presented a way to sign star players for their entire careers without making the team completely responsible for the agreed upon tens of millions of dollars. But to date, no other team has followed the Royals' example.

Most of today's contracts are for two or three years at the most, which means the "salary drive" is gone. Years ago, if you were with a second-division team, you really had to come up with some good numbers if you hoped to get a raise. So August and September were the big push months, the salary drive. You knew your contract would be based on where the team finished in the standings. Your only bargaining power came from having good individual numbers. Baseball is a team game played by individuals, and if you were on a second-division team, you really understood what that meant, especially in August and September.

I don't think even an Einstein could have argued success-fully with the reasoning of Branch Rickey on the subject of contracts. "Look at this list of players, my boy," he would boom out as he pointed to his chalkboard. "We finished last with you, and we can finish last without you."

George Weiss, as general manager of the Yankees, once answered Tony Kubek's request for more money with what I'm sure he thought was very practical advice. Kubek had been chosen Rookie of the Year, and he thought he deserved a raise. But Weiss didn't agree with the size of the raise Tony wanted and sent him a lower figure. Tony wrote back, saying he thought he could make more money than that shoveling snow where he lived in Wisconsin. Weiss's reply: "Get a big shovel."

If you have a guaranteed contract, you don't have to worry about a salary cut if you have an off year. In some cases that's good. Yet some players won't play as hard until they're into the final year of their contract.

Players with a lot of pride will play hard no matter what. They're the greats who would be great in any era. But for many, with the security of a guaranteed contract, you sense the attitude "Why play when you don't feel like it, why give an extra effort when you don't have to worry about a pay cut (and you don't have the incentive of getting a raise)?" Says Whitey Herzog, "There's nothing in the world that's tougher on a manager these days than to be out of the race on August 1 and have a team full of long-term, guaranteed, no-trade, up-your-bucket contracts."

Some players have even more security, with some type of guaranteed postcareer employment, maybe as coaches or broadcasters. Yet today those clauses aren't unusual. These days, just about anything is liable to show up in a contract.

Pitcher Mike Armstrong had a clause in his contract giving him an extra $30,000 if he'd agree to periodic drug testing. For $30,000, they could have watched me shower every day. Players have clauses awarding them as much as $100,000 for maintaining their weight. Pitcher Don Robinson went so far as to renegotiate his weight clause, getting the limit raised 10 pounds.

Many players have attendance clauses, which guarantee them a certain amount of money for every fan over a million or a million and a half. Bonuses as high as $250,000 are standard for making the All-Star team or for finishing first, second, or third in the MVP voting, or for any of the other postseason awards. One player had a clause giving him a bonus if he *failed* to win the MVP Award after a certain number of years. I try to imagine what I could have done with that kind of clause written into my contract.

Harold Baines of the White Sox has a clause guaranteeing him $200,000 if he's traded to a Canadian team and $100,000 if he's traded to a team in the United States. Forget the annual salary; I could have made a much more successful career out of being traded.

Three of my favorite clauses show up in the contracts of players who have to be admired for their ability to think ahead. The Mets' Gary Carter has a clause specifying a

$100,000 bonus for winning the MVP for the regular season, the League Championship Series, or the World Series. Standard, right? Well, he'll also get the $100,000 for being named "third-tier playoff MVP." Of course, there isn't any third-tier playoff, but if expansion or another strike-shortened season makes one necessary, he'll be ready.

Pittsburgh's Larry McWilliams has a clause guaranteeing that if he's traded or if the team moves to another city, the ballclub will buy his house from him. My favorite, though, is pitcher Rich Dotson, who will earn a $25,000 bonus for winning one of *The Sporting News*'s Silver Slugger Awards. Of course, as an American League pitcher, it's kind of tough to win a hitting award. But if he's ever traded to a National League team . . .

Aside from the money, incentive clauses have created a whole new set of rules and tensions. Managers say some pitchers with complete game clauses in their contracts complain a lot more about being taken out of games and will do just about anything to stay on the mound. The reverse is the pitcher who looks to get out of a game he can't win, unless there's a clause somewhere that'll make him some money.

Players aren't the only ones aware of the significance of incentive clauses. Former Seattle Mariner pitcher Dave Heaverlo was in the bullpen near the end of the 1980 season when the phone rang. The bullpen coach answered and, after a brief conversation with the manager, turned to the pitchers and said, "Skip wants to know which of you guys don't have incentive clauses in your contracts." Heaverlo and one other pitcher raised their hands. "Okay, then you two start warming up," he said.

Today, when a manager sits a player down on the bench, he or the general manager can expect a call from the player's agent asking what's going on. Look at the grievance filed by pitcher Dennis Lamp against the Toronto Blue

Jays. Lamp's incentive clause was based on a point system, and he needed a total of 100 points in 1985 and 1986 combined in order to have his $600,000 contract extended for 1987. If he failed, the Blue Jays could buy out the contract for $100,000. Lamp fell 4 points short of the required 100, after making only 12 appearances after the All-Star break in '86. He filed a grievance against the team, claiming the manager, knowing the situation, purposely didn't use him. The arbitrator found in favor of the Blue Jays.

Manager Chuck Tanner says, "I try to avoid learning about bonus clauses because I can't manage to accommodate them. But the players do make me aware of them." Yet a manager might want to know about any clause affecting the future of his team. If a player no longer figures in the team's plans, yet he's guaranteed another contract based on his current-season appearances or times at bat, a manager might be forced to think more carefully about putting that player in a game.

Incentives can even put pressure on the trainer and team physician. The trainer's job is to keep players in the lineup, but that's no longer enough. For example, a player has a clause guaranteeing his contract for the following year if he doesn't go on the disabled list with "back, groin, shoulder, or elbow" problems. Now he gets one of those injuries, and the trainer has to wrestle with his conscience. Tell the team, you lose the player. Don't tell the team, you lose your job.

All these factors add up to more tension between the player and the manager, one more reason it's tougher to manage today. Today's manager has to be much more diplomatic and a better handler of people and personalities. Former big-league manager Herman Franks, who's not exactly going to win the Mr. Smooth contest, says: "It used to be that you could kick a player's butt; now you have to kiss it."

The manager may be the boss on the field, but he usually

makes a lot less money than the players he's managing. In 1987, only three major-league managers made more than their team's average player salary. How can you fine a player for breaking hotel curfew when he probably owns the hotel? Besides, a player can't be fined more than $500, or the fine goes to arbitration. Leo Durocher used to say, "I don't want to fine a player an amount he can reach into his pocket and pay." Yet to players making anywhere from a quarter-million dollars a year to more than two million, any fine less than $500 probably won't mean much.

Job security? No way. Today's manager has a contract with both an option and an attendance clause: his option is picked up day to day, and the attendance clause guarantees he must show up. While Birdie Tebbetts was managing the Cincinnati Reds, he agreed to sign a one-year contract, provided the Reds announced it was a multiyear deal. "I don't want the players to think I'm only going to be here one year. I want them to believe I'm gonna be here awhile."

Today's manager also has to worry about motivating players. While I was playing, our motivation was *The Sporting News*. Every week I'd look to see what the catcher in Double A was doing. If he got five hits, I headed for the batting cage.

Maybe these tensions are the reason you often hear that today's players don't seem to have as much fun as we used to have. That's hard for me to believe, because I subscribe to the theory from the book of Isiah—not the biblical one but the basketball one. When Isiah Thomas decided to turn pro, his philosophy was simple: I'll still have a lot of problems, but I'd rather be rich with the problems than poor."

I think if I had a guaranteed contract, with renegotiation and arbitration available, I'd make it a point to have a lot of fun. Maybe players are afraid to look like they're having fun because they're making so much money. They think that to justify their salaries it has to look almost painful.

Maybe it's harder to have fun because there's so much pressure on them to succeed, to be worth all that money, or worse, to single-handedly bring home the pennant because the team is paying them so much money.

When Don Mattingly won his $1.975 million contract in arbitration, Yankees owner George Steinbrenner said Mattingly "can't play Jack Armstrong of Evansville, Indiana, anymore. He's like all the rest of them now. He goes into the category of 'modern player with agent' looking for the bucks. Money means everything to him." Steinbrenner also implied that Mattingly had better be another Mr. October like Reggie Jackson, and for all that money, had better make sure the Yankees win the pennant. It gets to the point where you're talking about players' "numbers" not in terms of 30 home runs and 115 RBIs, but as one or two million dollars.

A lot of people ask me if I think today's players are overpaid. No, not the good ones. When Dave Winfield signed with the Yankees in 1981, somebody figured out he'd be paid the equivalent of $170 an hour, 24 hours a day, until 1991. That's a phenomenal amount of money. Yet if good players can get a million dollars a year, or several million, I don't begrudge them that.

Baseball players are entertainers. They bring people into the ballpark, which means a lot of money for the team, and they entertain almost every day from March to October. They've paid their dues in the minor leagues, moved their families around, lived out of suitcases. Once they're at the top, they're not there for that long. And they live with a lot of pressure; big salaries make the fans less sympathetic to mistakes and slumps. Fans don't complain when Joan Rivers gets $50,000 a show in Las Vegas, but when Lance Parrish signs a multimillion-dollar contract as a free agent, he'd better be Superman in wristbands. Fans probably feel Joan Rivers is doing something they can't do—get up in front of people and make them laugh—but a baseball player is just hitting and catching a ball. "Anybody can do that," they think. "I do it every Thursday night at the weekly softball game."

Former Cubs owner Phil Wrigley said, "Baseball is too much a sport to be a business and too much a business to be a sport." Baseball is both, though, and accepting that fact has always been hard for players, owners, and fans.

Owners are finding out how some of their "good business" tactics can backfire. Teams use statistics to make their players look better, to keep the fans' enthusiasm going and keep them coming out to the ballpark. But when it comes time for arbitration or renegotiation, you can bet the players and their agents use those same statistics to get more money.

The Mets put out this stat on pitcher Ron Darling in 1986: "Although Darling has won only 15 games to date, he was taken out with a lead or tied in 9 other starts and wound up with no-decisions." The Mets had created an "almost" stat for Darling, and he ended up using it to get a million-dollar contract.

Statistics have become a big part of the negotiating strategy. Games played, hits, RBIs, and home runs used to be the main statistics for the nonpitchers. The pitchers worried about games won, earned run average, and complete games.

Now we have quality starts, game-winning RBIs, and dozens of other complicated statistics. The most important new negotiating tool, though, is using the salary of a player in your position as a basis for comparison. That's a big change from the days when we hardly ever knew what anybody else was making. There's a well-traveled story about the negotiations between a player and a general manager. After a bitter session filled with threats ranging from a salary cut, outright release, or trade, to being sent to the minor leagues, the player signed. "Great," the GM said. "Now just don't tell anybody what you're making."

"Don't worry," the player answered. "I'm as ashamed of it as you are."

Today a player's logic for determining what he's worth is simple: he's making a million, I'm only half as good, so I'm worth half a million. Simple, maybe, but in an arbitration session that logic works.

High, guaranteed salaries have made players into bigger investments for the team; there's greater financial risk than there was years ago. To keep pace with that change, scouts have improved the way they work. Their job is still the same: find a player and evaluate his ability. The technique used to be to sit in the stands and watch. The "high tech" was a gut reaction based on years of traveling back roads and seeing sandlot games. But now they have more modern ways of evaluating, including stopwatches, radar guns, and a whole new language.

Sitting with a group of scouts at a game can be a strange experience. As soon as a player hits the ball, you feel like you're at a cricket convention, with every stopwatch clicking to time the runner from home to first.

They used to say, "He's got good speed," or "He's got above average speed," or "He can't run." Now it's all numbers. Tell a scout a prospect is 6'4", 185, from No Name, Nebraska, and the scout can probably tell you the kid's name and that he's "4.3 seconds to first on a routine play, 3.9 trying to beat one out." The scouts who aren't busy clicking stopwatches are clocking the pitcher's fastball with radar guns.

Scouts used to evaluate pitchers with phrases like "He can really throw" or "He's got a live arm." Now "He's in the 90s" or he needs another pitch because he's "only in the high 80s."

Pitching prospects used to "throw hard with good control." Now they have "good velocity and location," which can lead to the observation Whitey Herzog made about one of his pitchers: "He has a location problem with his pitches. They wind up in the bleachers."

Catchers used to "get rid of the ball." Now they have "a quick release." If a catcher has a great arm and a quick release, he'll get the ball to second base in 1.8 seconds. This is the Johnny Bench model. The average is 2.1. The pitcher can give him some help, if *his* first move is clocked at no more than 1.3 seconds. A good base stealer takes 3.5 seconds to get from first to second. Add another .4 of a second for the tag and you've got a close play. One scout turned in this report: get the job done in 3.2 seconds or less to catch Vince Coleman or Tim Raines. When either one of those two is on base, you even have to wait in a hurry.

Some scouts still use the simple approach. I was sitting with Walter Shannon, who was scouting for the Milwaukee Brewers, and after we watched a catcher for four innings in a spring training game Walter said, "Can't play in the big leagues."

"Don't you know how you'll screw up an organizational meeting when you tell them that?" I asked. "What about his speed to first, his bat speed, or his release time when a man's stealing?"

"All they want to know is if he can play in the big leagues," Walter said. "He can't."

One story all scouts tell is about Dave Philley, a former major-league outfielder. Dave is on record as having filed the shortest, strongest, most definitive scouting report ever. It simply said "K.P." When Dave was asked what "K.P." meant, he said in his best Texas drawl, "Cain't play." He might have had some problems with spelling, but not with scouting or making a decision.

The biggest change in scouting over the years is the addition of the "super scout" or "advance scout." He watches the team that his team is going to play next and files a detailed report about who's hot, who's hurt, how the team pitched, and how they set up their defense.

All clubhouse strategy meetings used to sound the same: pitch him high and tight, then low and away. If you can do that every time, you're in the express lane to the Hall of Fame. They're probably saying it better now with more information, but I'd bet it still ends up "high and tight, and low and away."

Willie Mays once said: "When they throw it, I hit it. When they hit it, I catch it," but now it's a little more complicated than that. Teams have the "eye in the sky" to get an edge on defense, somebody up in the press box with a walkie-talkie, often a former player or coach. He sets up the defense with a coach who's in the dugout: the "eye in the sky" watches and communicates, and the dugout coach moves the players. It looks like a bad Flash Gordon movie when the "eye" contacts the coach, but he can't get the player to move. The "eye" is shaking the walkie-talkie, holding it up to his ear to see if it's working, the coach is waving towels, the player isn't looking, the pitcher's pitching, and the manager's wondering what the hell is going on.

As clubs look for more efficient ways to use information, it's only natural that computers have joined the scouting staff. At one point, the Cubs were using those punch-out computer cards to evaluate their players, as well as gather information on the opposition. One day, the story goes, some of the cards fell to the dugout floor, and outfielder Bob Thorpe stepped on them with his spikes. The next day four players were released.

Manager Davey Johnson, one of baseball's foremost computer users, says a computer is just like an extra coach. Then he adds, in his best computerese, "I like to go with the favorable chance deviation, otherwise known as the hitting streak."

Actually, I like Sparky Anderson's simple attitude toward computers. "I think computers are useful," Sparky says. "I just don't use them."

Despite all these modern advances, one aspect of the game that will never change is the unwritten, unspoken motto of the clubhouse: what you see here, what you say here, stays here. The clubhouse man probably understands that better than anybody else.

He'll always be one of my favorite people. He's kept up with the changes, but he hasn't changed. He's still the guy who gets the job done and keeps his sense of humor.

The biggest change in the clubhouse man's job must be the postgame meal. When I was playing, we rarely saw food in the clubhouse. Now when you go into the clubhouse you don't know if it's the end of the game or the start of an Italian wedding.

Several managers have done serious damage to food tables after losing a game. I'm surprised we haven't seen a statistic for "most food tables overturned after a tough loss." A clubhouse man better have a sense of humor, especially when he sees more calories on the wall than on the food table.

Clubhouse men also have a great talent for being able to keep players humble. Yogi Berra was already a star when he sat talking with teammate Charlie Keller in the Yankee clubhouse, and Yogi wondered if Keller remembered the first time they met.

"I sure do," Keller said. "I remember seeing you walk through that door in your navy uniform."

Yogi nodded and said, "I'll bet you didn't think I was a ballplayer." At which point clubhouse man Pete Sheehy said, "I didn't even think you were a sailor."

The clubhouse man has always had the uncanny ability to give an important message without saying a word. You know something's up: if the clubhouse man asks you to give up your uniform number to someone else, then gives you a number so high only a defensive lineman would wear it, he's sending you a message. When your T-shirt is left in the dryer so long that it's too small for your eight-year-old, and the clubhouse man says nothing, he's telling you something.

I knew I was in trouble when I made what I thought was a logical request, "I'd like to order some bats," and heard "Why don't you use some of the ones Musial doesn't like?" When the clubhouse man answers your request for new bats with "What for?" you might as well start packing, and be sure to get same-day service on your laundry.

If your "game shoes" aren't shined, and he says, "I'm really sorry, but I got jammed up," that could be a warning. These days, though, he could honestly mean it. Now a player's shoes have become a wardrobe accessory; cleaning just the regulars' shoes has become a monumental job.

The progression of the "shoe parade" over the years shows how much things have changed. I bought my own shoes, three pairs: a good game pair, a pair of "mudders," for wet fields so I wouldn't ruin the game pair, and another pair to break in. That was it. They were all black, and they all had metal spikes.

Stage Two of the shoe parade came when sporting goods companies began signing players to contracts. After you signed, the company usually supplied you with two gloves and two pairs of shoes each year. Still black shoes with metal spikes.

Then came the "Gold Shoe Rush." The foreign sporting goods companies began competing, and now players have color-coordinated shoes with all kinds of spikes: rubber, metal, or none at all. More than 20 manufacturers compete to sign players, and besides shoes, the deals might include unlimited sporting goods for the player and his friends plus that ever-important item, CASH.

Tom Lasorda, who broke in with the "buy-your-own-shoes crew" like I did, was able to take advantage of today's shoe bonanza. Lasorda accepted a fee to wear a certain shoe when the Dodgers were in the World Series. Then another manufacturer made a similar offer, and now he had a problem. How could he wear both? He thought maybe he could wear one brand at home and the other on the road and get two fees, but neither company would go for that. Well, if you know Tom Lasorda, you know he figured out a way to get both fees. He simply wore one shoe from each manufacturer.

I sometimes wonder what effect those endorsements really have on sales. I can't tell you what brand of shoe Tim Raines or Vince Coleman wears, and they both have advertising campaigns built around them. I know basketball star Bob Lanier sold some athlete's foot treatment, but I don't remember what brand. I only remember that he wears a size 19 shoe. Can you imagine athlete's foot on a size 19? That's an epidemic.

Another color-coordinated addition to the baseball wardrobe is the "designer" wristband. I believe these were once called "sweatbands," and I imagine their purpose was to keep perspiration off the player's hands. Now they're another accessory to the player's uniform, like his stockings or his belt.

To some, wristbands are almost as important as a bat—and almost as big. Some are more than six inches long, going three-quarters of the way up the arm to the elbow. They look like the latest style in Ace bandages. They come in different colors to coordinate with the uniform and often feature a player's picture. I like this: you can stare at your own face, or the face of your favorite player, or maybe you can even trade with other players. They're like bubble-gum cards for rich kids.

Some wear them because they look good; others actually like them because they're good for wiping the sweat off their foreheads. Shortstop Rafael Santana wears them hoping they'll make him look more like a ballplayer. "I'm just trying to sweat," he says. Kevin Bass of the Houston Astros has the best reasoning for wearing wristbands: "I have a small arm complex."

When I was playing, I always got excited about new equipment, and I'd try to find out everything I could about it. Today that's a real challenge; you could go crazy in the on-deck circle alone. Here's a list of what you might see, and I don't guarantee it's complete: weighted ring to make the bat heavier, a resin bag, a metal-weighted bat, a sledgehammer to swing, a piece of metal pipe, an attachment for the end of the bat that opens like a parachute to add more wind resistance, and, of course, the pine tar jar and rag. You don't know if the hitter's just bought a chain of sporting goods stores or if he's taken a job with a railroad.

All of this stuff could have spared me from my most embarrassing moment in baseball. I was with the Chicago Cubs, and we were playing the Brooklyn Dodgers at Wrigley Field.

I was in the on-deck circle swinging two bats to make the one I was going to hit with seem lighter. Bill Serena, our third baseman, got a base hit, and I was the next batter. I took one last, good warm-up swing with the two bats, then flipped them aside and walked up to home plate. Problem was I had just tossed away both bats, and now I'm standing at home plate empty-handed. I'm asking the Dodgers' catcher, Rube Walker, "Did you steal my bat? Where is it?" You can imagine the rest. I took the long walk back to the dugout to get a bat, returned to home plate, and proceeded to take three pitches right down the middle. I never even swung the bat.

Today's on-deck hitter reminds us that grass and daylight aren't the only natural elements to go out of style. Remember when your hands were sweaty and you wanted to get a better grip on the bat? You'd rub your hands in dirt, right? Well, today, dirt is obsolete. Now players rub the bat handle with pine tar or spray adhesive or a goo from a stick. But this advancement isn't without problems. You can't let the goo on the bat build up because it will actually weigh the bat down, forcing you to switch to another bat, which might affect your swing. I'm waiting for some player to use too much of this sticky stuff, get a base hit, and realize he can't let go of the bat.

George Brett has put up some impressive numbers in his career, but he'll always be well known for the infamous "pine tar" game against the Yankees, in which he was accused of having too much pine tar on his bat. Brett had the stuff about halfway up his bat, and his theory was simple: if you don't connect with the pitch, just reach up on the bat before the next pitch and it's "instant stickum." You can easily get a new grip. It's one way of carrying your pine tar with you. Like Brett later said, "You can't keep it all on the handle."

Dirt used to be important for several reasons. If you weren't sure of a signal from the coach, all you had to do was back out of the batter's box and pick up a handful of dirt. This would tell the coach you didn't get his signal. Let's see you try that with pine tar.

In the classic poem "Casey at the Bat," we're told "ten thousand eyes were on him, as he rubbed his hands in dirt, five thousand tongues applauded, as he wiped them on his shirt." Pine tar would never have made it with mighty Casey.

Some players avoid messing up their bats with pine tar by putting it on their gloves. Gloves are another thing Rip Van Winkle might have to get used to. When he was a fan, only the defense wore gloves, and that was to catch the ball. Today a player might wear one glove for batting, take it off when he gets to first and put a different one on, then maybe wear another one *under* his fielding glove.

Ask 20 players why they wear a glove to bat, and you'll probably get 20 different answers. "To ease the sting if I hit one off the handle" or "I get a better grip on the bat." Sometimes it gets scientific:

"To generate power you need bat speed, and for bat speed you need a thin-handled bat. But I don't like a thin-handled bat, so I wear batting gloves and they give me the feel of a thick-handled bat when in reality I'm using a thin handle and generating good bat speed."

I really liked that explanation, but the player was hitting .207 at the time. A for bat speed, A+ for looking good with the gloves, F for hitting.

Players wear gloves on either hand, for no particular reason. Left-handed batters who wear one on their right hand say, "It just feels better that way," while left-handed batters who wear one on their left hand say pretty much the same thing. And those who have doubts about which hand to wear it on wear gloves on both hands.

Some players wear different gloves for batting and baserunning. Most say they put on a thicker glove to run the bases so they don't skin their hands when they slide, but former Mets outfielder Rusty Staub gave a much more practical explanation: "The gloves I wear to hit are expensive, so to run the bases I wear the cheapies."

A lot of batters carry their batting and running gloves in their back pockets, a subtle change in style that once forced a league directive. Cleveland outfielder Mel Hall used to put three batting gloves into each back pocket before he'd go to bat. The reason was logical . . . to him. "I let the fingers hang out, so after I hit a home run I'm waving at the infielders as I circle the bases." The league president asked him to be less friendly.

When I was playing, I didn't worry about batting gloves; I just worried about bats. There was always something mysterious and exciting about bats. Simply ordering them was an adventure, mostly because I never knew if I was going to get any. I always got the feeling they were checking my batting average before I could place an order. Of course, the Musials and the Kiners could reject any bats they didn't think were made right, which usually meant guys like me would soon be switching to that model.

Louisville Slugger (Hillerich and Bradsby) was the big-

gest company, and if you signed with them you got a dozen
bats with your signature on them, plus a set of golf clubs
and cash. The competition is greater now, so players make
better deals and almost everybody can order bats, including
pitchers, although theirs should be stamped, "Continuous
use may be hazardous to your health."

The bat companies are always looking for that big hit
that'll mean a newspaper picture or a TV close-up showing
their label. Sometimes they get a big surprise, because a
player's loyalty lasts the length of the contract or until his
first slump, whichever comes first. So when the big hit
comes and the pictures follow, it's not unusual for the
player to have a competitor's bat in his hands.

Yet in spite of what the .300 hitters say, the most
important piece of equipment is still the fielding glove. It's
amazing to see how much time has been spent changing and
developing it. Today, the baseball glove is a whole industry.

With all the competition among sporting goods companies, gloves are almost always custom-made. Vans full of
hardware pull up to the spring training camps to repair
gloves or take measurements so new gloves can be designed
individually. It's like "glove room service," and as always,
the bigger the player's name, the better the service. Players
now have gloves for games (their "gamer"), gloves for
practice, and even backup gloves for practice.

Until 1954, we used to keep our gloves on the field while
we batted. When the third out was made, the defensive
players (except for the pitcher and catcher) would flip their
gloves into the outfield grass, then come in to hit. Makes
me feel like I played with Abner Doubleday.

All gloves were brown then and very much the same.
There were three basic models: big ones for pitchers (to hide
the ball better) and outfielders; small ones for second
basemen (get that ball on its way to first quickly for the
double play), and medium-sized ones for shortstops and
third basemen. Over the years they haven't changed much.

But consider the first baseman's glove and the catcher's mitt. The first baseman's used to be a polite little mitten you might have worn for driving; now it's a fishnet. Snag the ball, flag it down. The catcher's mitt used to be a big pillow with a small pocket and just two strands of leather for webbing. Today the webbing is probably the most important part of the mitt.

Catchers don't "hold on" to foul tips. The ball just happens to come to the right spot, and the glove closes in on it. You can't practice that: how can you prepare for a ball deflected off the bat? Catching a foul tip is just luck. If you catch it, you can thank the webbing.

In my day, if you were lucky enough to have somebody on the team who could work on gloves, you could get a good webbing. Harry "The Cat" Brecheen may be remembered most for winning three games in the 1946 World Series, but I remember him as my glove doctor. He knew how to add a bigger webbing to help hold those foul tips.

Les Moss was another good player glove doctor, although his work once got him in trouble with his teammate Early Wynn and got the opposing catcher, Clint Courtney, kicked out of a game.

One day Moss was working on a glove, and Wynn asked him whose it was. When Moss told him it belonged to the "enemy," Courtney, Wynn really got mad. First he got all over Moss, then he decided to do something about the glove.

The glove was already cut open, and Wynn put little hunks of Limburger cheese in the padding. Then he had Moss sew it back together. The glove felt great, and that's all Courtney cared about.

Then it was game time. First it was just a sniff here and a sniff there. Umpire Ed Hurley noticed the smell only when Courtney was behind the plate.

"Don't you feel well?" Hurley wanted to know.

Courtney said he felt fine. A few more sniffs, and as the

day grew hotter and the game longer, the smell got worse.

"If you don't stop it, I'm gonna throw you out of this game," Hurley said.

"I ain't doing nothing," Courtney shot back. "I think it's you and you want the batter to think it's me."

Another inning, a few more sniffs and several accusations later, Hurley threw Courtney out of the game with an order to see the trainer about his "problem." And Wynn never said a word. Of all the umpire reports turned in to the league office, that's the one I'd most like to see.

Today's catcher's mitt is like a big, soft pair of pliers. But with the small pocket we used, you really suffered the sting when you caught the ball. So you had to stuff some kind of padding into the glove to cushion the blow.

While most catchers, including me, used a sponge, Walker Cooper was a little more exotic. He used falsies. I've always tried to imagine how surprised the saleswoman must have been when this big guy, more than six feet tall and over 200 pounds of rawbone, looking like he stepped out of a John Wayne movie, asked for a D cup.

One day Coop made a tag play at the plate, and his glove was knocked off. The falsie rolled out, made a perfect little turn, and landed right in the middle of the plate. The next day the fans sent him a lifetime supply.

During one "NBC Game of the Week" broadcast with Vin Scully, the conversation got around to sponges and falsies.

Vin: Joe, did you use a falsie when you were catching?
Joe: No, I used a sponge.
Vin: Why didn't you use a falsie?
Joe: I got used to the sponge.
Vin: But falsies were supposed to be better than a sponge.
Joe: I always used a sponge.
Vin: Did you ever think about using a falsie?
Joe: No, I didn't want to get emotionally involved.
Dead air.

When I meet somebody who was a catcher on the sandlots or his town's team, he'll almost always say, "Let me see your hands. Mine aren't too banged up." He'll show off his twisted finger or busted knuckle like a badge of honor and blame it on a foul tip. I grew up thinking those breaks and bruises were just part of catching.

I remember the old catcher Gabby Street telling me about the time he got hit on his bare hand with a foul tip and it knocked a finger out of joint. He went to the mound and told the pitcher, "Snap it back in, just pull on it." With panic in his voice the pitcher asked, "Which finger?"

A catcher today has a good chance of seeing his fingers last almost as long as he does. One reason is the claw-type mitt, which lets him catch the ball in the webbing between the index finger and the thumb. He might use a small sponge for more protection, but since the index finger is already outside the glove, he doesn't have to worry too much about a bone bruise. Add the fact that a catcher almost always keeps his bare hand behind his back, and you can see why his fingers are much safer. Today's catcher can just about replace Madge in the Palmolive commercials.

Catching the ball in the webbing, however, has just about done away with the loud pop from a good fastball. As a rookie, I remember veteran catcher Ken O'Dea telling me to rub some shoe polish into my glove to make it pop. "Pitchers like that. Makes 'em sound faster than they're really throwing."

That was good advice until I was warming up a prospect in Pittsburgh under the watchful eye of Branch Rickey. "Go get a different glove, Joe," was his order. I knew what he meant: get one that didn't pop. If he was going to sign this guy, he didn't want to hear "I want more money! Didn't you hear me make that glove pop?" A good application of shoe polish could make a pitcher sound like he was stacking two-by-fours at the lumberyard.

One glove that hasn't changed much is the oversized

glove used to catch the knuckleball pitcher. This "special" glove is basically two big hunks of leather sewn together to help a catcher stop a knuckleball. Two stale, jumbo pizzas could do the same job. This glove is big enough to sleep four. Maybe it helps, but as former catcher Bob Uecker once said, "The way to catch a knuckleball is to wait until the ball stops rolling and then pick it up."

Managers and players are always trying to think of new ways to help catchers with their glove problems, but they don't always work. Paul Richards, during his White Sox days, came up with a great idea to help catchers on tag plays.

Richards's plan was that when the pitcher ran behind home plate to back up the catcher on a throw home, the pitcher and catcher should exchange gloves. This way, the catcher would have the use of a fielder's glove with the added help of a good webbing. Great plan: base hit, exchange gloves, catcher makes a one-handed grab with the fielder's glove, quick tag, easy out.

So in the late innings on a base hit, pitcher Bill Wight ran to back up Joe Ginsberg behind the plate. They executed the plan perfectly, smoothly exchanging gloves. They just overlooked one small detail. The throw was on its way, but Ginsberg couldn't get the glove on. Everybody forgot Wight was a left-hander.

Gloves may be custom-designed based on new theories and statistics, but they're still catching basically the same pitches. Only the names have changed. On the sandlots, I remember calling for a fastball, a curve, a drop, a fade-away, an inshoot, an outshoot, and even a riser.

Today it might be the cut fastball or the sinker. The modern curveball covers everything from the sidearm curve to the overhand curve. You even have a back-door curve, where a pitcher tries to hit the corner by "going in the back door"; a right-handed pitcher will throw the curveball to a left-handed batter, starting it way outside, hoping the batter gives up and the ball catches the outside corner. But my favorite high-tech pitch is Tommy John's do-fer: "It'll do for now until I get my good stuff," he says.

I'd never seen the slider until I got to the big leagues. A good one is a bat-breaker. A bad one is what the pitcher throws just before the batter hits a triple. A good slider looks like a fastball, and just as the hitter reacts to what he thinks is a fastball, it breaks down and across.

Then there's the knuckleball, which will never change. Most pitchers throw it off their fingertips, but it's still called a knuckleball. As for how to hit it, Charlie Lau, the man who helped players like George Brett and Hal McRae hit .300, had this advice: "There are two theories on hitting the knuckleball," he said. "Unfortunately, neither of them works."

I once asked umpire Augie Donatelli why he had called a knuckleball pitch a strike. He gave me an answer I'll never forget. "The pitcher doesn't know where it's going, the hitter can't hit it, the catcher can't catch it, and it's all over the ballpark before it gets here. It's been enough places that I figure sometime on the trip it must have crossed home plate for a strike." Okay, you win.

The pitch of the eighties is the split-finger fastball. Its "guru" is San Francisco manager Roger Craig, who began teaching the pitch at his baseball camp in 1974. Craig tells his pitchers to "think fastball." So it's kind of a fast forkball. The key to being successful with the pitch is arm speed. It's thrown with the same motion as a fastball, comes in looking like a fastball, but then drops down.

Some people say it's just a forkball with better publicity. Elroy Face, the great forkball pitcher and Pirates' relief ace of the 1960s, was once asked the difference between the pitch he threw and today's split-finger fastball. His answer? "The money."

On some teams, what a pitcher throws is not as important as how fast he throws it. The radar gun has become a full-fledged member of the pitching staff. The gun is a great tool to help scouts, managers, and players get down to a basic measurement to compare pitchers. A lot of things are more important than speed, but you have to start somewhere.

The gun becomes a detriment when coaches and managers use it as the sole basis for judging a pitcher in a game. For every pitcher knocked out of the box by opposing hitters, there's one knocked out by a radar gun. A pitcher can have a three-hitter going, and if the gun says his fastball is five miles an hour slower than it was in the third inning, some managers are convinced he's losing his stuff. The gun can't tell you a thing about movement on the ball (the hitter will tell you that), but if it says the pitcher's slowing down, that's enough for some managers.

The number of pitches thrown is another yardstick. The Houston Astros put a limit on Nolan Ryan's pitch totals in 1987: 110 pitches was his cap. You don't hear the old baseball advice to "go as hard as you can for as long as you can" anymore. Specialists have made the complete game almost obsolete.

No longer does a pitcher from the bullpen try to work himself back into the rotation. Now he's *trained* to be a reliever, and some are among the highest-paid players on the team. Relief pitchers have moved from urban renewal to the high-rent district.

Depending on the game situation, you might see a short man, a middle-short man who works only an inning, an early-long man, a setup man, and a closer. It sounds like a new sport: "What position do you play?" "I'm the closer." These can be misnomers, though. As pitching coach Billy Connors says, "If my long man doesn't have his good stuff, he becomes a short man in a hurry."

Even the way pitchers come in from the bullpen has changed. Some come in by car or truck, which can be embarrassing if you need a new set of tires after a home stand. Relief pitchers used to walk in; some, very slowly, like Joe Page, Jim Konstanty, and Hugh Casey, to intimidate the hitter. Now a lot of pitchers run in, and just like a pitcher who strolls in from the bullpen looks like he has a whole load of confidence growing with each step, a pitcher who runs in looks all pumped up.

Another relatively new intimidation tactic is the high five. Like dirt, the old-fashioned handshake is out of style. The high five has taken over.

A lot of teams today could probably use a handshake coach. We have "low fives," "finger touches," and whatever that was that Kirby Puckett did after Minnesota won the 1987 World Series. Watching Kirk Gibson give a high five, you hope a paramedic is standing by. His teammate Rusty Kuntz said, "When he gets on a roll, you stand back. The first time he gave me a high five, he drove my shoulder back about two feet. After getting into the dugout, I headed for the whirlpool."

Along with the high five you can add the "curtain call" out of the dugout. I'll give the Mets' fans credit for this one. Is it good? I'm sure the player making the curtain call enjoys it, but you can bet the opposing pitcher is making plans to avoid it next time.

In this era of specialization, there's a job for everyone. A pinch hitter used to be a broken-down catcher or an old outfielder who couldn't play anymore but could still hit the ball once in a while. Now pinch hitters are specialists. Some are experts at drawing a walk to start a rally. Some hit under the ball with a man on third to get a fly ball to drive in the run. Some hit down on the ball, behind the runner, to pick up a base. Former Met Ron Hunt had his own specialty: getting hit with a pitch to start a rally or getting hit with the bases loaded to force in a run.

Don't think that's too farfetched. I'll never forget what my manager, Phil Cavarretta, said to me one day in Wrigley Field, as I went up to try to hit left-hander Curt Simmons.

Cavarretta, a real competitor, filled me with confidence when he said, "He's wild. If he wants to hit you, let 'em." Hit *me*? I was so careful I wouldn't even let him hit my bat.

You can talk about how baseball has changed, but I'm sure of one thing. If you stay around long enough, you're likely to see that the things that have changed the most eventually return to the way they were. People like tradition, and nowhere is that more obvious than in today's uniforms.

Baseball uniforms started out as hot, woolen suits, which some players wore loose to make it easier (and less painful) to get "hit" by a pitch. Then, gradually, they became skintight and tailor-made.

The waist and shirt size used to be the only two pieces of information anybody asked for, and you just hoped it would come close to fitting. Now you find as many tailors at spring training as you do palm trees, and it's not just size they're interested in. Now they take special fitting instructions. Some players want a loose calf band, and others like it tight. Some want the pant leg to the ankle, and others want it to the knee. Some like to wear heavy fleece-lined jackets to take infield practice, while others wear cloth jackets, light jackets under their shirts, warm-up shirts—the wardrobe goes on and on. The locker of a major leaguer looks like he chose the right door on a game show.

Uniforms used to be white at home and grey on the road. Period. Then it was multiple choice: robin's egg blue, kelly green, Fort Knox gold, you name it. But those choices didn't begin to describe the Astros' uniforms. Pitcher Don Sutton said his uniform made him feel like he was on the Hilton Hotel softball team. Umpire Nick Bremigan claimed he prepared himself for a game with the Astros by sitting up all night "looking at test patterns on TV."

At one point, the Pittsburgh Pirates were wearing nine different combinations of uniforms. While that may have been confusing for the fans, it was even worse for the players. "We never knew what we were going to look like," Phil Garner said. "One day we'd look like bumblebees. The next day you couldn't see us, and then we'd look like a bunch of taxicabs running around the field."

Today, the old is new again, and many teams have gone back to the way uniforms looked years ago. Even the Chicago White Sox, who for a while didn't tuck in their uniform shirts and had the option of wearing shorts on hot days, are wearing traditional-looking uniforms. Pinstripes, belts, and shirts with buttons have returned. The grand tradition of white and grey is back. So what if the tradition was started because grey uniforms were easier to keep clean on the road?

Sometimes I think that the only thing about the game that'll never change is the baseball itself. When you look at today's ball, the only change seems to be the signature of the league president. Rip Van Winkle might have trouble figuring out, though, how the National League went from a president like Warren Giles, who was a lifetime baseball man, to A. Bartlett Giamatti, a Renaissance literature scholar and a former president of Yale. And yes, the same Bobby Brown who played for the Yankees is the American League president.

Okay, Rip, you know about the signatures. Now, the ball. First let's take batting practice. Different teams have different methods. In the minor leagues, it's not unusual to wash the old, dirty balls so the players can at least see them. The Cardinals' Louisville farm club took that idea one step further. According to Cardinal pitcher Joe Magrane, they washed the baseballs with milk. The balls turned white all right, but when one of those balls found its way into the game, by the eighth inning the pitcher needed a strong stomach even more than he needed a good fastball. The smell of sour milk on a hot summer day isn't exactly ballpark tradition.

Whitey Wietelmann, a former major-league infielder,

used a "ball eraser machine" when he was coaching for the San Diego Padres. The machine rubbed the balls clean, actually erased them, just like your best Woolworth's back-to-school special.

Most clubs used to start batting practice with two dozen old balls. When the balls were gone, batting practice was over. Today some teams start batting practice with six dozen new balls. Batting practice used to mean a tryout kid throwing to the extra men and the extra men throwing to the regulars unless a starter was trying to work out a problem. Now the batting practice pitcher and catcher are hired specialists: their only job with the club is to work batting practice. Most teams use former major leaguers to give the regulars "good B.P."

One thing about the ball that never changes is the occasional claim that it's "juiced up." When home runs increase or a little singles hitter like the Mets' Howard Johnson connects for a tape measure homer, all you hear is "The ball is juiced, it's hot."

The "lively ball" was the talk of the 1987 season, but it wasn't anything new. Back in 1948, Tiny Bonham of the Pittsburgh Pirates said he knew there was a rabbit in the ball when he saw the ball lying in the outfield eating grass. He was sure when he picked it up he could feel the heartbeat.

Almost 40 years later, Milwaukee Brewers pitching coach Chuck Hartenstein said, "We don't have to buy baseballs this year. We just put 'em in the ball bag and let 'em multiply."

The "lively ball" theories in 1987 ranged from the stitching not being raised high enough to a different kind of center in the ball. Mets pitcher Bob Ojeda blamed the so-called livelier ball on the night shift in Haiti, where the balls are made. "I think the night shift doesn't like pitchers, so they juice the ball, while the day shift likes pitchers, so they just make the normal baseball."

Dodger pitcher Don Newcombe's complaint always was

"It's live when I throw it, but it's dead when I hit it." Said Branch Rickey: "It's not the rabbit in the ball but the quail in the pitcher." Move to 1987, and Don Carman of the Phillies said, "It's not a matter of the lively ball. It's my dead arm."

The names change, the jokes may get better, and the ball may or may not be "juiced." But still the ball remains the most important part of the baseball puzzle. Nothing happens until the pitcher turns the ball loose. What follows might look as smooth as a well-choreographed dance or as weird as trying to put toothpaste back into the tube.

Former umpire Ron Luciano said about baseball, "When I started, it was played by 9 tough competitors on grass in graceful ballparks. By the time I was finished, there were 10 men on each side, the game was played indoors on plastic, and I had to spend half my time watching out for a man dressed in a chicken suit who kept trying to kiss me."

A lot of things have changed in baseball, and who knows what might be next. Maybe lasers to call balls and strikes or real grass in domed stadiums. The next innovation for players will be whatever somebody thinks is helping him hit or pitch better. (And it doesn't look like corked bats and scuffed balls are the answer. Manager Gene Mauch said it as a joke, but there's more than a little truth in it: "When you take a pitcher out of a game now, you want to ask, 'What kind of scuff did you have out there today?' ")

Transcendental meditation was once the solution, then some clubs hired hypnotists. In the first game of a double-header, Minnie Minoso went hitless in five at-bats. Between games he took a shower in his uniform, claiming he was washing away the evil spirits. Everybody laughed, but in the second game Minnie got three hits. After the game, eight players took showers with their uniforms on.

In spite of the changes, baseball is still baseball, and it still means all of the things it always has to players and fans. But it *has* changed. And even though Rip Van Winkle would discover that the mound is still 60 feet, 6 inches from home plate, and the bases are still 90 feet apart, the next time he goes to sleep, I think maybe he'd better leave a wake-up call.

"Whitey Herzog gets special Hall of Fame consideration because of this sign hanging behind his desk: 'A slick way to outfigure a person is to get him figuring you figure he's figuring you're figuring he'll figure you aren't really figuring what you want him to figure you figure.' He wrote it himself."

○

2

"The Wrong Foot on the Base": My Hall of Fame

"I AM NOW a catcher for the Chicago Cubs. It's my third trade and there are only eight teams in the league, so how can I have any goals?"

That's the way I answered a questionnaire in 1953, but I was just kidding around. Sure I had goals. In fact, I've had three specific goals all my life: to be elected to the Hall of Fame, to meet the pope, and to sleep in the White House. Those have always been my goals, although not always in that order.

The older you get, the more your priorities change. I always thought I had a chance for the first goal, but the other two were the direct result of daydreaming. In religion class, I'd imagine myself in a private audience with the pope. Trying to stay awake during history class, I'd find myself spending a night in the White House. When you realize my father became a naturalized citizen, it seems the chances of my doing *anything* in the White House are remote. But that's one ambition I did fulfill. I'm glad my father's papers were in order.

I've been to the Vatican, taken the tours, and stood in St. Peter's Square to hear the pope speak from the balcony. And in 1987, Pope John Paul II came to the United States and to Phoenix, where I live. Now I can say I've met the pope. We didn't exactly go over the hitters, but I did shake his hand.

If someone had told me I'd sleep in the White House *and* meet the pope, I'd have helped him into the shade because the sun was getting to him. But as Casey Stengel used to say, "You could look it up." Both those things have happened, and two out of three ain't bad.

When you get right down to it, I'm not in the Hall of Fame with Babe Ruth and Ty Cobb because pitchers pitched to me. My figures don't lie. I was a .257 hitter, and as Mr. Rickey would say, a .257 hitter "on merit alone." But I have an idea for another wing in the Hall of Fame.

Players would get into my Hall of Fame not by hitting, catching, or throwing, but by what they say or do that can't be measured by statistics. The quick answer under pressure. The player who can put the words together while the manager is incoherent. The runner who can actually respond when the umpire calls him out at third and the third-base coach is yelling, "What the hell were you thinking about trying to come over here on that hit!"

My Hall of Fame would call for a different kind of induction ceremony, too. I'd put in a whole team at the same time. A whole lineup of players who said the "right thing," led by their manager, Casey Stengel. He belongs in any Hall of Fame. But he gets my special vote not for what he said and did for the Yankees but for what he meant to the Mets (assuming, of course, that you could actually figure out what he meant).

Asked about the potential of a particular player, Casey

said, "He's 19 years old and in 10 years he's got a chance to be 29." When a spring training trip took the Mets to Mexico for an exhibition game, a visiting reporter interviewing Casey ran out of questions about the team, so he went to the weather. "Do you think the high altitude will bother your team?"

"No," said Casey. "We can lose in any altitude."

Casey makes it into my Hall of Fame for the unique way he'd tell a player he was traded. Casey always came out to the park early, and on one particular day, outfielder Bob Cerv was also at the park several hours before game time. He was sitting at the far end of the Yankees' bench, which has always been one of the longest in baseball (good for the player in a slump—he can hide from the manager, practically in another time zone).

Casey walked down the ramp from the clubhouse, got to the dugout, looked out over the field, and acted as if he were the only one around. He and Cerv were probably the only two in the ballpark. After surveying the field, Casey looked at Cerv, then directed his attention back to the field. He took a deep breath and said, "Ain't that something what happened today. One of us got traded to Kansas City."

Casey once had an outfielder, Lou Skizas. If Lou were playing today, he'd be the player who's taken out in the late innings for defensive purposes. But he was a good hitter and Casey knew his strength: "I'll tell you why he's a good hitter. He's a good hitter because he hates the ball, and when the pitcher throws the ball he wants to hurt it. In fact, he hates the ball so much that when he's in the outfield and they hit one towards him, he won't go near it."

And you have to appreciate Casey's philosophy: "There comes a time in every man's life, and I've had plenty of them."

Yet Casey isn't the only manager I considered for this prestigious Hall of Fame. After a tough loss to the Yankees, Sparky Anderson said he felt a very strong wind had slowed down some hard-hit balls by the Tigers. "We lost because what was real didn't happen." Sparky also made this interesting diagnosis of Alan Trammell's shoulder injury: "There's nothing wrong with his shoulder except some pain—and pain don't hurt you."

Oh. Okay.

Earl Weaver, during an Orioles winning streak, made this helpful observation: "In order to do what we've done, we have to keep doing what we've done in the past."

Pete Rose, talking about the Reds during spring training: "The lineup is set; it's just a matter of who's going to play."

Tony LaRussa, when his Oakland Athletics got off to a 3–10 start in 1987: "When you're not winning, it's tough to win a game."

Good one, Tony.

And how about this for confidence? The Yankees' Lou Piniella, when asked if pitcher Rick Rhoden would take his next scheduled turn after being drilled by a line drive: "There's no doubt about it, but you can never be sure."

The Cardinals' Whitey Herzog also gets special Hall of Fame consideration because of this sign hanging on the wall behind his desk: "A slick way to outfigure a person is to get him figuring you figure he's figuring you're figuring he'll figure you aren't really figuring what you want him to figure you figure." He wrote it himself.

And how could I leave out Billy Martin? While he deserves a spot just for all the times he's managed the Yankees, he came up with an ad lib that automatically qualifies him for my team.

He was doing a radio interview that suddenly began to sound a little like a roast, only the interviewer was using a meat ax to carve up Billy. About halfway through, the reporter said, "Billy, next to being on my show, what has been your biggest thrill?"

"Getting *off* your show."

End of interview, and you could have picked the interviewer up with tweezers.

The first baseman on my team is George "Catfish" Metkovich. His great suggestion not only broke up a Pittsburg clubhouse meeting; it also secured his spot in my special Hall of Fame.

Now, this was the 1952 Pirate team that lost 112 games out of 154 that year. We had just finished a terrible series against the New York Giants. Our centerfielder, who made three throwing errors, also let two balls get through his legs, and when that happened in the Polo Grounds you could run for a weekend. Things got so bad that when he picked up the ball we'd all holler, "Duck! He's got it again!"

We barely finished the series and moved over to Ebbets Field to play the Dodgers, odds-on favorites to keep our losing streak alive. At the end of the clubhouse meeting our manager, Billy Meyer, asked if anybody had anything to say. "Maybe somebody can think of something to help us win a game," he pleaded.

Metkovich had the answer. "Yeah, I'd like to make a suggestion. Let's try this against the Dodgers. On any ball hit to center field, let's just let it roll to see if it might go foul."

My backup first baseman is Dick Stuart, alias Dr. Strangeglove. Right away that nickname tells you fielding was not his strength, and he admitted it: "Errors are a part of my image," he'd say. When he was with the Pirates, he once grabbed a hot dog wrapper out of the air and the crowd gave him a standing ovation.

Stuart makes my team because of his use of logic. One day a ground ball got by him, one that manager Johnny Pesky thought he should have caught. "You have to catch that ball, at least knock it down. It can't get by you; that run can't score." Stuart had a different way of looking at it. "Aw, c'mon. I cut off the throw from the outfield, so I caught one out of two. That ain't too bad."

My second baseman is Rocky Bridges. He made my team by being the only second baseman ever to scream to the pope to throw him the ball.

This happened in Yankee Stadium, where several monuments to the memories of Yankee greats, like Babe Ruth and Miller Huggins, stand just behind the outfield fence. Before the renovation, though, the monuments were actually on the playing field.

Rocky was covering second with two men on when Mickey Mantle hit one over Albie Pearson's head in center field. The ball rolled out to the monuments, and soon Pearson had completely disappeared behind them. Two runs are in, Mantle is digging hard for third, and Rocky, completely frantic, hollers, "Get the ball, get the ball. Huggins, Gehrig, Ruth, the pope, *anybody*, throw me the ball!"

Actually, Rocky had already made my team, and not for anything he did in a ballpark. This was on a street corner.

It was the middle of the afternoon, not yet time to go to the ballpark, and he came walking toward me with a big wad of tobacco stuck in the side of his mouth.

"Where're you going, Rock?"

"No place important. Gotta mail this letter to my wife. But she'll be mad at me anyhow."

"Aw c'mon, you wouldn't give her a blast in a letter that would make her mad, would you?"

"Naw, that ain't it. She'll get mad because with the zip code, there's more writing on the outside of the envelope than on the inside."

The Dodgers' Pedro Guerrero was playing third base when he made the comment that earned him a place in my Hall of Fame. In 1984 the Dodgers were in fourth place, 14 games out of first place. Second baseman Steve Sax was having trouble making throws to first. First basemen were diving, screaming, signaling for a fair catch. Selling a ticket behind first base for Dodger home games was tough—it had become a war zone. At the same time, Guerrero was also making a few plays that weren't exactly soothing to manager Tom Lasorda's stomach. Lasorda decided it was time for one of his famous motivational meetings. He started on Sax, then zeroed in on Guerrero.

"You're a better player than what you've been showing. How can you play third base like that? What the hell are you thinking about out there? You've gotta be thinking about something besides baseball. What are you thinking about?"

"I'm thinking about only two things when I play third base," Guerrero said.

"Two things? What are they? Tell me," Lasorda yelled.

"First, I think, 'I hope they don't hit the ball to me.'" The players all snickered, and even Lasorda, who was still upset, had to fight off a laugh.

"Awright, that's one thing. What's the other thing?"

"Number two, I think, 'I hope they don't hit the ball to Sax.'" Meeting's over, and Guerrero is on his way to my Hall of Fame.

I also have to consider the Detroit Tigers' third baseman Jim Walewander, for his original answer to an often-asked question. When Walewander hit his first home run, someone retrieved the ball and gave it to him, knowing it would mean a lot to the rookie. When he was asked, "What did you do with the ball?" he said, "I put it in my glove compartment." Why? "Because that's where I put the other one," he said, meaning his first major-league hit. "When I fill up the glove compartment, I'll buy a new car."

Shortstop was an easy position to fill. I considered only two players: Rabbit Maranville and Ernie Fazio. Maranville made it to *the* Hall of Fame as a player, but he gets only an honorable mention on my team. The choice was tough, but remember, it's not the way you play—it's what you say.

I didn't know Rabbit Maranville, but one of my managers, Fred Haney, was a teammate of his. During spring training in California, the two of them headed for downtown Los Angeles one day by trolley car. The trolley was actually just one car pulling another. Maranville and Haney had just finished a long workout and they were tired. They went immediately to the back car to look for a seat.

The car was jammed, hardly leaving room to stand, and since neither one was more than 5′6″, it looked like it was going to be a tough ride. "Like riding inside Babe Ruth's sweatshirt after a doubleheader," Haney said.

After a few minutes, Maranville leaned over to Haney and said, "If you've got the guts, I can get us some seats."

"How?"

"Never mind. You got the guts?"

"Yeah, sure. Do it."

Maranville maneuvered his way to the front of the car. The next thing Haney sees is Maranville in a conductor's hat, bellowing, "We are having some mechanical problems with this car, and it will have to be detached. You can stay and it will be repaired, or you can move up to the other car, which will continue to downtown Los Angeles." Slowly the crowd began moving up to the front car, and Haney and Maranville had all the seats they wanted.

So they sat down and enjoyed the ride in a practically empty car. As they rode along, though, many of the people who had moved to the other car began wondering when the "repairs" would begin. First a few curious passengers drifted in, then a steady stream, and finally a crowd.

Rabbit turned to Haney and said, "Remember when I told you, if you've got the guts I can get us seats? Well, look at that mob coming at us. Here's where the guts come in."

Ernie Fazio deserves to be the number one shortstop on my team because of a quick and honest answer. Ernie was in a slump, and when a player's in a slump he'll try anything. Somebody once said a slump is like the common cold: it doesn't make any difference what you do; it'll last for two weeks.

Fazio had just tried cure number 299, a new bat. So someone asked the obvious question: "Ernie, why did you go from a 35-inch, 33-ounce bat to a 34-inch, 32-ounce bat?"

He didn't go into all the usual reasons, like "They're jamming me and I can't get around on the fastball," or "I'm opening my shoulder, and a lighter bat will help."

Fazio's answer was much simpler. "I went from a 35-inch, 33-ounce bat to a 34-inch, 32-ounce bat because it's lighter to carry back to the bench after I strike out."

Induct that man.

Every team has to have a utility infielder, someone who must always be ready. For my team, Alfredo Griffin is the easy choice.

When baseball started inviting wives of All-Star players to the game and paying their way, the single players complained. Soon they too were allowed to invite their fiancée, a parent, or a good friend.

Damaso Garcia was selected to play for the American League team in San Francisco in 1984. Having nobody to take to the game, he asked Griffin, his teammate and good friend. Griffin went, and when he got there, he found out Alan Trammell had hurt his shoulder and the American League needed an infielder. Since he was already there, Griffin was asked to substitute. Now, Griffin had absolutely no chance of being voted or chosen as an All-Star, but he certainly "made" the team. And he had a clause in his contract that said that if he made the All-Star team he'd get a $25,000 bonus. He made the team and collected his bonus.

One other utility player deserves recognition for his special contribution to the game. When I was playing, we had what we called the Three-Inch Club. Becoming a member was easy. Every Sunday you'd get a newspaper and a ruler and measure up from the bottom of the list of batting averages. Every player listed in that three inches was a member. Then, a few years ago, the Mendoza Line was created. Mario Mendoza was an infielder whose lifetime batting average was .215. A struggling hitter who'd pull his average above .200 was said to be getting ready to "cross the Mendoza Line." Mendoza has to be in my Hall of Fame.

My catcher? I might have to put in more than one. Consider Bob Kearney and his unique ability to handle baseball's changes. When he was asked why he objects to drug testing, he said simply, "I hate needles."

My first choice, though, is Joe Azcue, who showed how fast he could think when he was a catcher for the Cleveland Indians. It was spring training, and in a bunt situation Azcue bunted the ball right back to the pitcher, who ran over to tag him. Azcue got caught in a run-down between home and first base. He had one chance to get out of it, and he grabbed it. He took off back to home plate and made a sensational hook slide. He was out, but how many guys have you ever seen slide into home plate from *first* base?

Former Dodger catcher Bob Stinson also makes the team, not because of something he said, but because of his honest effort to follow the manager's directions.

Back in the Rookie League, Tom Lasorda asked Stinson to bring the catching equipment from Mesa to the park in Scottsdale where they were scheduled to play. When Stinson got to the Scottsdale ballpark though, he realized he forgot to bring the catching stuff, so he went back to Mesa for it. But unfortunately, he forgot where his team was playing, and instead of going back to Scottsdale, he went to Tempe's Diablo Stadium.

Now the team scheduled to play in Tempe pulled up, saw Stinson in uniform, figured they were at the wrong park, and headed for Scottsdale. As they pulled up there, so did the umpires scheduled to work the Scottsdale game. But when the umpires saw the team bus, they figured *they* went to the wrong park, so they took off because they didn't want anybody to know they went to the wrong place. So they headed for Tempe, and for the next hour team buses and umpires were crisscrossing Phoenix trying to find the right park, all because Bob Stinson forgot his shin guards.

Three of the starting pitchers in my Hall of Fame made it on their ability to communicate. When manager Jim Leyland told Jose DeLeon he had to pitch inside, he asked, "Did you trade me to Houston?" Joaquin Andujar began one season by announcing to the press, "There is one word in America that says it all, and that one word is 'You never know.'" After a tough year, he came to spring training the following season and announced, "I got a new word this year: 'no comment.'" Curt Young wouldn't let a home run by Rickey Henderson bother him, although he admitted, "He hit it a lot further than it went."

Burt Hooton, who had several good years with the Dodgers, makes my team for his mathematical abilities. Manager Tom Lasorda was lecturing the pitchers on the importance of helping yourself win games by being a better bunter and a better fielder.

"If your record is 10 and 10 and you learn how to bunt properly, you can win maybe two more games and you'll be 12 and 8. If you learn to field your position, you'll win two more. So if you do both well, instead of being 10 and 10 you'll be 14 and 6."

After the session, Hooton asked Lasorda what his big-league record was. "Oh and four," answered Lasorda. "See," Hooton said, "if you'd learned to field and bunt, you'd have been four and oh."

My first-out-of-the-bullpen relief pitcher is Satchel Paige. Not only could he pitch, but he'd be on my club just to keep everybody loose. He could tell his favorite story about how he came in with the bases loaded, no outs, 3 and 2 on the hitter, and got out of the jam without even throwing the ball to the batter. Satch insisted he picked the lead runner off third base, then picked the runner off first, and did it so deceptively the batter swung and missed for strike three and the third out. "So I got 'em all and didn't even make a pitch," old Satch would say.

I've also got a spot for former Texas Rangers reliever Jim Kern, since every good bullpen needs a flake. On a plane trip, he noticed a sportswriter really involved in a book, down to the last chapter. Kern walked past the writer, turned, and ripped the last 10 pages right out of the book. The writer came unglued and went after Kern, who flipped the torn pages to Sparky Lyle. Sparky flipped them back to Kern, who stuffed them all in his mouth and ate them. Recalling the incident a couple years later at an Old-Timers Game, Kern said, "It wasn't that tough. It was a paperback. Hardbacks are a little tougher to chew." He also added that the best part was seeing the writer in the back of a bookstore the next day, trying to read the end of the book without having to buy it.

My centerfielder is Mickey Rivers. He'll be in charge of the "kangaroo court," which fines players for missing signs, failing to bunt, and any number of other things, since he handled the job so well while he was with the Texas Rangers. One day the "court" fined Buddy Bell for breaking batting helmets, and Mickey announced the fine: "That's three helmets at two dollars each. Since three and two are five, you owe me five dollars, Buddy."

Actually, Mickey Rivers is probably overqualified for my team. Any one of these beauties assures him a spot on the roster:

Describing an opposing player: "He is so ugly that if you walk by him your clothes wrinkle."

"My goals this season are to hit .300, score 100 runs, and stay injury-prone."

His opening question in a trivia game: "What was the name of the dog on 'Rin Tin Tin'?"

Right next to Mickey is outfielder Dave Henderson, who picked up the telephone on a team flight and called

Domino's Pizza. "I'd like to see them deliver a pizza up here," he announced to the guys.

Brandy Davis, an outfielder and teammate of mine with the Pittsburgh Pirates, is my choice for team captain. In the bottom of the eighth, Cincinnati was beating us 3–1, and I led off the inning with a walk. Standing on first, I was thinking about all the things I'd been told about my speed. Like don't ever try to go from first to third on any hit.

Gus Bell was our next hitter, and he hit one hard to right field. I took off. Feeling the wind at my back, I rounded second and kept going. I was flying. When I slid safely into third base, Sailor Bill Posedel, our coach, dusted me off, congratulated me, and said, "Stay here; don't get picked off." Was he crazy? "Bill," I said, "I can't even remember the last time I was here. Where do you think I'm gonna go?"

So now with runners at first and third, Ralph Kiner came to bat. Kiner was the only person in our entire organization, including scouts, secretaries, and vendors, who could hit the ball out of the ballpark consistently. A home run now and we'd win.

Billy Meyer, our manager, making all the moves, put in a very fast Brandy Davis to run for Bell at first. And even with Kiner hitting and a chance to win the game with a home run, Brandy took off for second. The whole ballpark, including the fans in the rest rooms, was wondering, "Where the hell is he going?"

All managers have their own habits when things are about to go wrong. Some whistle; some repeat the same phrase, like "I don't believe it, I don't believe it." Billy Meyer was a grunter and a repeater. From where I was standing on third base, I could hear Meyer: "*Grunt, grunt*—stop him! stop him!" But Brandy made it, and now we had runners at second and third.

With first base open, I thought the Reds would walk Kiner. But they decided to pitch to him.

I'm standing at third, looking right at second base, and I see Brandy start to take a lead. I know I'm not going anywhere, so I'm thinking, "Where is *he* going?" Now he's taking a little bigger lead, and I'm thinking, "But we're on the same team—I know I've seen him in the clubhouse." Soon it's an even bigger lead, and I'm checking my uniform. *Mine* says Pittsburgh on the front, *his* says Pittsburgh on the front.

All of a sudden, here he comes. He's about four feet from the bag, and I'm rooting, "C'mon Brandy, c'mon Brandy!" He makes a great slide, and since I'm positive by then that we're on the same team, I scream, "Brandy, where in the hell are you going?" He looks up and shoots back this Hall of Fame answer: "Back to second if I can make it."

My Hall of Fame has a special place for baseball's unsung heroes, and the player I've picked is really an "unknown," because nobody ever found out who he was. Lefty Gomez tells this story as an eyewitness and the opposing manager.

Our "hero" was on second base when the batter hit a single to center field. The runner took off at the crack of the bat, trying to score. It was going to be close. Our man beat the throw home but missed the plate sliding in.

Gomez saw this and hollered to his catcher to tag the runner, who was on his way back to the dugout. But the catcher had forgotten who the runner was, and now all he saw was a bench full of players. So he ran into the dugout and routinely began tagging everybody sitting on the bench. He was just two men away from the guilty runner when our man jumped up and raced to the plate, thinking he could beat the catcher.

However, second baseman Jerry Coleman, who later played for the Yankees and is now a broadcaster for the San Diego Padres, was standing at home plate watching all of this. The catcher saw him, gave him a perfect throw, and our man was out, ending probably the first and maybe the only run-down ever between home plate and the dugout.

I'd also add a special coaching staff to my Hall of Fame. First, to teach humility, there's outfielder Gorman Thomas. An older woman once asked him to sign her baseball, which already had the signatures of Babe Ruth, Joe DiMaggio, Hank Aaron, and Mickey Mantle. After Thomas added his name he told her, "No telling what that ball was worth before I signed it."

Rocky Colavito could be a big help with positive thinking. Regardless of the statistics, Rocky was never in a slump. "I'm not hitting," he'd say, "but I'm not in a slump."

Bobby Valentine was a coach with the Mets when he showed his players the value of honest communication. "The workout is optional," he said of an off-day practice in Atlanta. "Whoever doesn't come gets optioned."

The first broadcaster I'd choose would be Jerry Coleman. His line speaks to the philosophy of my Hall of Fame: "I've made a couple of mistakes I'd like to do over."

Actually, choosing one broadcaster is tough, because Al Helfer, who did the "Mutual Radio Game of the Week," is certainly eligible with this line: "And that's what makes the game of baseball so great. The expected is always happening when it's least expected and vice versa."

Broadcaster Ralph Kiner would agree: "That's the great thing about baseball: you never know what's going on."

Phil Rizzuto also deserves credit for really making his listeners think twice. On a ball that was hit so hard into the air it acted like a knuckleball, Phil said, "That ball took a bad hop in the air."

Fred White, the Kansas City Royals' broadcaster, makes the choice even tougher. The wire machine giving the scores of other games had been having problems all night. Wrong names, wrong spellings, wrong scores. At one point, Fred looked at the latest information and said, "This thing has been acting up all night, and now look what it says. Felton started the game in Minnesota, and now they've got him relieving himself on the mound."

The television producer and director who've earned spots in my Hall of Fame are two men I've worked with for many years, Larry Cirillo and Harry Coyle. I've known Harry as long as I've been at NBC. Nobody knows more about telecasting a baseball game than Harry—he has literally "written the book." Yet he has another side, a way with words that puts him beside some of the greats. Nobody ever misses a Harry Coyle meeting, not because he's so strict, but because Harry always has something unique to say, and he says it like nobody else can. He mixes a little Yogi with some pure Sam Goldwynisms, and on a good day, even some Norm Crosby.

After reading a newspaper article about himself he said, "This is a good story. Usually they just take your biology and rewrite it."

And if Harry asked you to do this, how would you go about it? "Take a lotta pictures and make a nice emblem for him." I once walked into a meeting in Los Angeles, and Harry asked me if I remembered a particular cameraman. I told him I didn't. "Oh, you'd know him if you met him," Harry said. "He's dead, died yesterday."

Larry Cirillo, an NBC producer, will have a plaque right next to Harry's. How can I not include a man who finishes a statement by saying, "and that goes for all you guys in your Eiffel Tower." Most large hotels have a concierge, but Larry was once late for a meeting because he had to stop by the "consommé's desk."

My team's chief scout is Ellis Clary, who worked for the Minnesota Twins for more than 40 years and then went to work for the White Sox. "Every 40 years I change jobs," he said.

Ellis has his own way with words. "I cain't unnerstand

why they done let me go. Calvin [Griffith] always said I done the work of two people, Laurel and Hardy.

"Let me tell you about where I live," he says about his home in Valdosta, Georgia. "I really live in the boondocks. In fact, to go hunting I have to walk towards town."

Ellis once scouted a pitcher who was so bad that "when he came into the game the ground crew dragged the warning track."

Talking about his own career with the old Washington Senators and St. Louis Browns: "My coordination was so bad, I had to pull my car off to the side of the road to blow the horn. The only record I'm part of is 10 pop flies in one game. Hit four and dropped six."

Ellis is in my Hall of Fame because he can come up with the answer in clutch situations. Talk about pressure? As he was having a heart attack and being put into an ambulance to go to the hospital, he turned to another scout, Atley Donald, and said, "Get the mileage on this ambulance so I can have it for my expense account."

Two other scouts who've earned a place are Russ Sehon of the Yankees and Carl Blando of the Royals. The two of them were scouting a high school pitching prospect when Blando told Sehon that the Royals don't rely on the radar gun; they just use it to back up what they see when they watch a pitcher.

"There are truck drivers who throw 90 miles an hour but can't pitch," Blando said.

"You got the names of those truck drivers?" Sehon asked.

Electing umpires to my Hall of Fame is tough. I have to consider Scotty Robb and Artie Gore just for the headline they created. They were umpiring an International League game in Toronto, in which a number of calls went against the home team. In the next day's paper, the headline read, "Maple Leafs Jobbed, Robbed and Gored."

I've always wondered why more umpires don't do what

Jocko Conlan once did. Pitcher Jack Sanford kept throwing the ball back to Jocko because it didn't feel right. After Sanford tested three balls and threw them all back, Jocko hollered, "Hey, Jack, here," and, emptying his pockets of baseballs, rolled them all out to the mound.

When the designated hitter rule was new to baseball, umpire Nestor Chylak appeared on my "Baseball World" pregame show to help fans get a better understanding of the change. This is his word-for-word explanation: "Well it's really simple. Actually what it is, is a designated hitter gets a designated spot in the lineup, 1 through 9, and, if I may project a line, and the pitcher is down below the line, which is the number 10 man, which means he doesn't participate in the game with a bat. And as long as they switch that designated hitter either for another pinch hitter or for a pinch runner, but as long as that man in that position does not take a defensive position, then you go along with the next man as a substitute becomes a designated hitter. But the minute he takes a designated spot on the field of play, or on the field of battle, whatever the case may be, then you throw out the designated hitter spot, he becomes an active member, you bring the pitcher up over the line into the open spot of where he's going to be, right field, second base, shortstop, whatever the case may be, and then you go along with the natural rules of baseball." Thanks, Nestor. I signaled for a fair catch and went right to a commercial.

I don't know whether Tom Gorman or Beans Reardon came up with the best answer to an impossible question, but both belong in my Hall of Fame. Tom Gorman was a good umpire and a funny man—you always felt better around him. He once used my catcher's mask for nine innings and I didn't even know it. I go out to catch, and when I finish warming up the pitcher I'm looking everywhere for that mask and I can't find it. Finally I figure I didn't bring it out with me and I send the batboy back to get one.

After the final out of the game, Gorman hands me my

mask. "Thanks, Joe. I forgot to bring mine out, and I wasn't going to give those bench jockeys ammunition by going back and getting it." After that, he was one of my favorites.

In a collision at first base between Al Oliver and Paul Popovich, Gorman got blindsided and broke his leg. He was lying on the ground waiting for the stretcher when Leo Durocher came tearing out to see what was going on. When Leo saw Tom was conscious, he started screaming, "What is he? Safe or out? Safe or out?"

In spite of his pain, Gorman answered, "He's out; he had the wrong foot on the base." So Leo headed back to the bench. Not until the next inning, with Gorman on his way to the hospital, did Leo realize he'd been had.

"What did Gorman mean, 'wrong' foot? There's no 'right' foot," he screamed at the other umpires.

"Too late, Leo," they said. "You'll have to ask Tom."

My number one Hall of Fame umpire story involves Beans Reardon. I told this story in *Baseball Is a Funny Game*, but I can never leave him off my team.

Reardon was working third base, and Richie Ashburn of the Phillies was the batter. Ashburn hit a ball down the left-field line, and it looked like an easy two-base hit. The throw came in to Billy Cox, who put the tag on Ashburn. Reardon, on top of the play, hollered "Safe," but his arm was high in the air, indicating "Out."

"What the hell does that mean?" Ashburn yelled.

"Richie," Reardon began calmly, "you know you're safe. Billy, you know he's safe. But 30,000 fans see my arm. Richie, you're out."

Just as with Cooperstown's Hall of Fame, my list of possible inductees is long, and I'm sure it doesn't include everybody who's worthy. Like Joe Lis, for example, who explained why it was tough to maintain his playing weight: "I don't know what my playing weight is. I never play."

And Joe Grzenda, who spent 11 years pitching in the

minors before making it to the big leagues. His ambition? "I'd like to stay in baseball long enough to buy a bus and then set fire to it." Or better yet, he could burn half the bus, then let a relief pitcher come in to finish the job.

I'd also have to include Milwaukee infielder Dale Sveum, just for his realistic attitude toward life. His name is Norwegian, pronounced "Swaim," and people are always asking, "So what does 'Sveum' mean?" His answer: "It means a lot of people mispronounce your name." I can relate to a guy like that. And if Sveum made it to my Hall of Fame, next to his plaque I'd put up one for catcher Doug Gwosdz (pronounced Goosh), just to hear fans try to pronounce both names.

Outfielder John Lowenstein also deserves recognition for being an "idea man." He once recommended moving first base back a foot to "eliminate all close plays."

I'd find a place for Joe Ferguson for being the only man ever to leave Tom Lasorda speechless. With men on first and third and two outs, the batter hit a ground ball to the Dodgers' third baseman, Mickey Hatcher. Everybody expected Hatcher to throw to first and get the easy out, or maybe throw to second for the force out. Both routine, easy plays. Instead he threw to the plate, the hardest way to get the out. Yet there was Ferguson, waiting for the ball. He made the catch and tagged the runner.

When they got back to the bench, Lasorda, who couldn't believe what he'd just seen, asked Hatcher why he threw to the plate. "I lost track and thought there was only one out," Hatcher said. Okay, Lasorda could understand that. What he couldn't understand was how Ferguson made the play.

"That was a dumb play," said Lasorda, "but you were dumber because you were ready for it."

Ferguson had a Hall of Fame answer: "Hey, Skip, when you play with dumb players you have to think dumb."

Birdie Tebbetts also deserves consideration for his managerial advice to Bobby Bragan. Bragan succeeded Birdie as the manager of the Milwaukee Braves, and when he took over he found two envelopes in the manager's desk, labeled "A" and "B." Birdie had told him to open "A" only when things first began to look bad.

"After a year and a half I opened 'A,'" Bragan recalls, "and the note inside said, 'Blame it on me.' So I did, pointing out that I had a bunch of old players like Spahn, Burdette, Logan, etc.

"A year and half later, things were *really* bad, so I opened envelope 'B.' The note inside said, 'Prepare two envelopes.'"

I even have a fan I'd like to induct, just for his honesty and sincerity. During spring training in St. Petersburg, Florida, announcer Lindsey Nelson was leaving his motel for the ballpark when an older man stopped him and said, "I'd sure like to watch the game today, but I guess they don't want us out there."

"Sure they do. What gave you that idea?" Lindsey asked.

"Well, it said in the paper, 'No admission.'"

The induction ceremony for my Hall of Fame would be simple. Only one speech. I'd have a massive ceremony with the whole group going in together. A "designated speaker" would make the acceptance speech on behalf of the group, and in keeping with the spirit of the occasion, it could only be someone who's distinguished himself as a great speech-maker. I pick former Milwaukee Braves infielder Johnny Logan.

Logan is the player who heard manager Fred Haney's "footprints" coming down the hall for bed check. He once introduced Stan Musial as "one of baseball's immoral players." And to say thanks on behalf of all the inductees in my Hall of Fame, he could use the acceptance speech that got him into these not-so-hallowed halls: "Thank you very much for this honor. I will perish it forever."

"Trying to make the best of a terrible season, I said, 'We may not be very high in the standings and we don't win many ballgames, but you've got to admit we play some interesting baseball.' A voice from the back of the room yelled, 'Why don't you play some dull games and win a few?' "

○

3

"Our Speaker, Joe Giardello . . . No, Gorgonzola . . . er, Grigiologa . . . um, Joe the Catcher."

EVER HEARD OF "flop sweat"? I'm sure you've experienced it. When you have it, you know it. "Flop sweat" takes over your whole body. I'm sure there's a medical term or explanation for it, but when it hits you, you know "flop sweat" is the perfect description.

I learned about "flop sweat" on the banquet circuit. The banquet circuit was my training ground, my Communications 101 course straight through to my postgraduate degree in working behind a microphone.

I was working for the Yankees when I had my first experience with "flop sweat." Dan Topping, one of the team's owners, asked me to do a banquet during spring training. That seemed simple enough. Topping was a baseball owner, he wanted a banquet—I figured it had to be a sports-oriented affair. Sounds easy—two umpire stories, what the catcher says to the pitcher, finish with some Yogi stories—just tell me the time and place and I'll be there. Simple, right? Wrong.

What they forgot to tell me was this "sports banquet" was the Flamingo Stakes Ball, the big jet set social event of the year. Instead of names like Sparky and Buck, the guests had names like Ogden and Conrad. Half the names had Roman numerals after them, and they weren't batting averages.

They also forgot to tell me it was a black-tie affair. When I pulled up to the Carrillon Hotel in Miami Beach and saw all those limousines, black ties, and long dresses, I figured the fancy party must be in the big room and my dinner would be in one of the smaller rooms next to the kitchen.

It didn't take me long to figure out we were all going to the same party. I took two steps into the lobby and ran into an unmistakable program-chairman-type straight from Central Casting. He was already hollering at me.

"Where the hell is your tuxedo?"

"What are you talking about?" I asked, not at all sure I wanted to know.

"This is black tie. Where's your tuxedo?"

"It's back in New York. Nobody told me this was black tie." He wasn't at all satisfied with my answer. "What do you want me to do?" I asked.

"We've got to get you a tuxedo."

"How're you gonna do that?" I asked, afraid to hear the answer.

"Follow me," he said, and we went straight to the kitchen and grabbed the restaurant's maître d'.

"Have you got an extra tuxedo here?" my "friend" said to the maître d'.

"Yes, for what?"

"I need it for *him*," he said, pointing at me. I didn't even have a name anymore. I was *"HIM."* Even Leo Durocher never referred to me like that.

"You gotta be kidding," I said. "I can't wear his tux. Look at the difference in our builds." The maître d' was maybe 5'4", 200 pounds, and built like the Pillsbury dough boy.

"With suspenders to hold up the pants, it'll fit. Look, do you want me to call Topping?" he threatened.

"You couldn't make it fit if you called Oral Roberts," I said.

He got the tuxedo and I put it on. I took one quick look at myself—long enough to know this wasn't going to work—before I heard "Come on, they're introducing you." And out I went.

This "sports banquet" not only wasn't sports-oriented, it wasn't even a banquet. It was an auction. My job was to auction the items during and between the courses of the meal. Well, I'd already learned from speaking at Boy Scout banquets that when you compete against the food you end up the big loser. Add to this the fact that I was wearing pants four sizes too big and six inches too short, and you get an idea of how self-conscious I was. My only hope was that as long as I kept the jacket buttoned, the pants wouldn't be too noticeable.

My first couple of "funnies" didn't get any reaction. Great. The only thing I knew about this function was that Dan Topping was there, so I went into my New York Yankees material.

Nobody was listening. Nobody cared. They were eating. And I was starting to panic.

I went right to my "A" material, surefire stuff that had always worked before. Not even a smile. Nothing. Now I could feel the "flop sweat" starting. You know, that sudden warm feeling, those little beads of sweat that form on your forehead. Your brain goes into neutral.

The auction was the main event anyway, so I figured it would get me off the hook. Since I'd hardly moved, I felt I was hiding the tuxedo pretty well. Then it happened. As I reached from the stage to a front table for the names of the donors, the button on the coat popped, the coat flew open, and the pants rode up to my collar. I felt like Bozo the Clown. Then I heard a big laugh from the crowd. I'd like to think it was something I said, but I doubt it.

By now the "flop sweat" spigot was turned on full blast. Big beads of sweat popped out around my forehead (which is worse when you're bald because your forehead is your entire head). You know how this goes: a cold trickle begins behind your head at the base of your neck and runs down the middle of your back. No matter how you move, it's still a cold trickle, and as the Mississippi separates east from west, this little trickle cuts your body right down the middle.

All you think about now is survival. You're hoping for a call from the governor to save you. Keep it moving, just get it over, and get out. If I'd been making a speech, I would have thanked them and sat down. But this was an auction. I stood there as straight and as rigid as a foul pole and took my beating. No jokes, no ad libs—just give me your bids.

The committee members were going to auction the grand prize, so once they were introduced I was able to escape. I tore out to the kitchen, got my clothes, and returned the soaked shirt and tuxedo. I scrambled into my own clothes, happy to see they still fit. I was sure the "flop sweat" had shrunk me so small I'd be buying my next suit in the boys' department.

"Flop sweat" is not terminal. You do recover. In fact, everyone should have it once in his life. It gives you some perspective.

When I was playing for the Cardinals and living in St. Louis, the team's publicity department convinced me public appearances were not only part of my contract but a great opportunity for me. I thought they were spreading it a little thin with the "opportunity" approach, because in the early days I had no thoughts of broadcasting; I was going straight to the Hall of Fame. But they told me I "owed it to the fans." I found out later the team's stars must not have owed the fans anything because they were getting paid for their appearances.

Stars like Stan Musial, Red Schoendienst, and Marty Marion got the "high-rent district" appearances. I was working church basements. I saw all the Junior Chambers of Commerce, the scouts, and, of course, the Little Leagues.

You really need a game plan, or maybe more like a combat strategy, for attending a Little League banquet. They're the toughest because these "players" have a combined attention span of less than 30 seconds. The little guys are all dressed up to get their awards, and they've been excited for two weeks. Mom is always right there, usually helping to serve dinner (she's the real hero who should get an award, balancing plates of food while trying to keep her guy from throwing a dinner roll at his best friend).

So you might as well forget the stories. No story can compete with a pitiful voice saying "I have to go to the bathroom." When you hear that line in the middle of your speech, you know it's over.

The best strategy is to bring the loot. Lots of it. Team pictures, stickers, bubble-gum cards— anything you can hand out. If you have a dozen baseballs, you're home free. If the baseballs are autographed (and the kids usually don't even care if the ink is smudged), you may be voted onto the team as an honorary member. Then you get to go to *all* their meetings. Free.

The kids don't want speeches, but you can have some fun with a question and answer session. Just be prepared to answer questions that come straight out of left field. Like "How much money do you make? How old are you? When did you get bald? Do you have two cars? What kind do you drive?" Reading baseball record books doesn't help you here at all.

While I was playing with the Pirates, I made a speech

before the Pittsburgh Junior Chamber of Commerce that turned into an informal question and answer session. Trying to make the best of a terrible season, I said, "We may not be very high in the standings, and we don't win many ballgames, but you've got to admit we play some interesting baseball." A voice from the back of the room yelled, "Why don't you play some dull games and win a few?"

The second-toughest audience may be the service clubs. Groups like Kiwanis, Optimist, and Rotary have the same goal for a speaker: get finished by 1:30 so we can get back to work. The philosophy is "I'm here only to keep my attendance record going, but I'll listen to you as long as you're finished by 1:30."

When you're the guest speaker at a service club luncheon, you can go to your best material early, but don't count on it to work. The audience sits there like a painting. Even if they haven't heard your story before, they like to give the impression it's old news. So many times I've wanted to borrow from the great put-down artist Jack E. Leonard, who would walk out on stage and say, "Hello, opponents." With the service clubs it isn't speaker and audience but "Well, I'm here—make me laugh."

I don't want to be too hard on the service clubs—it's tough to maintain a decent standard for speakers when you have to get one every week and you don't pay a fee. But I always seemed to be scheduled the week after a lecture on why the plastic paper clip is more efficient, and the audience was still ticked off because the speaker wasn't Bob Hope. The service club circuit is well scouted, though, so as Casey Stengel would say, if "you did good," you could depend on a flood of invitations.

When I first started out on the circuit, I did mostly sports banquets. I'd be out as many as six nights a week. During the winter I averaged about 20 speeches a month. One year I actually kept track: more than 100,000 miles and more than 200 hours just flying to and from banquets. I never knew there were so many ways to cook chicken.

Television, especially the "Today" show and "The Tonight Show," widened the banquet circuit for me. Once I could be introduced with "You've seen him on the 'Today' show," it no longer had to be a sports banquet. Retirement dinners, fund-raisers, conventions, outings, lecture series, roasts—you name it, I did it. And from all that "experience" over the years, I've come up with a few working banquet survival rules.

Rule 1: The Biggest Aren't Always the Toughest.

I've seen five people in a banquet hall and I've seen thousands. The banquet for five was a mistake, but the remedy was even worse. The secretary had sent out the wrong date, but instead of just canceling the "banquet," he invited two couples at the last minute. What do you do? You thank the two couples and hope the battery in your car isn't dead so you can make a quick getaway.

I once got a fee for speaking to only 15 people, at a board of directors' dinner meeting. My instructions were simple: have dinner and tell some baseball stories. Tough night—I felt like I'd been invited to be the main speaker at the Wax Museum.

Rule 2: Don't Ever Think You've "Seen It All" on the Banquet Circuit.

In Pittsburgh one night, it wasn't "flop sweat" but pure panic. I was making a speech at a men's club, and I wasn't getting any reaction. Zip. Zilch. I'd usually get at least a few laughs with my opener: "When I played with the Pirates in 1952, it was a tough year. We lost 112 games that season . . . but not in a row." Nobody even smiled.

I went on. "Well, we got off to a slow start. We lost 10 of our first 11 and then went into a slump." More silence. "I'll tell you how bad we were. After we lost the next four we had a rain-out. Our manager brought in a cake; we had a victory party." Even more silence—and I started to panic.

"But at least I was a catcher. I didn't care what the manager said, and I got to hang around some great guys—the umpires." Still no reaction. Not even the chairs were moving. Dead silence. I went right to my best shot.

"Ever wonder what goes on when the manager, pitcher, and catcher are out there talking? I remember one game when our pitcher just couldn't get anybody out. Our manager, Fred Haney, finally came out to the mound and asked for the ball. The pitcher didn't want to give it to him. "I know I can get this guy out," he said. "I know," Haney answered. "You proved it when he led off the inning." Still nothing. Not even somebody clearing his throat.

By now I was feeling complete panic, with symptoms of flop sweat, when I looked down at the table and, for the first time, saw a copy of the evening's program. In big, bold print on the front cover it said:

DON'T MISS THIS MEETING!
HEAR ONE OF THE GREAT BOXERS IN
HISTORY!—JOE GIARDELLO

Once I explained to them who I was and what I did, they switched their brains from boxing to baseball and we got along great.

Rule 3: All Writers' Dinners Are Not Created Equal.

Baseball Writers' Annual Dinners draw some of the biggest crowds on the banquet circuit. Organized by the writers in each city, these dinners usually honor either the World Series hero or the "hot" player, whomever the fans want to see: the home run king, the MVP, the Cy Young Award winner. See who had an outstanding World Series and you have your talent for the banquet, an automatic lineup for the awards. I should clarify that—see who had an outstanding World Series *and* is able to be there to accept the award. If you can't be at the banquet, your chances of being named Man of the Year are slim.

All baseball writers' dinners I've attended begin with a cocktail party. That's good news and bad news. The good news is you see players and writers you haven't seen for a while, so there's lots of talk, with line drives and shutouts all over the place. The bad news is that some of the guys get so much booze in them, they ought to have "bottled in bond" signs around their necks. I've been to more than one writers' dinner that was spiced up by a former player who suddenly remembered— loudly—how a writer had blasted him when he was still playing.

Later, everyone makes a speech, usually thanking the writers for the award. One of the great "thank you" speeches I ever heard was by Art Shamsky, who played for the Mets at the time. After receiving an award at a St. Louis dinner he said, "I'd like to thank you for this award, and I'd like to thank my manager, but that would be silly because he never played me."

A lot of the dinners have themes *and* entertainment. Picture a pack of New York writers who can't sing, can't

remember the lyrics, and can't even stand up, saluting
Casey Stengel by singing "Old Man Casey" to the tune of
"Old Man River," as if they were the Mormon Tabernacle
Choir. And what about these lyrics, set to an old, familiar
tune, about batting against Sandy Koufax:

You better be quick, you better watch out.
You better act sick and sit this one out.
Sandy K. is pitching today.

You swing at Sandy's fastball
It turns into a curve;
But looking for his curveball
Takes an awful lot of nerve.

There's nothing to do, there's nothing to say,
Right after strike three just holler "oy, veh!"
Sandy K. is pitching today.

When I was growing up in St. Louis, my team was the
Gashouse Gang Cardinals. These were the guys on the
bubble-gum cards we flipped in the schoolyard. If you've
ever had heroes like that, you can imagine how I felt when
I was asked to emcee the banquet celebrating the 25th
anniversary of the Gashouse Gang's 1934 World Series
victory. Dizzy Dean, Joe "Ducky" Medwick (my hero),
Pepper Martin, and Leo Durocher were all there. So was
Branch Rickey, the general manager in 1934. Mr. Rickey
could describe people and events in such a way that even
when you couldn't understand him he still sounded great.
    The Gashouse Gang may have been Mr. Rickey's favor-
ite team. How proud he sounded when he said, "The
Gashouse Gang . . . [pause, and I mean a long one—it

was "church" quiet with 1,200 people in the room] was a group of ferocious gentlemen, willing to embrace the hazards of rational chance." Who else could come up with a description like that for a baseball team?

Mr. Rickey talked about all his "boys," then brought the house down when he "praised" Leo "The Lip" Durocher, for his "great facility in making a bad situation immediately worse."

When it was Pepper Martin's turn, he became sentimental and said, "I would have played on the 1934 team for nothing." And then, with a pixie grin, added, "I guess Mr. Rickey knew his players pretty well."

One of the most emotional nights I've ever had on the banquet circuit was when the St. Louis writers honored Wee Willie Sherdel, a member of the 1926 Cardinals. I knew it was going to be special because the purpose was to honor a hero from the past, not a player who had just had a great season and was being honored in every major-league city across the country. A banquet can't go wrong if the theme is "We Remember You."

I met Willie Sherdel at a luncheon the day before. He was about 5′6″ and had been using crutches since having a leg amputated. In the course of our conversation, he talked about how often he thought about his playing days in St. Louis.

"Lotta days, when there was snow on the ground, I'd sit by my window and think about St. Louis and wonder if they remembered the left-hander. Lotta people have told me they do, and that makes a guy feel good."

A great thought, right from his heart. But when lunch was over, Willie said to me, "I don't have no speech for the banquet, and I really don't know what to say."

"Are you kidding?" I said. "Tell those people what you told me about wondering if they remember you and how good you feel because they do."

"You think that's okay?" he asked me.

"It's perfect."

When I saw him at the banquet, he had on his best brown suit, white shirt, and a walnut-colored tie. It's a picture I'll never forget.

I introduced him, and as he started up to the microphone, the 1,500-plus people in the audience stood up and gave him an incredible ovation. He stood at the mike, just watching the crowd. When the applause died down, he started.

"There were plenty of days . . ." His voice cracked. "I was . . ." and that was all he could say. His heart overflowing, the tears came in a rush. He was crying, the people at the head table were in tears, and more than 1,500 people in the audience were in tears. He just waved and slowly made his way back to his seat.

As the emcee, I let the emotion in the room play out, not really knowing what to do. For me, to have been a part of this long, long love affair between a left-handed pitcher and a city was very special.

Rule 4: If the Story Fits, Use It.

Most players try to tell a story about their team because they think that's what the fans want to hear. The most popular one is the catcher-pitcher-manager story. Just fill in the names with the World Series hero or big-name pitcher. Every year the names change, but the punch line stays the same. Here's what I mean—the 1987 version, told by a Cardinal player.

"During the season we're playing the Cubs. We've got our ace, Danny Cox, going against them. He could beat Chicago by just throwing his glove out on the mound.

"This day was different. The first hitter doubles, then the next guy singles, then the third guy up hits a home run, then a triple, then another double. By now Herzog's had enough, and out he comes." (If you're an infielder, you tell the story as though you were standing on the mound listening. If you're a pitcher, you found out when the manager came back to the bench.)

"Herzog asks Tony Peña, our catcher, 'What's going on? Is he throwing hard? What kind of stuff does he have?'

"And Peña says, 'I don't know, I haven't caught one yet!' "

I've heard that story told about Yogi and Casey Stengel, Earl Weaver and Rick Dempsey, Whitey Herzog and Darrell Porter, and many other combinations—and it works every time.

The other banquet "regular" is the umpire argument. You can build this one up any way you want. The punch line stays the same.

Umpire: "I've had enough. Be quiet or I'll bite your head off."

Player: "If you do, you'll have more brains in your belly than you've got in your head."

Wonderful Casey Stengel had some great stories, but he could make them into a continuing series. I once followed him on the program at banquets in Kansas City and St. Louis. In Kansas City, he told a story in which he worked his way to a man on third base. But then he suddenly switched himself to another story, and his speech ended with the guy still on third.

So when we got to St. Louis, I mentioned this, and he said, "Yeah, yeah, I'll remember." He promised to do the right ending. So he started that same story, worked the guy to third, switched again in the middle, and to this day Casey's man is still on third.

Rule 5: Don't Look for Humor Where There Isn't Any.

Too many times I've seen an athlete feel obligated to tell a story, but he only knows the ones he's heard in the locker room or the bullpen. And he quickly finds out what's funny in a locker room isn't funny in a ballroom. Nobody pays the price of a banquet ticket to listen to a dirty story. It's that simple.

Physical handicap stories aren't for the podium either. A story about a pitcher who had a harelip drove home for me a lesson I'll never forget. The player who told the story considered it one of his best, and he did tell it well. This night was no different, and because of his delivery he got big laughs all through the story. When the banquet was over and the youngsters were getting their autographs, a kid about 12 years old asked for the pitcher's autograph, saying, "I can't help this, but I still like you." The boy had a harelip. I remember hoping that his class would rub off on the player. I'm not sure it did, but that night, it was the youngster who was the real champion.

Rule 6: Expect the Unexpected and You Won't Be Disappointed.

Following the great double-talk comedian Al Kelly gave me one of my most memorable "nights to forget." I'd seen Kelly work and I'd heard so many stories about what he did to people, I asked to be moved from the spot following him. The banquet organizers wouldn't change the lineup. The argument they gave me was that the program had already been printed, and I wasn't strong enough to make them change their minds.

Al Kelly could totally confuse even the most intelligent person. He would always be introduced with some official title pertinent to the affair—if the audience was all doctors, he'd be chairman of some medical society. He didn't really know anything about the subject, just enough key words to make his new title sound legitimate. Then what a job he'd do on the audience. People would solemnly nod their approval; some would be taking notes. And once they figured out what was going on, they'd spend the next 20 minutes trying to convince the person next to them that they knew all along Kelly was a double-talker. All this while I'm trying to make my speech.

My favorite Al Kelly story involves former baseball commissioner Happy Chandler. Kelly was using an official-sounding title, which must have sounded good to the commissioner, because he agreed to schedule a meeting with Kelly.

Kelly started off with just enough baseball terms to be confusing: "Mr. Commissioner, I love baseball and have been a fan for many years, but when I think of the spratigan of players with coaches thrown in, and you hear so much about mawking and cleetsville to expansion, then it's only remous that agents get involved in pergaminations of schedules that freepap the entire season." (Hopefully you get an idea of what he might have sounded like.)

The commissioner said his ideas sounded interesting but asked if he could speak a little louder. Kelly kept it up, to the point where Commissioner Chandler, claiming to be just getting over a cold, wasn't hearing well at all. He asked Kelly to pull his chair a little closer so he wouldn't miss anything. With this Kelly knew he had him and went into high gear. The commissioner got up and closed the window, saying the traffic was making too much noise. Kelly kept it up. The commissioner finally agreed Kelly had some valid points and asked him if he'd put them down in a letter so they might be studied further.

I learned a lot following Al Kelly at a banquet, but believe me, his act wasn't even the hardest one to follow. Just as you don't want to follow an Al Kelly, you don't want to follow a magician unless you know his last trick.

At a banquet in Milwaukee, a magician was put on the program to fill the time from dessert until my speech. He was very good, filled the time perfectly, the tables were cleared, and the crowd was in a good mood, thanks to him. I thought it was a great idea to use a magician in that spot. Wrong.

For his last trick, his grand finale, he released a couple hundred balloons in the room. The crowd loved it and gave him a great ovation as he left. Terrific. Then the emcee introduced me, and for the next 20 minutes, while I was trying to make a speech, 600 people were sticking the lighted ends of cigarettes into floating balloons. All you could hear was *Bang! Bang! Bang!* It sounded like a war movie. You couldn't give a punch line, you heard it.

Follow Al Kelly and a balloon-releasing magician and you think you've seen it all. You haven't. If you're making a speech at an Elks Club, you better be sure you have a watch and a good grasp of the time.

One night I was telling the Elks one of my favorite banquet stories about my old experts-on-losing 1952 Pirates team, about a couple of baserunners. I do a long buildup and get one runner to third base before the punch line. The key element is the baserunner getting to third.

So this night I get my runner to third and I start to go for the punch line when all the lights in the room suddenly go out and a bell begins to toll. I'm not talking about the bells of St. Mary's either. This sounds like Quasimodo is doing the ringing. Eleven long chimes, major-league somber. All the Elks get to their feet, face the west, and speak in unison about their departed brother Elks. I found out later it was an Elks' ritual, always done at exactly 11:00 o'clock, to honor the members who have died. They could have added me to the list that night.

The bell finally stopped, the lights came back on, and there I was with that guy still on third base, wondering what had just happened. My story was finished, but I tried to regain the mood by telling the audience they had just been a part of history—that was the longest any Pirate ever stayed at third.

It was also on the banquet circuit that I gave a former president a direct order. In Sikeston, Missouri, I was the emcee of a banquet to kick off the campaign of Governor Warren Hearnes. The main speaker was Harry Truman. I was seated between him and the program chairman.

When the crowd was seated, the program chairman stood up and introduced the National Anthem. Somewhere between the rockets' red glare and the bombs bursting in air, I saw the program chairman start to slump over. He looked like he was having a heart attack. I sat him down and quickly grabbed the microphone. But when I broke in asking for a doctor, everybody thought it was some kind of joke and started laughing. Pleading, I yelled, "This isn't a joke, is there a doctor here?" All I got was more laughter, and with that I grabbed President Truman and told him, "You ask for a doctor; they don't believe me." He went to the microphone and asked for a doctor, and one immediately came up. The program chairman was indeed having a heart attack and was rushed to the hospital. The story has a happy ending, though. The man recovered, and now I can tell people I once ordered around a president.

Another audience that had a hard time taking me seriously was a scholar-athlete group in St. Louis. The maître d' came up to me, visibly shaken, and said, "Don't panic [even though he looked like he could use a change of underwear], but there's a fire in the hotel, and the fire department thinks we should get these people out of the ballroom."

More than a thousand people were in the room. I announced to the crowd, "Don't be alarmed, but I've just been told to ask you to leave the ballroom. Everything is under control, but please start filing out through the south door." It got a big laugh. And nobody moved.

I tried again. "This is no joke. There's a fire in the hotel, and the fire department has asked us to vacate the room." Another laugh.

Finally, my third try worked. "This is not a joke. If you want to stay here, you can. But I'm grabbing those nuns seated by the exit and leading them out because my mother would never forgive me if something happened to them." With that, I stepped down from the dais and, flanked by four nuns, left the room. I guess everybody believed me then, because they followed me out of the ballroom like I was the Pied Piper.

Rule 7: Prepare Everything—Even Your Ad Libs.

Real, bona fide ad libs seems to happen only when you already have your ad libs prepared. Then you don't worry about what you're going to say and your brain is free to react to what's going on around you.

My favorite example involves a lovable rogue named Halsey Hall, a sportswriter-turned-broadcaster from Minneapolis. Everyone who played in the American Association or knew Halsey from his Minnesota Twins days has his own Halsey Hall story.

Halsey was an example of how somebody really can look like an unmade bed. He loved green onions and had this habit of always carrying a supply in his pocket. Combine the scallions with his ever-present cigar, and you realize that when Halsey said something, you could practically read it. He was a human skywriter. He knew it too, so to offset any problems he always carried Clorets, the breath fresheners.

Halsey's classic ad lib happened one year at the Minnesota Writers' Dinner. The emcee introduced him, and as he spoke his first words, "Good evening," a beautiful floral piece right in front of him toppled to the floor. Without skipping a beat Halsey said, "But I just had my Clorets." A perfect ad lib.

But in order to have your mind free enough to come up with an ad lib like that, you have to be prepared. I usually find out what the banquet chairman expects me to do at the event and who's going to be there. Then I break down that information into categories and try to come up with some "ad libs" appropriate to the people:

Rich:

"He's got so much money, he doesn't count it. He measures it."

"He catches a cold and the IRS sends him a box of Kleenex."

Big Guys:

"He went to [name the university] on a scholarship. He was the team bus."

"He's got so many muscles under those pants he has to wear prescription underwear."

Skinny Guys:

"He went to Jack LaLanne's to work out, and they put him on the critical list."

"He has the perfect build to model a one-iron."

Traffic:

"I have a St. Christopher medal on my dashboard, and when I made a left turn at [name the town's busiest intersection], he covered his eyes."

One trick is to try out your prepared ad libs before the banquet and watch the reaction. If they work in a conversation, they'll work at the microphone. But give yourself a chance. Don't try it with the IRS agent while he's doing your audit.

Rule 8: Learn to Tell the "Good Guys" from the "Bad Guys."

The word "around" is a red flag for me. As soon as I hear "The banquet starts *around* 7:00," a warning bell goes off in my head and I know I'm in trouble.

Good banquet organizers are honest and tell you the exact time events will get under way. "Cocktails are at 6:30, the banquet starts at 7:00. Will you be able to come to the cocktail party?" They give you a choice. Unless you agree up front to be at the cocktail party, I think it's an option.

The sharpie (the bad guy) will tell you the banquet starts "*around* 6:30." When you arrive you find the cocktail party just starting, and dinner isn't until 8:00. "I thought the people would like to meet you," the sharpie says.

The danger, of course, is that by the time you're ready to give your speech, the audience is almost tired of you. The novelty of seeing you is gone. If you repeat anything you said at the cocktail party, you can practically hear the audience say, "Doesn't he have anything new?" The zinger you came up with just last week is now a hundred years old because you used it at the cocktail party two hours ago.

Beware also of the banquet organizer who picks you up at the airport and casually says, "I have to stop by the office [plant, church, home, etc.] to get something." No doubt a crowd is waiting for you and you'll shake more hands than a politician in an election year.

After the banquet the "bad guy" might say, "Let's stop by the house to relax and have a quiet drink." That usually means everybody from the neighborhood and/or office is waiting. If the crowd is "just relatives and good friends," be prepared for a slide show that includes (at no extra charge) the reason he didn't make it to the big leagues and why he's a better hitter than you. The more freely the drinks flow, the longer the night, and the farther he hit the ball.

Your biography in the hands of some emcees is a weapon. The "good guy" emcee takes the highlights from your bio, puts them into his own words, and asks you if there's anything specific you need or want in your intro-duction. The "bad guy" reads your bio with all the enthusiasm of the tax man on April 16 and then closes with "He's a very funny man, and I'm sure he has some *new* stories."

The "frustrated jock" emcee is also dangerous. He can turn a great mood into a temple of gloom. He uses what he thinks is locker room jargon to tear you down. And make a fool of himself.

"Our speaker wore the tools of ignorance. That was his major in high school. He couldn't get into college, and now he's in the broadcast booth because he couldn't hit Uncle Charley (curveball) and couldn't catch it either. He could get wood poisoning from the way he handles the hickory (bat)." You get the idea. It's completely embarrassing to listen to and even worse to act like you enjoyed him.

The worst thing an emcee can do is make the introduction an outline of the speech he wants to hear. "Ladies and gentlemen, Joe will tell us tonight what he really thinks of Barbara Walters, and I know we're all anxious to hear what she's like at seven o'clock in the morning, and I want to know what happened that time on [a game show or ballgame] when Joe did [some obscure incident the emcee remembers]."

You have no chance after an introduction like that. By the time you've tried to cover his ground and get to your own speech, the clock tells you it's time to sit down. An introduction like that usually guarantees a severe case of flop sweat.

The second-worst thing an emcee can do is set a booby trap for you with an introduction using your own stories. "I know Joe'll tell you, and you're going to love this story, about the guy on second, and when he rounded third he said . . ." and there goes your punch line. "I couldn't believe it when I heard it! He's gotta tell that one." Meanwhile, your brain is frantically reshuffling your speech to cut the story he just ruined.

Rule 9: Don't Let the Awards Go to Your Head.

The awards don't seem to change much from year to year, although the names vary from the "Nostalgia Award" to the "Good Guy Award." But there's always an "Out-standing [you fill in the blank] of the Year Award," whether it be the athlete, the rookie, the comeback, or the humanitarian being honored. If you're a big enough name and agree to attend the banquet, you might even get the "Meritorious Service Award" or "The Man of the Year" award.

After my first year on the "Today" show I could have put a new entry in the *Guinness Book of World Records* for "Most Times Awarded Italian-American of the Year." I thought it was strange because I hadn't done anything except sit next to Hugh Downs and Barbara Walters. I probably could have been the "Italian-American of the Decade" if I had accepted the award on the "Today" show.

I try to keep in mind what football coach Joe Paterno said: "Praise is like poison; it doesn't hurt unless you swallow it."

Rule 10: Get a Hall of Fame Agent and You'll Get Paid.

Times have changed for athletes on the banquet circuit. Teams are now willing to pay players for off-season appearances. Speakers' bureaus are common among the clubs, with former players serving as speakers year-round. So even a "spear carrier" (utility player) can do all right on the circuit. Of course, the bigger the name, the bigger the payday, and in this day of agents, everything is negotiable.

I had two Hall of Famers as my first "agents." In my case, an "agent" was somebody who made sure I didn't go around talking for free. My first "agent" was Frankie Frisch, the Fordham Flash. The year was 1946, my first year in the big leagues, and we were in the World Series against the Red Sox.

In the fourth game, in Boston, I had four hits, along with Enos Slaughter, Whitey Kurowski, and Boston's Wally Moses. Me. Four hits. One game. I was 20 years old, and suddenly I'm holding two World Series records: for being the youngest catcher ever in a World Series and for getting four hits in one game.

These days, the list of players who've gotten four hits in a World Series game is about as exclusive as a listing in the Yellow Pages. At the 1967 World Series, when official scorer Bob Addie announced in the press box that Lou Brock had just tied the record, he added, "But don't get too excited—it's a long list. Even Joe Garagiola did it."

But this was 1946, and in 1946 this was news. With no television, radio was the vehicle for players to make extra money at World Series time. A program called "We The People" sent a representative to the hotel in Boston to talk to me, a man named Sherman Feller, who's now the Red Sox's public-address announcer.

Sherm was going to pay me $300 for the interview. That seemed like a lot of money to me. After all, Branch Rickey gave me only $500 for signing, and he owned me. Not knowing too much about these kinds of deals, though, I went to see our traveling secretary, Leo Ward. Leo had been around. He once got me a case of shotgun shells for a speech I made at Olin Industries. Of course, I didn't hunt and didn't even have a gun, so I thought it was sort of a bad deal, but Leo, Red Schoendienst, and Enos Slaughter thought I'd done great. They got the shells.

When I went to tell Leo about the $300, Frankie Frisch happened to be in Leo's room, and he said, "Tell that guy to come up here. I wanna talk to him."

So I brought Sherm to the room, and Frisch, sounding completely insulted, said, "This kid is a Series hero, and you're only gonna give him $300? Not enough."

Now I'm starting to worry because I can see the money going out the window.

"Who's on the show with him?" Frisch asked Feller.

"A dog," he answered, "a dog that sounds like he's talking when he barks."

"A dog?" Frisch gasped. "A dog!!! Are you kidding? Is the dog on before or after Joe?"

"I don't know," Sherm said, looking nervous. "I think after him."

"How much is that dog getting?"

"I'm not sure. . . . I think $500. But they told me I can pay Garagiola only $300."

With that, the Old Flash went right to his best umpire-baiting stance, and I knew Sherm Feller was overmatched.

"How many hits does that dog have in the World Series? That dog might be able to talk, but this kid can talk *and* he can hit. You call your people and tell them my man [now I was 'his man'] won't go on unless he gets at least as much as a dog they *think* can talk."

Sherm Feller left. Sherm Feller came back. And he gave me the $500. My "agent" had done a Hall of Fame job.

Stan Musial was the "business manager" who really got me into the talk-and-get-paid-for-it league. Stan was always being offered money for appearances. That's what happens if you hit over .300. And that's why I wasn't getting any money offers.

In those early days, Stan wasn't too sure about standing behind a microphone. A scouting report on his speaking style would say: "Dresses well, stands straight, tells great 'middles.'" He could never seem to get to the end. So he'd make me an offer. "Come along with me and we'll split the money."

Stan would make the deal, we'd use his car to get to the affair, and the crowds were always friendly because everybody wanted to see Stan. I'd just sit there in the audience until he'd bring me up to talk. So I got paid *plus* I got the exposure, which meant hopefully someone who had heard me at the dinner would call me about another appearance.

Stan had a favorite joke he used to introduce me, and he still uses it today. It's his signal to me to get ready. Imagine a big drum roll . . . here it comes. "You know, Joe and I both have mike fright. I'm afraid to get the mike, and he's afraid he's not going to get it."

Then he breaks up with that great Musial laugh. He really loves that line, even though it's not true anymore. Stan's over his mike fright now, and if you have any doubt about that, just ask the folks of Meadville, Pennsylvania.

Stan was making his "I'm tough" speech in Meadville. Standing at the microphone, he'd look around, spot one of the famous athletes on the dais, and then spend 10 minutes explaining how tough he was when he played that guy's sport. Like Pavlov's dog, the bells would go off when he'd see a star player—his juices would start flowing. And he didn't just take on the sport; he took on each player's position, which really shows the Musial confidence when you consider some of the athletes seated at the head table that night: Pittsburgh Steeler middle linebacker Jack Lambert, Miami Dolphin quarterback Dan Marino, boxer Boom Boom Mancini, NBA center James Edwards, and baseball's Chuck Tanner and Tom Lasorda.

Stan was really on a roll. As the emcee I tried twice to stop him, but he kept on going. He figured since he was from Pennsylvania and was on his home turf, he was safe. Finally Chuck Tanner got up, walked over to Stan, dropped a set of keys on the podium, and said, "Stan, you lock up. I'm going home." It brought down the house.

In spite of the mishaps and the potential for disaster, the banquet circuit is a lot of fun. When the group doesn't have a budget for a speaker, it usually provides a gift, and the list reads like a Sears catalog: a pocket watch, a camera, rosaries, a jug of cider, sunglasses, a wristwatch, gift certificates for everything from hamburgers to tacos, a yarmulke, a portrait, a novena, and a custom-made toilet seat with a furry cover.

Banquets are really the people who organize them and make them happen. Television has made us friends, and a banquet is one of the best ways for us to meet, although I do get some strange greetings.

I don't remember the town, but I'll never forget the incident. I arrived in the morning for a sports banquet that night, and as soon as I stepped off the plane, a guy put a microphone in my face and said, "Joe, say hello to all your friends on wop radio."

"*What* radio?" I asked.

"Wop radio. W-A-A-P. Those are our call letters." I felt a whole lot better after he said that.

Such memories are the biggest reward from the banquet circuit. The memories and the feelings you hang on to long after the program organizer and the audience have told you they're glad you came.

"Jimmy Piersall would reach across the plate with his bat, and make a cross in the dirt. One day Yogi was catching, and when Piersall finished, Yogi stepped across home plate, rubbed out the cross, and said, 'Why don't you just let God watch the game?' "

○

4

God in a Sweatshirt

"IT IS EASIER to play the game of baseball, as well as the game of life, when you have God as your partner."
—Mike Schmidt
"Don't worry about it; it's the Lord's will."
—Darrell Porter
"If God let you hit a home run the last time up, then who struck you out the time before that?"
—Sparky Anderson

Hairpins, lucky clothes, stepping on the same base when running in from your position, making sure not to step on the foul lines—superstitions have been a part of baseball since the catcher used to stand behind the plate and grab the ball on one bounce. More than 30 years ago Yankee great Phil Rizzuto regularly stuck the piece of gum he'd been chewing onto the button on the top of his cap. In 1986 Boston's Wade Boggs ate chicken before every single game.

They do it to get a psychological edge, a little control over all those things beyond their control when they're on the field. It's a way of asking a "higher authority" for help. Now a new way of "asking for help" has come into sports. All of a sudden, God is the Greatest Sports Fan Ever.

The first religion-in-sports story I ever remember hearing involved Waite Hoyt and Joe Dugan while both were with the Yankees. They were walking to Fenway Park one day when Dugan stepped into a church and lit a candle. That afternoon he hit 3-for-4 and the next day 4-for-5. The following day Hoyt went into the church with him and lit enough candles to start a forest fire. Later that day he was knocked out in the third inning.

"How do you explain it?" Hoyt asked Dugan. "You light candles and get a bunch of hits. I do the same thing and get knocked out."

"Easy," Joe said. "I saw you light all those candles in church, but right after you left I saw two gamblers come in and blow them out."

God has been around ballparks and stadiums for a long time as another form of superstition. Players who haven't stepped inside a church since they were altar boys step into the batter's box and are so busy making the sign of the cross you don't know if it's their first at-bat or the beginning of Lent.

Once Tracy Stallard was pitching to Willie Davis when Davis stepped out of the box and crossed himself. Stallard watched, backed off the rubber, then crossed himself and hollered at Davis, "Who's He going to help now?"

When Jimmy Piersall was playing, he'd step into the batter's box, reach across the plate with his bat, and make a cross in the dirt. He did this one day against the Yankees while Yogi was catching.

Yogi watched very patiently, and when Piersall was finished, Yogi came out of his crouch, stepped across home plate, rubbed out the cross, and said, "Why don't you let God just watch the game?"

Now players are more serious about asking God to take an active part in the game. Today, God is a teammate. A lot of players are becoming Christians, and many have been very outspoken about their beliefs. Some, having given their problems and worries to God *off* the field, have decided He can probably help them *on* the field as well. Why not hand Him a batting slump or a losing streak? For many, God has come off the bench and into the lineup as an everyday player. And what used to be superstition or maybe luck is now "God's will."

Baseball Chapel seems to have started the whole thing, and it has definitely added a new dimension to the clubhouse. Watson Spoelstra, a former *Detroit News* sportswriter, started the chapel after promising God he would serve Him the rest of his life if He would save his daughter from a brain hemorrhage. She recovered completely, and the baseball chapel was Spoelstra's way of saying "Thanks."

The chapel is generally a positive addition to the game. Getting to church before the game can be a problem, and the chapel makes it easy. Of course, some players wouldn't go near a church if it was on the room service menu. That hasn't changed for years.

Typical is this story I've heard about the great Yankee manager, Joe McCarthy. His team had just pulled into Philadelphia during a tough road trip. They'd just lost a couple games, and arriving very early in the morning during a bad rainstorm didn't make things any easier. But McCarthy ordered the bus to drop him off at a church so he could go to Mass.

As he got off the bus, he turned and asked, "Anybody else want to go?"

Silence.

Then finally, "No thanks," came a voice from the back of the bus. "I'd rather get some sleep."

So McCarthy walked off alone, and just as the bus started to pull out, the player shouted out the window, "Hey, Joe, I want to ask you a question. What if your guy is wrong? Look at all the sleep you're missing."

Baseball Chapel eliminates the player's excuse that he can't get to church because of bad weather or he can't get up so early in the morning after a night game. The players meet at the ballpark before the game for a nondenominational worship service. The original purpose of the chapel was to provide services for the visiting team, but once chapel leaders found out the local players had just as much trouble getting to church, they started services for them too.

Originally the services featured a motivational talk, and the speakers ranged from prominent Christian businessmen to reformed addicts or former gang leaders. Recently, though, the focus has shifted away from the motivational speakers toward speakers who strongly emphasize the Bible and relate to the players as men first and not primarily as baseball players.

The services are usually well-attended, and like most things in the baseball world, they've led to some good stories.

Pat Kelly, a free-swinging outfielder with the Baltimore Orioles, found himself the target of an Earl Weaver zinger because of the chapel. Kelly's a very friendly, sincere player who married a minister's daughter. Chapel was very important to him.

In this particular game, Kelly was batting with the bases loaded, and he swung at a pitch that could only have been called ball four and forced in a run. Instead, he struck out.

The next day as he was leaving the chapel service, the first person he ran into was his manager, Earl Weaver. With typical Kelly enthusiasm, he said, "Earl, I feel great. I've just left the chapel, and once again I've learned to walk with the Lord."

Weaver just looked at him. "Too bad you didn't learn how to walk with the bases loaded," he snapped. But Kelly didn't give up on Weaver. A few days later he asked him when he'd last read the Bible.

"Aw, I guess maybe I picked it up once or twice this winter," Weaver said.

"When's the last time you really got down on your knees and prayed, Skip?" Kelly wanted to know.

"I'll tell you the last time I got down on my knees and prayed," Weaver shot back. "The last time I sent you up to pinch hit."

The chapel has been a good influence on a lot of players, but when they get too serious about bringing God into the game, it causes problems. Instead of "I took a bad swing" or "I really misjudged the ball," the new expression is "It's God's will."

We were in Montreal to do the "NBC Game of the Week" between the Expos and the Cardinals, and I was talking to the players and coaches, ending up with manager Whitey Herzog. He was giving me a rundown when his catcher, Darrell Porter, walked by.

Whitey pulled him aside and said, "Darrell, I don't care if you strike out every time. I don't care how bad you miss the ball. Swing the bat, just swing the bat. Quit trying to feel for the ball. Just find the damn thing and have a good cut—that's all I want you to do."

Porter waited until Whitey finished and then said, "Don't worry about it; the hits will come. It's the Lord's will."

Whitey replied, "Lord's will? Hey Darrell, let me tell you something. The Lord knows a lot about a lotta things, but He don't know a damn thing about hitting." The gospel according to Herzog.

Whitey's not against religion in the clubhouse. He just

doesn't want his players to use it as a crutch if things go wrong or allow it to take away from their aggressiveness.

One spring he hired the Reverend Andrew Jumper of Central Presbyterian Church in Clayton, Missouri, to come to spring training to support the players with advice and weekly services. Reverend Jumper knew exactly who was really swinging the bat on the field. A player came up to him after a service and said, "God gave you a great sermon today." "Yes," Reverend Jumper said, "but I want you to know I typed it."

God probably does know something about hitting, but I don't think it's His top priority. I don't think a strikeout with the bases loaded is God's will. Give the pitcher some credit, or maybe you took a bad swing. And if it's both, then it's certainly not God's will; it's a slump. I grew up going to Catholic schools, but I still believe an hour or so in the batting cage with a hitting coach will help more than lighting a dozen candles and making a novena. I just can't believe with all the problems available to Him, God is worried about whether a baseball player strikes out or a football player catches a pass.

A few seasons ago, the Seattle Mariners' management felt the chapel was causing some strain among its players. General manager Dick Balderson felt some of the players were falling back on God as the reason for their immediate success or failure—especially failure. He said that too many players believed a loss was the way the Lord meant it to be.

Several players agreed with Balderson that others weren't getting fired up enough, that being Christian was keeping them from getting mad or physical and was giving them an excuse for making mistakes. They sensed an "If we lose, we lose; if we win, we win" attitude and felt it was helping them lose.

During the Mariner controversy, team management was accused of equating Christianity with weakness. Dick Balderson said, and I agree, that the issue was not religion, but mental toughness. "I think God would be mad if He got beat," Balderson said, "not 'Well, I did my best, and that's the way it was meant to be.'"

The last word, though, came from Steve Largent, the veteran Seattle Seahawks wide receiver and a regular at pro football's chapel services. Suggesting that decisions by the front office—not religious beliefs—were responsible for the Mariners' losing so many games Largent said, "It doesn't surprise me that the Mariners want to get God out of their locker room. They've gotten rid of all their other good players, too."

The players have their own response to the accusations that they cause morale problems for the team with passive, noncompetitive behavior. When pitcher Gary Lavelle was asked how being a Christian helped him on the field, he said, "Christian athletes can handle a bad day better. They don't go around kicking things. You don't have to come in and break up the clubhouse when you don't do well."

John Werhas, a former major leaguer who now coordinates chapel services for the Los Angeles Dodgers, agrees that being a Christian should make it easier for ballplayers to keep defeats in perspective. But he also says that if being Christian "doesn't add to their aggressiveness, the guys don't understand what the gospel's teaching." Werhas believes it should "make you better at what you do, and if that means getting mad sometimes, do it; let it serve a purpose, get it over with, and put it behind you." Dodger pitcher Orel Hershiser adds simply, "Being a Christian doesn't mean you have to be a wimp."

San Francisco Giants manager Roger Craig agrees. When pitcher Dave Dravecky shut out the St. Louis Cardinals with a two-hitter in the second game of the 1987 League Championship Series, Craig said, "They say Christians don't have any guts. Well, Dave Dravecky's a Christian, knows how to pitch, and he ain't afraid of nothing." Added Dravecky: "What people don't realize is if you put Jesus

Christ in my shoes, He would be the most intense, aggressive performer on the field. He would win every time. As far as I'm concerned, Christians are the most aggressive, intense athletes who perform today."

I don't think there's anything un-Christian about being aggressive or even getting angry occasionally. Says Billy Martin, who should be an expert on the subject by now, "A temper is an asset. If you use it, then it doesn't use you. The good Lord had a temper. Christ says you have to be aggressive in your job."

I don't know exactly where He said that, but He showed more than once He knew how to get mad. What about in the temple, when He tore the place up and threw out the people buying and selling? If Jesus had been a big-league manager and blown a doubleheader, He might have tipped over the food table in the clubhouse just like He turned over the tables of the money changers and the sellers.

God is everywhere, including the ballparks and stadiums; I just don't think He has a bat in His hand or is dropping back to throw a pass. Watching, yes; playing, no. God has given us all skills. He's interested in what we do with them. I don't think He's interested in who wins the game. I do remember a day, though, when I felt He really helped me.

Things were going along pretty normally for me—I hadn't played in about 10 days. I had done everything but call "Dial-a-Prayer." Then one afternoon in the clubhouse meeting, our manager, Eddie Dyer, named the starting lineup against sidearm pitcher Ewell Blackwell, and I was in it. Dyer's logic was to start as many left-handed batters as possible against the right-handed pitching of Blackwell.

Dyer got a kick out of doing me favors like that. He wouldn't let me hit against left-handers like Dave Koslo, Ken Raffensberger, and Johnny Schmitz, although I could have taken some good cuts simply because they didn't throw as hard. But Dyer gave me the "opportunity" to play against right-handers like Blackwell, Newcombe, Sal Maglie, and Robin Roberts because I batted left-handed. This is the kind of logic that makes you decide to go to either air-conditioning school or the broadcast booth.

Blackwell had a way of making right-handed batters feel like he was throwing from behind the third-base coach. Keeping your front foot attached to the rest of your body in the batter's box was a constant battle. Roy Campanella referred to it as the "jelly leg."

Batting from the left side only made it less painful to make an out. So it really didn't make much difference which side you batted from against Blackwell. He was an equal opportunity slump-maker. He made you feel like the guy who was asked which ocean he would prefer to swim across, the Atlantic or the Pacific. Either way, you're going to drown.

So on this bright Sunday afternoon, there I was in the lineup, thinking, "Great, what a break. I'm hitting what, .212 right now? So by the end of the day I should be hitting at least .199."

I walked out of the clubhouse and ran into two close friends, Father Boul and Father Scheffer. Both priests were supreme optimists, and both were hoping I was in the lineup.

"You playing?"

"Yeah, great," I said. "I haven't had a hit since Ash Wednesday, I'm 0-for-16 right now, and with Blackwell pitching, I should be 0-for-20 by 4:30, Central Daylight Savings Time."

"No, no, we've got the answer," they whispered. "Let's go over here for a minute where we can have a little privacy."

We went into the runway leading to the dugout, where Father Boul whipped out a bottle of holy water from Lourdes (which made sense because I figured it would take a miracle for me to hit Blackwell) and started to sprinkle it all over me. Actually, it was more like drenching than sprinkling. I looked like an innocent bystander at a four-alarm fire where the hose broke.

"Straight from Lourdes, that means at least two hits," Father Boul said.

I'd been armed with industrial-strength holy water.

Then Father Scheffer said, "Wait, I've got something, too." He reached into his pocket and took out a crucifix, the big, heavy kind with a screw on the end that you could remove so you could see the relic inside.

"Here, put this in your back pocket. It's got to be good for at least two hits," he promised.

So out I went, as wet as Jacques Cousteau on a good day and armed like a Crusader. "Blackwell doesn't have a chance," I thought. "I just hope somebody warned him."

My first time up, Blackwell threw me a high fastball, which was rare for him. He could throw low strikes to Toulouse-Lautrec. But I nailed it, a line drive into the gap in left-center field, a definite extra-base hit.

I dug hard and took off for second. I could see a double all the way. The throw came in, I went into one of my best tryout camp slides, and reached second sounding like a wounded elephant, bleeding from my pocket to my knees. I had slid on the crucifix. Funny thing, I was safe, the play wasn't even close, and it all looked completely routine. Yet there I was lying on the ground with a six-inch gash in a very bad spot. Everyone's looking around wondering what happened, and I'm wondering, "How're they gonna apply a tourniquet to stop the bleeding?"

Doc Weaver, our trainer, ran out to me and hollered, "What in the world happened?"

To which I gave the honest answer, "God just helped me."

Maybe I have St. Paul to blame for thinking God would help me get a hit off Blackwell. When I was a kid, St. Paul convinced me God was a sports fan.

The two biggest factors in my life then were the church

and baseball. Going to parochial school made it seem like I was spending all my time in church. Lent was always the worst for me because it was right around the beginning of baseball season. I wanted to hear about Joe Medwick, Pepper Martin, Dizzy Dean, and the Cardinals, but I had to listen to Matthew, Mark, Luke, and John instead. I had a tough time keeping my mind on what the "Big Four" were saying because they never wrote about sports. But St. Paul was different. If anybody in the Bible wore a sweatshirt, it was Paul. He was the "jock apostle."

I didn't think he could help me swing the bat any better or kick the soccer ball any harder; it's just that when I heard the priest read from the letters of St. Paul, I thought, "Here's a guy who knows something about sports." After all, he's the one who told Timothy, "I have fought the good fight, I have finished the race. . . ." You could find that on the sports page.

St. Paul wrote a lot of letters, and I always wondered about that. The Corinthians seemed to be his favorites, but I never heard about even one letter *to* Paul *from* the Corinthians. Didn't they ever write back? And what about Timothy? Wouldn't it be great to go to church on Sunday and hear, "Today we have a letter from Timothy to St. Paul. Dear Paul, about that good fight . . ."

When St. Paul wrote to the Romans, he must have been thinking about umpires and referees: "Everyone must submit himself to the governing authorities . . . the authorities that exist have been established by God." Later I met some National League umpires who must have been anointed to the job. At least that's what they told me.

Whenever I'd hear Paul's letter to Timothy advising him to "be prepared in season and out of season," I'd always think of spring training. Paul also wrote to Timothy, "For physical training is of some value. . . ." Hey, if you've got a weight clause in your contract, it's of a lot of value.

St. Paul told the Philippians: "Forgetting what is behind

and straining toward what is ahead, I press on toward the goal to win the prize. . . ." The great philosopher Satchel Paige may have been only paraphrasing St. Paul with one of his famous sayings. In fact, according to some, Satch knew Paul personally and probably told him, "I think my way of saying it is better: 'Don't look back; somebody might be gaining on you.'" If you ask me, I'll take Satchel's version.

I've heard my share of locker room pep talks, but I don't know who got the message across better, St. Paul or Tom Lasorda. Seeing those two names in the same sentence should be enough to send you running. But actually, Lasorda is famous for his one-of-a-kind, fire-and-brimstone speeches.

I don't know what the situation was when St. Paul told his favorite pen pals, the Corinthians, "Do you not know that in a race all the runners run, but only one gets the prize? Run in such a way as to get the prize." I don't know whether they got the prize or not, but they would've been a lock if they'd heard what Lasorda had to say.

Los Angeles was battling Montreal in the League Championship Series in 1981, which the Dodgers eventually won in the fifth game on a two-out, ninth-inning home run by Rick Monday. A long, tough season was finally coming to an end. Everybody was tired, and the Dodgers had had a lot of injuries. So in the clubhouse before the fifth and deciding game, Lasorda began.

"Guys, I know we're coming to the end. Montreal seems to be in a better position to win this game and go on to the World Series. I'm proud of all of you. I'm proud of the way we've fought to get this far. I wish I could think of the proper words to express myself, but I can't."

Dropping his voice lower, he continued, "I will simply quote from the Holy Bible, from Romans, Chapter 26, verses 5 through 7 [Okay, Romans has only 16 chapters, but did the players know that?].

"From tribulation comes strength, and from the depths of

strength comes character. . . ." Raising his voice a few decibels to the Jimmy Swaggart level, Lasorda went on, "and from the depths of character comes hope," and now reaching the volume of Gabriel's horn, he screamed, "and I hope all of you jackasses realize that if we don't win this game, we go home!"

Is God wearing a sweatshirt? The answer depends on whom you ask. Tom Lasorda's long association with the "Big Dodger in the Sky" tells me the Dodgers' manager has a sense of humor when he calls on some extra power from his bench.

Then there are those who want the extra power but feel they have to dress their prayers in batting gloves, shoulder pads, and sneakers. Take a look at this prayer of Niagara University's basketball team before a big game with St. Bonaventure several years ago. It went, in part, like this:

Dear Lord, we dedicate this game to you.
Please regard each dribble as saying "We worship
     you!"
Please regard each assist as saying "We need You and
     our fellow man!"
Please regard each intercepted pass as saying "We be-
     lieve in you!"
. . . each loose ball recovered as saying "To hell with
     you, Satan!"
. . . each blocked shot as saying "We hope in You!"
. . . each personal foul as saying "Forgive us, Lord."
. . . each point scored as saying "We thank You!"

The prayer concluded with "We don't ask for a 'miracle'—just a victory over the Bonnies! Mary, Queen of Victory, pray for us!" By the way, Niagara won the game 80–74.

Pregame invocations have also brought God and the game a lot closer. Years ago a priest or minister would get up and just say a simple prayer. Now they've turned them into speeches, and the idea of sports-as-religion doesn't seem so farfetched.

Like this prayer, said at a football banquet in Alabama several years ago:

> Heavenly Father: When you sent your backline coaches from the Old Testament, and your frontline coaches from the New Testament, into the huddle of human life, we members of the team kept receiving the same signal: "Love the Lord your God with all your being and your neighbor as yourself." Your son, our quarterback, knew the play by heart.
>
> Even though we fumble sometimes, being blitzed and tackled by the devil in such plays as making passes and then holding, we know that if we come to obey the plays as you call them and do our best to carry out our assignments, the whole stadium of angels will finally cheer as we cross the stripe of death with the precious touchdown of a holy life. Help us Lord, to carry the ball. Amen.

Or what about this invocation given before the American Zone finals of tennis's Davis Cup matches? Father George Tribou asked God to "Grant to the referee, the linesmen, and the umpires sharpness of vision and fairness of judgment that they may see from the sides with the same clarity with which You will be watching from above." I like that prayer because it doesn't ask God to take sides. If we're going to make Him a fan, let's at least make Him impartial.

I don't think I've ever gone to Mass during a World Series that I didn't hear the priest pray for "our team." What if you're a player on the visiting team attending that Mass? What do you do during that prayer, ask for equal time or call a time-out?

When it comes to asking God for help during a game, the fans don't hesitate to use Him as some kind of cosmic lucky charm. Like the enthusiastic congregation of a church in Boulder, Colorado, that ended its service on Super Bowl Sunday in 1987 by "toasting" the Broncos with glasses of Orange Crush while praying and "blessing the Broncos to victory."

Before that game, Denver head coach Dan Reeves was asked if he thought it was out of line for fans to pray for a win. "I just don't think God chooses sides," he said. "At least I hope God doesn't choose sides. After all, they [the New York Giants] may have even more people praying than we do."

Penn State coach Joe Paterno tells a great story about the power of prayer. Penn State was in Miami getting ready for the Orange Bowl game against Kansas, and Paterno was talking with Green Bay coach Vince Lombardi and Pittsburgh Steelers owner Art Rooney. That might sound like a Football Hall of Fame meeting, but actually they were discussing the impact of prayer and religion on their lives.

Rooney said he felt especially fortunate because he was able to buy the Steelers for practically nothing. But of course he had an "edge," he added, since his brother was a priest and his two sisters were nuns.

"Wait a minute," Paterno told them. "My mother's got something going with prayer, too. Listen to this. We're on a big winning streak, and my mother listens to every game, but if we're losing, she goes into the bathroom with her rosary. She won't come out until my brother tells her that we're leading. Does it work? For 18 games she hasn't been in the bathroom when she hears the final score."

Then came the Orange Bowl game. As Paterno tells it, "Kansas had the lead for most of the game, so I know where my mother is, and I know where our streak is going. But with a minute to go we score to make it 14–13, Kansas still leading. I decide to go for the win, so we try for the two points, but we don't make it. But wait, my mother must have been working overtime, because Kansas has 12 men on the field, they get a penalty, and we get another chance. We go for the two points again, and this time we make it to win the game and keep the streak alive.

"The next day I get a telegram from Art Rooney, and it reads: 'Congratulations. I'll trade you my brother and two sisters for your mother, straight up.'"

Some fans don't just pray, they make a TV career out of bringing God to the ballpark. The "designated preacher" has made John 3:16 famous. I mean, who hasn't seen that sign at every sporting event in America? Some think it's John Madden's weight, some think it's the time left on the clock, but most think it's a nuisance. I first noticed those signs because of the hairstyle on the guy who held them. His hair was all frizzed out to about 16 inches in diameter and dyed different colors. He looked like he'd had a hair transplant from the NBC peacock.

He was everywhere. At baseball games he was behind home plate so the center-field camera couldn't miss him. He was behind the golfer who was putting and behind the golfer on the tee. Wherever the camera was, so was "John 3:16." I was convinced there were at least a hundred of them. One person couldn't be in that many places.

During the 1986 World Series, the Mets vs. the Red Sox, "John 3:16" set a record for most appearances by anything in a seven-game series. A whole *team* of sign-holders was there, and what a system they had. High-tech religion had invaded the stands. Stationed behind both dugouts, with portable TVs so they always knew what the camera was showing, they were ready. With a right-handed batter, the first-base camera had the shot, and up would pop "John 3:16" on the third-base side. With a left-handed batter the routine would reverse. The only time I didn't see "John 3:16" on the screen was when the parachutist landed on the infield. And when I saw him coming over the fence, I half expected to see "John 3:16" written across his parachute.

John 3:16—"For God so loved the world that He gave

His only begotten Son, that those who believe in Him may not perish, but may have everlasting life." It's a beautiful message being turned into a gimmick by people who want to get on TV, like streakers or Morganna, "The Kissing Bandit."

I agree with the Dodgers' John Werhas, who thinks the messenger is overshadowing the message. Werhas says, "I'll try to tell guys, 'Do you know what it says in John 3:16?' and they'll say, 'Oh you mean that guy that holds up the sign at the ballpark? I don't want to hear about it.'"

For the fans, the "John 3:16" sign is annoying. I don't think it's going to make anybody run out to buy a Bible and suddenly turn to religion. And just as I don't think players should try to give God an active role on the field, I don't think "John 3:16" signs belong at the ballpark. Can you imagine going to church and holding up a sign that says "Let's Go Mets"?

What these rainbow-heads need is a sense of humor. I once saw a sign that read "Jesus Saves," and underneath someone had added "at the Chase Manhattan Bank." Or how about this one, where the message on the billboard said, "You must pay for your sins," and below was written, "If you have already paid, please disregard this notice." My favorite is one I saw on my way to Yankee Stadium. "Who is Jesus?" the sign asked. Underneath was written "Matty Alou's brother."

To some players, God is never in the losing locker room. Listening to interviews with the winners of a big game, you wonder if you made a wrong turn and ended up in a church revival meeting. Players thank God for all the gifts He's given them, including a crucial interception or a game-winning home run.

I appreciate those feelings, but I'm not sure they belong in a locker room. How should the losing team feel? Did God give them second-rate gifts? I believe God is in both locker rooms, but I think if He had to choose, He'd pick the losing one. Writer Lewis Grizzard said it best: "Losing hurts more than winning feels good." I think the Lord would be where the hurt is.

Besides, if prayers really helped teams win, clubs like the Saints, the Cardinals, the Padres, and the Friars would have the edge. Take care of your own, right?

God goes to the ballparks and the stadiums—that's for sure. The desperation pass is called the "Hail Mary," and everybody understands the meaning. Get the pass interference call, and the "prayer is answered." Could there be a more perfect description for the tipped pass caught by the Steelers' Franco Harris in the 1972 AFC Championship Game than the "Immaculate Reception"?

If you think about it, I'll bet you've even seen a miracle-healing at the ballpark. How many times have you seen a batter foul a ball off his foot and slump to the ground in great pain? Everybody from his agent to the trainer to a visiting nurse gathers around him to help him limp back into the batter's box. On the next pitch he tops the ball, and with a base hit in sight there's no limp now—he's flying down the baseline. A miracle.

Did I pray when I played? Yes, I think most players did, usually during the National Anthem. For me it was a time to meditate, a quiet moment when I would ask God to keep me from injury and let me do my best. I think most players today ask for the same things.

Since prayer and belief in God are so personal, I can easily understand how players, coaches, and fans occasionally let a prayer slip out for that base hit that'll win the World Series or a field goal that'll win the Super Bowl. But when it comes to a strikeout, an error, or a slump being God's will, then I think He's taking Yogi's advice and just watching the game.

"I picked up the phone, and all I heard was a series of clicks. Click . . . click . . . click . . . I imagined it had something to do with a sophisticated phone system at the White House. The I realized my wife and and kids were picking up every extension in the house so they could hear my conversation with the president firsthand."

O

5

It's the White House Calling

"CHEET-A-DEEN." That's the way my pop would say it in his Lombard dialect.

"Cheet-a-deen." That's the phonetic spelling for what my pop wanted to be.

Cittadino is the true Italian spelling. *Citizen* is the way we spell it in America.

In school we studied George Washington and Abraham Lincoln. On the streets we heard and read about Franklin Roosevelt. But the big political man in our lives was Midge Berra (no relation), the 24th ward alderman. We knew if Pop needed help he would go to Midge.

Giovanni Garagiola was a laborer who didn't speak English. That language barrier had a powerful effect on his life. It made him go to work when he was sick even though he should have stayed home. He was afraid he'd be fired if he didn't show up and afraid he wouldn't be able to get another job because he didn't speak English. My father did speak two other languages, though: Italian and straightforward. Like all immigrants, he appreciated the American political system and what it stood for. In our neighborhood, Midge Berra was the key to that system. Men like FDR and Harry Truman were idols to my father, but Midge Berra was a reality.

When people tell me they grew up in a neighborhood like mine, I always ask if they knew who their alderman was. That's the yardstick. In a neighborhood with a big immigrant population, the alderman is the relief pitcher, the guy you go to when you need help.

Pop came to America in 1911. He arrived with a sign around his neck that read "St. Louis." Several years passed before he could save enough money to send for Momma.

Sam Levenson, one of my favorite comedians, tells a story that reminds me a lot of my pop. Levenson says his father came to America because people told him the streets were paved with gold. When his pop arrived, he found out not only were the streets *not* paved with gold, but they weren't paved at all, and everybody expected him to do the job.

The only memories I have of my pop and politics are the "political discussions" he had with our neighbor, Mr. Columbo. This was during the Depression, so Roosevelt was the hero and Hoover got the blame for everything, including the wine-making grapes going sour.

My pop loved this country. America promised him opportunity and kept that promise. He was able to buy a house and raise a family. He saw his "children's children," and that's all he wanted from life.

Though he didn't live to see many of the good things that have happened to me (he died in 1962), he did share several wonderful moments with me. He saw me break into baseball and play in a World Series. And he saw his son appear on TV with an arm around a former president of the United States.

Now, it's not like I had a hotline to Washington. In fact, in those days I didn't have much contact with politicians at all, only those few who made an occasional visit to the broadcast booth to say hello to their "dear friend," Harry Caray. Almost every one I met asked me if I could get a ball autographed by Stan Musial. Occasionally I ran into Midge Berra the alderman, who always wanted to know how his "cousin" Yogi was doing. Once Yogi became a Yankee he picked up all kinds of relatives.

During this time, broadcasting baseball games was just part of my job, a "summer" job so to speak. In the winter, it was luncheons, dinners, or whatever Cardinal owner Gussie Busch needed. Stan Musial may have been a valuable piece of merchandise in Gussie's game plan, but he came in second to the Anheuser-Busch beer distributor.

At one of Gussie's dinners, I wound up experiencing one of the great moments of my life. Senator John Kennedy was campaigning for the presidency in 1960, and a dinner had been arranged in his honor in St. Louis. Gussie Busch was the dinner chairman, which meant a command performance for everybody but the Clydesdale horses. An appearance was not just mandatory; it fell into the category of job security.

A few days before the dinner, Al Fleishman, the man who handled Anheuser-Busch's public relations, called me into his office and told me he had a "protection plan" of which I was to be a major part.

"If for any reason Senator Kennedy is late," he said, "we can't just let the people sit there. We're after campaign contributions, and we don't want people to be upset when we ask them for money. So I want you to be ready. We'll pull you out of the audience, and you'll come up and fill in until the senator arrives." His plan sounded simple, at least to him. I wasn't so sure.

"Fill? With what?" I asked.

"There'll be a lot of sports fans there, so do your usual

thing for as long as it takes to get Kennedy to the microphone. We may not need you, but I want you to be prepared," he said.

"Okay, I'll be ready," I said, grateful for the warning. I just figured that with more than 2,000 people at the dinner, Kennedy would be on time.

When the big night came I was ready, although I wasn't expecting anything out of the ordinary to happen. I was having a great time when suddenly I heard Mr. Busch begin an introduction. Then I realized he was introducing me, and within two seconds there was a major hockey game going on in the pit of my stomach. I was prepared, but that didn't make it any easier. The room was jam-packed; I'd played doubleheaders in Pittsburgh with Bing Crosby singing the National Anthem that didn't draw as big a crowd. All the political powerhouses were there—three tiers of them to the side of me and behind me. And out in front of me were the "folks."

I launched into my speech, and after about 10 minutes, just about the time I started to relax, I remembered that Pop was watching on television. He wasn't able to do much else by that time. He was on his way out and we knew it.

Harry Truman was one of his heroes, and here I was standing right next to him. The problem was, I wasn't sure Pop could see him because the close-up shot was on me, and in the wide shot President Truman was lost in the crowd. Then I got an idea. When the thought first struck me I put it out of my mind, but then it came back, and I asked myself, "Why not? Do It." So I did.

Suddenly I said, "Mr. President, would you stand up here next to me?" He did. "Senator Symington, would you mind standing up next to the president?" He did. The crowd was baffled. You could almost hear them asking themselves what I was doing. "Governor, would you stand next to me on the other side?" He did. "Mr. Mayor, would you please stand next to the governor?" He did. Then I put one arm around President Truman and the other around Governor Dalton, looked right into the camera, and said, "Hey, Pop, I just want you to see who I'm hanging around with."

The room split with laughter. For the price of being a blowout patch, I had pulled one off for Pop. When Senator Kennedy finally arrived, I was yanked off the podium faster than Leo Durocher yanked a pitcher who'd given up five runs. But I didn't care. When I went to see Pop the next day, it was as if he had made a quick trip to Lourdes. He slowly got up out of his chair, put his arms around me, and couldn't wait to talk about the banquet. All he could say was he saw me with my arm around President Truman and he couldn't believe it.

He was so proud, his heart was filled to overflowing, and the big, happy, gumdrop tears began to fall. Here was this huge man, more than six feet tall with hands like snow shovels, fighting and losing a battle against an enemy that was shrinking him daily, weakening those once-powerful hands; here he was crying happy tears and trying to explain his overwhelming feelings. I was thrilled to have done something that meant so much to him, thrilled he was able to see it and to share it with me.

Not until the late 1960s, when I was a host on NBC's "Today" show, did I find myself again in the company of politicians. Being a host on one of television's most prestigious programs seemed to put me on the mailing list for state dinners. President Lyndon B. Johnson was in office when I received my first invitation, addressed to me at NBC, 30 Rockefeller Plaza, New York, NY. I figured it was just another letter until I saw, embossed in gold lettering in the upper left-hand corner, "The White House." When I opened it, I sat back, read it, then reread it. I guess I thought White House invitations were different; maybe a fancy letter delivered by a Secret Service agent while the Marine Band played "Stars and Stripes Forever." When it finally sank in, I let out a yelp, then called Audrie, and I must have sounded like an auctioneer because she had to slow me down to figure out what I was saying. We had seven days to get ready for the dinner, so guess what we talked about for the next seven days and nights?

In spite of all our planning we were still nervous, but once we arrived at the White House, everything was so well orchestrated I realized it would be impossible to do anything wrong. You went through all the procedures dictated by protocol. You were met at the door and escorted upstairs. You went through a receiving line and were introduced to the president and first lady. You were given a card with a number on it that told you not only where to sit but also who was sitting with you.

I'll never forget the first time I heard the band play "Ruffles and Flourishes" and a voice announce, "The President of the United States," followed by "Hail to the Chief." Believe me, you get terminal goose bumps. When the president walks into the room, the man you've seen every day on TV and in the papers, you stop to realize who he is and where you are, and it's staggering. Like Audrie said, "It's like a painting that suddenly comes alive; the characters start moving and walking off the canvas."

The invitation plainly said, "On the occasion of the visit of His Excellency, The Prime Minister of the Somali Republic and Mrs. Egal," but I really didn't pay any attention to whom the dinner was for until it was almost over, because I was so excited and so busy looking around to see who was there. I was trying to relax and act like I was having dinner at a friend's house, but that's tough. When they set the tables with the Truman and Wilson china, you know you're not at McDonald's. And the guest list doesn't exactly read like a roster of first-base coaches: Chief Justice Earl Warren, Vice President Hubert Humphrey, Secretary of State Dean Rusk, Sammy Cahn, Kitty Carlisle, Barbara

Rush—140 people were invited, according to the official list that I still treasure.

The menu sounded great—Consommé au Quenelles, Rack of Lamb Persillés, Cauliflower au Gratin, Broiled Tomatoes, Green Salad, and Mousse Shukri. The only thing I was sure about was "Green Salad," although I think I might have been on the same team with Mousse Shukri. Anyway, Catcher's Mitt Sauté would have tasted great to me that night.

After dinner, a marine guard quietly approached us to say the president wanted us to join him and a small group of people in a private room for coffee. And at the appointed hour the president and first lady left. It was a very formal, highly organized affair.

One of the more relaxed White House affairs I attended was the All-Star luncheon in 1969. President Richard Nixon was a big baseball fan, so I was at first surprised by how stilted and forced his "official remarks" seemed. Later I realized they were probably written by somebody else, because he was completely different as the All-Stars went through the receiving line. He had obviously watched a lot of games, and he won the guys over with his casual remarks. He told me he'd seen me hit a home run while I was with the Cubs. I knew he had to have watched that on TV, because in those days there were as many people in the stands as there were on the field. And, I might add, they got their money's worth because we almost always played the bottom of the ninth.

Being invited to the White House is an honor, no matter who's in office. To sit at a table with the president, Muhammad Ali, and King Hussein and his queen is like a fairy tale. But the state dinner I enjoyed the most was the last one given by President Gerald Ford and his wife, Betty. Since he was leaving office, this last state dinner was more like a big farewell party. Protocol seemed less important than sharing the evening with friends and longtime associates and having a good time.

The evening meant a lot to me because I was able to share it with two of my closest friends, Jack Paar and Yogi Berra. Although Jack had been very close to the Kennedys, he had never been invited to a state dinner. Once he almost made it to the "hollowed halls" of the White House, but not quite. His friend Pierre Salinger, President Kennedy's press secretary, had taken Jack to his office to wait to meet the president. While waiting, Salinger was showing Jack the ticker tape machine he had set up in his bathroom. But while they were admiring the machine, word came that the president had to leave immediately. Jack Paar's trip to the Kennedy White House never made it beyond Pierre Salinger's toilet.

So it was quite a day when the Paars, the Berras, and the Garagiolas set out to be entertained at the White House. Jack and Yogi's planning would have made a great army training film. Eisenhower during the invasion of Normandy couldn't have covered details like these two:

"What are you going to say to him when you see him, Yogi?" Jack wanted to know.

" 'Hello, Mr. President,' I guess, and if he wants to talk baseball, we'll talk."

"Tell me some baseball in case he wants to talk baseball to me," Jack said.

"He won't talk baseball to you, Jack," Yogi answered.

"Okay, that's right. Now, what time do you think we should start to get ready? You think we'll have any problem getting in, Joe?"

"No, they have our names at the gate, and we have a limo, and the driver will know exactly where to go," I reassured him.

"What if I forget my invitation?" If you're ever too busy to worry, give Jack Paar a call. He's a professional worrier.

This day he was so nervous he could have threaded a sewing machine while it was running.

As *The Washington Star* reported the next day, "Ostensibly in honor of visiting Italian Prime Minister Giulio Andreotti, the White House dinner last night turned into a farewell bash for (and by) the Gerald Fords."

What a night it was. Tony Orlando sang, Pearl Bailey sang, Johnny Bench sang, Rod McKuen sang; Peter Graves played the saxophone, and everybody danced all night. Pearl Bailey was teaching the Fords how to do the hustle, and Jack Paar had his arm around his friend Jerry. At previous state dinners given by Presidents Johnson and Nixon, I always made a note of the time the first family left. This night set the record: 2:03 A.M. It was quite a bash.

But actually, I'm getting ahead of my story. This one really begins, oddly enough, on a golf course. A lot of important things that happened to me after I stopped playing baseball seemed to have begun on a golf course.

I never played golf when I was a ballplayer. It wasn't that I thought golf might have a negative effect on my baseball ability; I just never got around to playing. Once on a road trip into New York, Yogi asked me if I was playing any golf on off days. That's when I realized why I hadn't taken up the game. The kind of teams I played for always took batting practice on off days.

Actually, hardly any teams work out on off days in September, because the contenders want to conserve their energy and the bad teams know by then they're not going anywhere. When I was with the Cubs, I got into trouble for publicly stating I thought it'd be a good idea to take batting practice the last week of the season because we didn't want to let overconfidence cause us to blow seventh place.

But anyway, back to the golf course at the beginning of this story. I was invited to play in a pro-am tournament in Hilton Head, South Carolina. The people in charge of pro-am events don't really care how you play if you're a professional athlete or in the movies or television. If you're in the "celebrity" category, all you need to do is show up. The way most of us in that category play, our golf clubs should be registered at police headquarters as dangerous weapons.

After playing in a few of these pro-ams, I knew the routine. The first thing I'm supposed to do is walk over to the putting green and practice missing a few putts. Usually it's pretty crowded, but on this particular day, only one other player was there: Gerald Ford.

Not long before, Spiro Agnew had resigned and Ford had become vice president, an instant world leader. No one knew then that Watergate would soon bring about Richard Nixon's resignation and Ford would become president, thrust into office during one of this country's greatest periods of turmoil.

But on this day he was just practicing his putting, with all these guys in dark suits standing around watching him. (I thought he was getting a lot of attention for a guy just trying to knock in four-footers.) I watched him for a moment, then I walked over and said, "How're you doin'? Can I putt with you?"

"Sure, why not," he replied. He wanted to talk about the Detroit Tigers, and I just wanted to talk, so I could tell people I had spoken to the vice president. Our conversation wasn't long, it certainly wasn't profound, and soon he left to play with his foursome. I didn't see him again at Hilton Head. I figured our brief conversation would be the extent of my influence on national politics.

A few months later, in August of 1974, Gerald Ford became president. Then in July of 1976 I received a telephone call from the White House. "The president is going to the All-Star game in Philadelphia and he would like you to join him. Can you make it?" You can bet I didn't bother to check my calendar. So from putting with the vice president I had been promoted to going to the ballgame with the president.

"Ernie Banks is going," I was told, "and also a couple of newspaper reporters. White House security will have your name at the guardhouse, and they'll direct you from there. Be at the White House by 5:30 P.M. so you can be helicoptered from the South Lawn." Then they added casually, "You know, you're one of the only people outside the residence to be 'coptered from the lawn."

Well, I knew this had to be important because I'd never been " 'coptered" from the South Lawn—or anywhere else for that matter. And I'd definitely be there by 5:30 because I was planning to leave the hotel at 8:00 in the morning. Never mind that I was two miles from the White House; I didn't want to hit bad traffic.

The day of the All-Star game I arrived at the White House security gate at 4:00 in the afternoon. The security guards directed me to a press room, with telephones all around and dozens of chairs. My attempt to make it look like this kind of thing happened to me every day must not have worked; soon I had two people showing me where to sit, where to wait, and telling me they would let the appropriate people know I was there. Not that I minded the wait. In fact, I was wishing somebody from my old neighborhood would pass by so they could see who I was hanging around with *now*.

Soon I was taken to the back entrance of the White House, where I sat waiting, holding the baseball I'd brought to get autographed by President Ford for my daughter, Gina. This was going to be like any other trip to the ballpark, except I was going with the president of the United States.

Finally President Ford walked into the waiting room, and it was as if a history book had fallen open. Suddenly it sank in: this wasn't just the guy I'd been putting with at Hilton Head or was planning a night at the ballpark with. This was the *president*, like Lincoln and Washington. Then he put out his hand, gave me a big, friendly smile, and with that, the history book closed and I felt like I was just going to the ballgame with a regular fan.

We took our seats in the helicopter, Ernie Banks and I sitting up front with the president. The engines started, and we lifted off the ground, with a lighter-than-air sensation that matched how I'd been feeling all day.

Before long the three of us were talking baseball, and Ernie had the president completely convinced it was a good day to play two. We told one Cub story after another, and the president enjoyed each one more than the last. Of course, being a Michigan native made him a Tiger fan, so he wanted to hear everything we knew about Mark "The Bird" Fydrich, whom he'd never seen play in person. Trying to describe "The Bird's" antics and gyrations was a story in itself, and the Tigers' highest-ranking fan loved it.

As usual with the presidential party, there was no waiting. When the helicopter touched down, cars were standing by to rush us to Veterans Stadium. The motorcade traveled a constant 30 miles per hour, and as crowds lined the streets along the route, the president waved continuously from the airport to the ballpark.

At the park's entrance, a huge crowd was awaiting our arrival. I couldn't wait for someone I knew to see me. Our car pulled up to the gate, and there, preparing to officially greet the president, was baseball commissioner Bowie Kuhn. I had to be the last person he expected to see getting out of the car. Kuhn opened the car door all smiles, and when he saw me step out, the expression on his face was . . . well, it was the same one I saw on Eddie Dyer's face in Brooklyn when he found himself in a tough spot in the ninth inning and discovered he had only one pinch hitter left—me. And as I hurried past the commissioner with Ernie and the president, I couldn't help gloating a little.

We went upstairs to a private room where a very private cocktail party was in progress. VIPs were elbow to elbow, each one jockeying for position to say hello to the president, shake hands, or get a ball signed. Husbands were setting up screens that would have made Red Auerbach proud, just to give their wives the chance to be introduced. I got a kick out of watching the "big guys" try to get next to the Big Guy.

Right now I couldn't tell you the score of that game—I'd have to look it up. But I have dozens of other memories of that night, a kaleidoscope of warm, sometimes funny, always genuine moments, particularly all the military personnel, the lieutenants, captains, majors, and—I've convinced myself—a few generals, too, saluting as we walked to and from the helicopter. Of course I pretended it was all for me, and I imagined myself getting even for all the PFCs in World War II who had to wait 18 months for a presidential order before being promoted from the rank of private. "Salute, soldier!" I wanted to holler.

I remember President Ford throwing out the "first balls," one right-handed to Johnny Bench and one left-handed to Thurman Munson. I remember the world-leader-turned-baseball-analyst asking how Cesar Cedeño could generate any power with his hands so high on the bat, and Cedeño answering the question a few pitches later with a home run. I remember how the most powerful figure in the country greeted the players in the clubhouse after the game, so genuinely happy to meet them, like a kid taking inventory, checking to make sure they were the same guys he had on his bubble-gum cards. And the simplicity of Mark Fydrich, asking the question any normal red-blooded American young man would ask a president: "How about fixing me up with your daughter?"

Flying back into Washington on the return trip, I sat across from the president, and there were two round windows behind him. Over his left shoulder I saw the Washington Monument and, a moment later, the Capitol dome. I expected to hear the "Battle Hymn of the Republic" and "America the Beautiful," and I was ready either to join up or buy savings bonds when all of a sudden I heard "Happy Birthday to you! . . ." Ron Nessen, Ford's press secretary and definitely not a singer, had a cake and was leading all of us in an impromptu song for the president, whose birthday was the next day.

When we landed, I was genuinely sorry to see the night end. As we stepped from the helicopter, the president spotted his wife and daughter on the balcony overlooking the lawn. "Hey look, Betty and Susan are still up," he said, waving to them and calling, "Be there in a minute."

Standing on the lawn, I kept thinking, "I don't believe this. I'm standing here with the president on his lawn, and there's nobody from the neighborhood to see me." I don't know what I expected—this was a big event for me, but he was just going home to his family. I knew I wouldn't see George Washington chopping down cherry trees or Abraham Lincoln splitting rails, but I at least thought Congress might be there to say good night. Instead, he was just like any other family man coming home—except home was the White House.

The car to take me back to the hotel was waiting in the driveway. The president put his arm around my shoulder and said, "Hey, that was great. Let's do it again."

"Well, I think I could work it into my schedule," I said.

As I lay in bed that night, like a kid I replayed the whole evening over in my mind many times. I never imagined I'd get that close to a president for even a moment, and there I was at a ballgame with him. I kept reminding myself to enjoy the memory because I knew it wouldn't happen again. At least that's what I thought in July of 1976.

On the morning of October 20, I was awakened suddenly by my wife, Audrie. She was very excited.

"Wake up, wake up," she said, shaking me. "It's the White House calling. The president wants to talk to you."

"Tell him to ask Henry Kissinger to solve his problem this time," I grunted, figuring it was some kind of joke.

"No," she said, in an absolute panic. "IT *IS* THE PRESIDENT . . . *wake up, it's him*!"

I picked up the phone, and all I heard was a series of clicks. Click . . . click . . . click . . . I imagined it had something to do with a sophisticated phone system at the White House. Then I realized my wife and kids were picking up every extension phone in the house so they could hear the conversation firsthand.

After a brief hello, the president became very serious. "I want to ask you a very important, personal favor," he said. "We have an extensive program outlined for appearances around the country during the last 10 days of the election campaign. It will involve quite a bit of television coverage, and in our discussions about who should moderate these programs, your were our choice. Will you do it?"

I was overwhelmed, first with the question and then with all the possible ramifications if I said yes.

"Mr. President, I'm flattered," I said, "but I may have some problems with it. I'll have to talk it over with the people at NBC first."

"I understand," he said. "I know what's involved and what I'm asking." Certainly he knew a lot of well-known people prefer not to antagonize any of their "public" by taking political stands. I told him I would discuss it with my bosses at NBC and call someone on his staff as soon as I had my answer.

"No," he said, "don't call my staff. Call me. I'll tell them to put you through right away."

I had to laugh, thinking of the time I asked Leo Durocher if I was in the lineup and he didn't even answer me. And he was sitting right next to me. Now I could get through to the president of the United States on the phone.

The excitement was still running high when my family and I sat down together to discuss our options. Although we realized that my taking a political stand beside Gerald Ford could open us up to a lot of criticism, we agreed I should do it. My next step was to call NBC.

They weren't exactly enthusiastic. While nobody at the network ever told me not to do it, they didn't make any secret of the fact they would have been much happier if I hadn't. Their attitude was clear: "We can't stop you, but you know there are just as many Democrats as Republicans out there, and the minute you join up, you know what you'll be getting into." I told them I realized all that, but still, it was something I wanted to do. I felt I knew Gerald Ford, and I believed in him.

NBC wasn't the only corporation with a stake in my political beliefs. I was doing commercials for Dodge at the time, so I felt I also had to consult the Chrysler Corporation. The American automobile business was in a tailspin, and I wasn't sure how they'd feel about my taking a visible political stand. I called Bob McCurry, a vice president at Dodge with whom I had a strong personal relationship.

"Bob, President Ford has asked me to campaign with him. I realize that not only Republicans buy cars, so I wouldn't do this without first getting your feelings about it."

"I think you ought to do it," he said, "but I'll run it by the right people here and get back to you."

A short time later he called back. "Go ahead and do it. Just make damn sure he wins so we can get this automobile business back where it belongs," he added with a chuckle.

I've since wondered what I would have done if either or both had said a firm "no." I guess it would have depended on their reasoning and how strongly they felt. Still, I probably would have done it anyway. I believed in Gerald Ford and what he stood for. I also knew he was offering me an opportunity I would have regretted passing up.

I called the president—I did get right through to him—and told him I was honored to be part of his team. I was told to fly to California for our first meeting, where John

Deardourff, who was in charge of the advertising campaign, met me at the airport. He drove me to the hotel, where I met with the people who would shape those next few exciting days for me: President Ford, his chief of staff, Dick Cheney, and Deardourff. They outlined the plan.

We were to travel to the major cities in the eight most populous states, states that accounted for more than three-fourths of the electoral votes needed to win the election. Added to these stops were nine other states in which the polls showed President Ford had a good chance of beating Jimmy Carter. In the large states crucial to his election—California, Illinois, Pennsylvania, Ohio, New York, and Texas—I would be the host of a 30-minute television program to be broadcast statewide.

The TV programs, taped just before they'd go on the air, would show highlights of President Ford's campaign appearances during the day, followed by a question and answer session. The questions would come from a panel made up of former Democratic congresswoman Edith Green, a well-known Republican with statewide or regional political clout at each stop (such as former Texas governor John Connally or Senator Charles Percy in Illinois), and me, who would also act as moderator.

Throughout this first meeting, I was impressed by the president's low-key firmness and control. He never raised his voice or talked down to anyone. He was never indecisive. He never said, "Maybe we should try this," but always "We'll do it this way." When the meeting was over, we had a chance to talk briefly. He thanked me, saying he'd never forget my willingness to help him.

Later that night, before he left his hotel room for an appearance, we talked as he dressed. I'll never forget the look of genuine sadness that came over his face at one point. He looked at me and said, "Isn't this something? I have to put this on." He wasn't complaining about the tuxedo. He was talking about his bulletproof vest.

Just a year before, in September 1975, two assassination attempts just two weeks apart in California made an ever-present danger all too real. He accepted the inevitable vest with calm resignation. Wearing it didn't anger or frighten him. It just made him sad.

The next evening we went to the studio to tape the first show. We had to tape it twice because the president became so involved in the discussion he didn't leave enough time for his closing remarks. After the show aired, I was accused by one newspaper of "tossing big, fat, slow questions, right across the plate." Guilty as charged. That's what I was supposed to do, help the president talk about the issues in an informal, conversational way. These weren't news shows or even interview shows, but paid political advertisements. That message appeared at the end of each show so viewers would have no doubt they were watching a political "commercial." I wasn't asked to be part of the Ford team to put the president on the hot seat, especially not on a television program he was paying for himself. I wasn't there to pitch a no-hitter; I was there to throw batting practice. I was there to be the caddy, to tee the ball up high and let him smack it as far as he could.

After the first couple of days I adjusted to the hectic pace of traveling with the president. It's an interesting, exciting, and exhausting experience. Everything was kept in the strictest order, from our complicated itineraries to who sat in which seat on the plane. When we ate a meal, we signed a voucher as part of an accounting of campaign fund expenditures. And the telephone service aboard *Air Force One* is even better than you'd see in a movie. They asked me to call Johnny Bench about appearing at a rally in Cincinnati. Without his phone number, I picked up the phone, told the White House operator to get me Johnny Bench in Cincinnati, and before the receiver was back in the cradle he was on the line.

There were several speechwriters on each trip, continually submitting ideas to the president about what subjects he should discuss in each television appearance. He made the final decisions, told me what questions he wanted to answer, and I put them into my own words.

When the speechwriters worked on a speech, they could anticipate the impact it would have. Sometimes they knew it would create a lot of interest and attention. "This one will get some headlines," they'd say. Sometimes they knew the opposite would be true.

I remember their confidence in a particular speech the president made in Pennsylvania, in which he distinguished his administration from the Watergate scandal and talked of how he'd led the nation in "an incredible comeback." They were sure it would grab a lot of headlines, and it did.

The writers were continually channeling ideas and rough drafts to "Passkey." I thought he was the head writer until someone told me "Passkey" was President Ford's Secret Service code name. Everyone had a code name: Betty Ford was "Pinafore," Susan Ford was "Panda," David Kennerly, the family's official photographer and one of my favorite guys, was "Hot-Shot." Even I had a code name. No doubt in recognition of my ability to hit with such power in my playing days, my name was "Ballbuster."

When *Air Force One* would land in a new city, the president would always ask me to come up to the front and stand beside him before he got off the plane. I think it was a sort of "breather" for him before facing the crowds and the glare of the press. We didn't discuss the campaign or the issues or anything very serious. We just talked. Soon he'd be down those airplane steps, with politicians and dignitaries waiting for him, along with a huge crowd anxious to see their president wave and smile.

Once we were on the ground, we didn't waste any time. While he would say hello to local officials, I'd head straight for our bus, because when his car left, that bus left. Nobody waited for anything, least of all me.

We never had to wait for a stoplight either, since all the intersections were blocked off for the length of our route. New York takes on a whole new look when you don't have to worry about the traffic.

The presidential limousine was equipped with a loudspeaker system that was like something out of Disney. With speakers hidden inside the fenders and a microphone in the back seat, "The Amazing Talking Car" (as it was nicknamed) allowed the president to speak to thousands lined along the motorcade route.

The Secret Service's job is made both tougher and easier by the rapid pace at which everything moves. When you arrive at the hotel, you walk through a corridor of people into the lobby, where a waiting elevator travels nonstop to your floor. When you get off the elevator, security guards are already posted at both ends of the hall. You must turn your luggage over to the Secret Service three to four hours before departing so they can make a thorough search. Even the infamous "hot line" telephone makes road trips. In fact, two boxes, nearly identical, traveled with us. One contained the red phone. The other carried a collection of President Ford's pipes.

And on we went. Dubbed "The Joe and Jerry Show" by the press, the TV programs came across as relaxed and informal, like a good talk show, but each one was carefully planned. Nothing in the campaign happened accidentally.

For example, Pittsburgh is a big football town, right? So who was in the party greeting the president there? Pitt All-American running back Tony Dorsett. And in Cincinnati, where the Big Red Machine was in high gear, guess who came early to a presidential appearance in Fountain Square? Johnny Bench, Tony Perez, and Pete Rose. That's a lotta RBIs.

The entire experience of campaigning with a president is unforgettable, yet certain especially warm moments stand out in my mind. I remember the congregation of a Polish

Catholic church in Buffalo, New York. As I watched the awe and respect on their faces, I couldn't help thinking that in spite of all our sophistication and cynicism, the experience of coming face to face with a president is unbelievably overwhelming.

I also remember a particularly tense situation that showed me a lot about what kind of man Gerald Ford is. It was the Sunday before election day, and after 15,000 miles of campaigning in 11 days, nerves were ragged and tempers short. In these last few days, everyone was feeling the pressure of a very tough campaign. That day, a black minister, Reverend Clennon King, and three other blacks tried to attend church services at Jimmy Carter's Plains Baptist Church. The deacons canceled the service rather than admit them. Word of the incident spread quickly through the press corps, and a couple of photographers told me they were sure the incident would finish Carter's chances. I began to wonder how the president would react.

In a meeting aboard the helicopter en route to our next stop, the president asked his chief of staff, Dick Cheney, what he knew about the incident.

"Like you, just what I've been told," Cheney replied. "I told our people to put a lid on it!"

In a strong, firm voice the president said, "I hope none of our people are involved in this. But if I find out we had anything to do with it, I will handle it myself." As far as I was concerned, it was the best speech he made during the whole campaign.

I do remember one other speech very vividly, one that led to the most exciting part of my association with Gerald Ford. I was riding back to the hotel with him after an appearance at a theater-in-the-round outside Philadelphia. I always went to the speeches, even though it wasn't part of the job. You think I wanted to miss anything?

The night before, he had practically lost his voice trying to be heard above a particularly excited, noisy crowd. So in

Philadelphia his voice was barely a whisper when he took the stage. He spoke dramatically for 30 minutes, turning constantly to the crowd encircling him.

During the ride back to the hotel he asked me what I thought. I grinned uncontrollably and felt I had to give him my honest reaction. "I kept watching you walk around that stage with that long microphone cord trailing you," I said. "The truth is, I spent more time watching that cord than I did listening to you. I've seen some big performers get in trouble trying to unravel themselves from microphone cords, and I kept waiting for you to tie yourself up or trip, and I could just see tomorrow's front page. When you got off the stage in one piece, I considered the night a success."

He smiled, yet I could see he was exhausted. We were making two stops a day now instead of one. The campaign had picked up speed and was racing at an unbelievably hectic pace. He turned to me and said in a slightly hoarse voice, "Betty and I wanted you and your family to spend election night with us in the White House."

My mouth dropped open. I was speechless. Hard to believe, I know, but I was astounded. I said something like "You don't have to do that" (imagine me telling the president of the United States what he doesn't have to do).

"But two of my kids are married," I said, not sure he knew he'd have a full house. He just nodded and said, "We want your family there."

I couldn't wait to phone home. I called Audrie to tell her the news, and at first she couldn't believe it either. Finally it sank in, and she asked the same question I did: how can we stay at the White House with seven people? We finally decided we'd get motel rooms nearby for the kids. They could be with us for dinner and into the evening, then return to the motel later that night.

The next night I told the president I had called home with his invitation. "We're all really excited. We had one small problem, but I think we've got it solved."

He smiled. "That's a twist, you solving problems for me." I told him Audrie and I planned for the kids to stay in a motel. "No, no," he said. "They're staying with us."

"But you're talking about three more bedrooms," I said. He looked at me, smiled, and said, "Well, I'll tell you. If we don't have enough beds, I think we can get some cots. Don't you think there are enough rooms in that place, Joe?"

On the afternoon of election day, Audrie and I, with our two sons, their wives and our daughter, took the Eastern Airlines shuttle to Washington's National Airport. Two marine sergeants met our plane and drove us to the White House. When we got there the curator was waiting for us and showed us upstairs to the Lincoln Bedroom, where Audrie and I were going to stay. I felt like I'd stepped into the pages of history. After all, this was the room where Abraham Lincoln signed the Emancipation Proclamation. Hanging over the desk was a handwritten copy of the Gettysburg Address.

At one point I was in the bathroom, and Audrie said, "How can you go to the bathroom at a time like this? This is the room where Abraham Lincoln slept." I pointed out that if Lincoln slept in this bedroom, he most likely used the bathroom, too.

Then our daughter Gina came to our room to see if we had any White House stationery. She had used her room's supply writing to everyone she'd ever met, and probably a few people she hadn't. It wasn't long before the supply in our room was also gone.

Around 7:00 we were ushered into the president's private quarters, and as if it were any old day to be giving house-guests a tour of his home, he showed us around the second-floor family quarters.

I don't know what I expected to see in the White House, but the family's rooms were nothing like a museum. Other parts of the house had pieces of history, like Francis Scott Key's original music for the National Anthem, but these rooms just had pieces of the family's life, like pictures and mementos. Just like I show my friends one of the bats I used (which is hardly marked), President Ford showed me the leather football helmet he wore playing for Michigan in the 1935 East-West All-Star game. Like most former football players he had an exercise machine to strengthen his bad knee. I walked away thinking, "Hey, a bed is a bed and a chair is a chair, even if they are in the White House. This is where they live."

Dinner was buffet-style, so everyone could eat while gathered around the television to watch the election returns. Other guests included Pearl Bailey, President Ford's running-mate Senator Robert Dole and his wife, Elizabeth, Edith Green and her family, New York Senator Jacob Javits, and several of the president's staff, including David Kennerly, Press Secretary Ron Nessen, and Dick Cheney.

I sort of expected that the president of the United States would have special teletype services and a battery of phones to follow the election results. The truth is, we did just what most people do: we watched it on TV. Actually, there were three TVs, each one tuned to a different network.

NBC colored the states Carter won in red and those Ford won in blue. As the reports came in, morale swung back and forth throughout the night. After losing both New York and Texas, a big blow, everyone was down. Then North Dakota went for Ford, and even though it meant only three electoral votes, it was a big psychological boost.

"Go big blue," I yelled, and soon everyone was hollering "Go blue," including the president.

But the encouraging news didn't last long. It was a tough night. Not only had I come to like and admire Gerald Ford; I also believed in my heart we were going to win.

I was impressed by the honesty in the room that night. Men like Dole and Cheney told the president what they thought, not what they thought he wanted to hear. At one point his pollster, Bob Teeter, reported to him, "We can do it if we win Hawaii and Texas, but Mr. President, we're not going to win either one of them." The president took all the news very calmly. There was no yelling, no display of temper. The truth is, I'd seen Enos Slaughter get more upset about an umpire saying "Strike two" than Gerald Ford did when he realized he wasn't going to win a presidential election.

Finally, around 3:30 A.M., the outcome was painfully clear. The president said, "Well, I'm not going to make any concessions tonight. I'm going to bed, and I'll do what I have to tomorrow."

Slowly the group drifted off, knowing sleep wouldn't come easily. It was like losing a pennant-deciding baseball game, except the next game was four years away.

The next morning as we prepared to go home, the president went before the press to make his concession speech. We watched on television as Betty Ford read the speech for her husband, who was too hoarse to speak. A moment later, White House physician Dr. William Lukash stopped by our room and said, "The president wants to see you before you head back to New York."

We walked into the Oval Office, and I threw my arms around him. With tears leaking out I said, "Dammit, we should have won, we should have won."

He said quietly, "Hey, there are more important things to worry about than what's going to happen to Jerry Ford."

"Not today, dammit," I said. "Not today."

And he looked at me and said, "Listen, Joe. I'm glad I can say I gave him the White House in better shape than I got it." Then he asked the White House photographer to take pictures of my family with him, mementos of a special night I know they'll treasure forever.

The campaign and becoming a friend and, in a sense, a coworker of Gerald Ford are experiences I'll treasure forever, too. I'd do it all again with no hesitation. I can't see why high-profile people shouldn't take political stands, as long as they're willing to accept the fact they're going to be criticized for it and alienate some people. (One television critic remarked about a World Series broadcast, "How could you believe a man who hit only .257 and campaigned for Jerry Ford?")

I was there as an attention-getter. Maybe somebody is flipping the dial on his television set, and he recognizes my face. He might stop to watch, just to see what I'm doing, and as a result he might hear what the candidate has to say. My role was to grab the attention of a lot of people who might not otherwise have tuned in to a political broadcast.

During the campaign, the *St. Louis Post-Dispatch* sent a reporter up to "The Hill," the solidly Democratic neighborhood where I grew up, to get reactions from people about my campaigning for a Republican. I couldn't believe it. The story painted me as a traitor to my roots, and that's complete nonsense. I later told the publisher of the paper I thought he'd taken a cheap shot at me. I told him about my memories of my father, sitting at our kitchen table poring over the dozens of facts about America he had to learn in order to become a citizen. He struggled through the questions and the answers. My brother and I would quiz him over and over, not so he could become a Democrat or a Republican, but so he could do the same thing I wanted to do now—stand up for himself and make a free choice in a free country. Those are the only roots that mean anything to me.

I'm not a Republican or a Democrat. I make up my mind on the basis of who's running. I've voted for many people in both parties, and I will again, as long as I believe in them.

In thinking about my experience with the Ford campaign, there are only two things I wish were different. One, of course, is the outcome. The other is that I wish my father had lived to see it. I try to imagine how he would have felt. He would have thought back to when he came to this country, unable to speak the language, with just the name of his destination hung around his neck. This land promised him opportunity, and he would not have believed how it delivered: his son flying in *Air Force One*, appearing on television with the president and other national leaders, and even spending election night with the first family in the White House.

He would have been grateful and happy and proud. He might even have bragged to his friends about me. But if he needed a favor done, he wouldn't have settled for the guys I hung around with. He'd go to the strength. He'd go to Midge Berra.

"He rubbed the top of my head and said, 'Man, that feels just like my wife's bottom.' Trying not to overact, I rubbed the top of my bald head and said right back to him, 'You know, it *does* feel like her bottom.' "

○

6

"You Losing Your Hair?"
"No, I'm Bald."

"CURE BALDNESS."

Those ads always bug me. It's not like athlete's foot or a headache—take two aspirin and it's gone by morning. What is there to cure? It's not contagious. Dr. Jonas Salk didn't spend any time trying to isolate dandruff.

I just wish there were a more glamorous word than "bald." Some good-sounding euphemism. "Prematurely bald" doesn't say it. Being born at seven months is premature, but losing your hair at any time is never premature. It's like an "untimely death." Is there ever a good time for it?

"Thinning" is another super concept. Did you ever hear of anybody's hair thickening? Or how about hearing yourself described as "young and balding"? I guess it's better than being called "*old* and balding." Some, trying to be kind, might describe "his depleted pelt," but any way they say it you're still *B-A-L-D, BALD*.

The toughest challenge in the beginning is to actually admit you are bald. For a long time you think you might be losing *some* hair, but you're sure that "by next week" the fuzz you see will be long hair.

The pattern is easy to follow. You're the first to notice, but you don't want to believe it. Even though your comb is hairier than your head, you keep telling yourself your hair's not falling out. You begin trying everything from pasta as a pomade to a novena. It's almost time to panic, but not quite. About this time hair cream ads start to take on a whole new meaning. The key phrase is "thicker hair." When you reach this stage, you don't care if it looks like a Brillo pad or an O'Cedar mop, just so it's thicker.

Athletes always wonder what's going to tell them it's time to retire. Will it be my legs? Will I lose my desire? Maybe my timing? With losing your hair, even though you're convinced it's only temporary, your "friends" will tell you when your hair is really going. The words you don't want to hear keep coming at you: "Hey, Joe, you losing your hair?" Oh, does that cut. Even if they don't say it, they sure send you the message.

They never look you in the eye anymore. When they talk to you, they focus on your hairline (which is moving daily), and you try to make eye contact by standing on your toes. Once you're on your toes, he's looking higher to focus on your hairline, and soon you need elevator shoes and elevator shorts to be at eye level. You're trying to have a conversation and end up looking like a bad dance team.

Then you start trying different hairstyles. Puffing it up, swirling the last few faithful strands, parting the remaining hardy hairs in the middle. I've seen some men part their hair so far down the side I thought I'd have to whisper into their nose.

Regardless of what you try, one culprit always stands between you and the truth and keeps you from making that final admission. One healthy strand, maybe an eighth of an inch wide, as healthy now as the day you graduated from grade school, always falls to the wrong side. You're combing it from right to left across the top of your head, and if you left it alone it would probably reach to your elbow. Just when you're thinking, "Boy, is my hair getting thick," the crisis comes. A gust blows up, and you have to play the wind to keep your strand on top. One wrong move, the "pigtail" comes down, and you look like the guy they worked on the first day of barber school.

When I finally got a good look at my pigtail, I knew I'd have to make a decision. It was at the Bob Hope Desert Golf Classic, and I was one of the commentators. We taped the opening shots, a panoramic view, followed by a shot of the announcers, as seen from a high camera.

When the opening was played back, I couldn't believe what I saw. My pigtail was in place, running from my right ear across the top of my head to my left ear, looking like a giant varicose vein. It looked like Highway 66 had found a new route across the top of my head.

People had already been suggesting I wear a toupee, but I didn't want to. So the following Tuesday, when I walked into the "Today" show dressing room for my usual routine of makeup, I knew this day would be different. As always, Barbara Walters's hairdresser was there, and I said to her, "Today I want you to style my hair." As I expected, she laughed. When she finally pulled herself together, I asked her to get a scissors so we could cut Mr. Pigtail and give him a proper burial. Getting rid of him was easy and painless. The tough part had been deciding to finally have my hair "styled."

Once you decide it's okay to be bald, it's interesting to see the completely new way people look at you. The same friends who couldn't take their eyes off your hairline now look you right in the eye, check what little fuzz you have on top, and say, "I'll bet if you let it grow you'd have a full head of hair." Would you believe they sincerely mean it?

When I was on the "Today" show, people sent me all kinds of suggestions about my head, like "Stay the way you are" or "At least wear a toupee or a head cover on TV," a suggestion that always made me feel like a 4-wood. My favorites included comfort from a lady in Ohio who didn't want me to give up hope. Her 80-year-old husband had been bald for 35 years, then started to grow hair. It had already grown an inch when she wrote. Another lady told me to put sulphur on my head. She had bought a bottle for her husband, and before it was empty he was going to the barbershop regularly (probably to get a shave and place a bet). A man wrote to tell me he rubbed a certain brand of toothpaste on his hair and it grew like crazy. And I'll bet his head didn't have any cavities, either.

I still have people tell me I should wear a toupee, but it's too late. Besides, I have my routine set for getting ready for a TV broadcast. Cover the beard and cut the glare on top with powder. Sometimes, in places like ballparks and racetracks where powder hasn't been available, I've improvised. Maybe you've never read it in "Hints from Heloise," but Ajax and Bon Ami gets the job done. That time you may have thought I looked pretty good, I might have been breaded with Bon Ami.

One of the hardest things about being bald is having to listen to all the dumb things people say. Why it is always the guy with a full head of hair, and I mean full to the point where a case of dandruff might be terminal, who says, "You're lucky because you have a great-shaped head. You look good. If I were bald I'd look awful"? Oh, yeah? And another thing. Why do people say, "He's standing next to the bald guy"? Why don't I ever hear anybody say, "He's standing next to the guy with hair"?

Actually, the worst thing about being bald is not the lack of hair. It's the jokes. I think in the years I've been bald I've heard only one new joke, credited to Senator Alan Simpson of Wyoming: "A bald head is a solar panel for a sex machine." Not too accurate, but it sounds great.

Bill Madlock wins first prize among major-league players for his needle: "Hey, Joe, is that sunroof standard equipment on that body?" From that day on he's always called me Sunroof.

Skin Head, Baldy, Onion Head, Chrome Dome—those are just a few of the regulars you hear constantly. Amazingly, people use those terms as if they just thought them up and they're so original.

I don't think I've ever walked into a ballpark or played in a pro-am golf tournament without hearing this original line: "Put a hat on, Joe. The glare is killing me."

Or:

"Hey, Joe, did you get a crew cut? If you did, the crew bailed out."

"You must have had wavy hair because it waved good-bye."

"Hey Joe, you know what stops falling hair? [Pause.] The floor." (That always gets a big laugh from him and a wish from me that he'll get a good case of heartburn.)

"You have to quit sleeping on those rubber pillows— you're erasing all your hair."

"Get a bigger bed—you must be rubbing up against the bedpost."

The oldest snappy one-liner is the one I always hear in the barbershop (some men now go to a "stylist," but it's still the barbershop for me). "You must have to pay double for your haircut—half to find it and the other half to cut it."

One of those clever lines gave me the chance to use a comeback I'd saved for four years. I'd read it somewhere, liked it, and practically prayed I'd someday get to use it.

I was at a party, and a guy with a perfectly combed, full head of hair just couldn't wait to start agitating me about my bald head. He was going through the usual routine when he rubbed the top of my head and said, "Man, that feels just like my wife's bottom."

I couldn't believe it. Four years of waiting, and finally, this was it! I almost choked up and blew it; I could actually feel my heart pounding faster. Trying not to overact, I rubbed the top of my bald head and said right back to him, "You know, you're right, it *does* feel like her bottom."

And being bald has other disadvantages, besides the verbal abuse. On a hot day the top of your head sweats like crazy. Hairy guys love it because it gives them a chance to fluff their flowing locks. If you're semibald, you can at least dab it dry. But we full-fledged members have to wipe it off as if we trained in a car wash. There's nothing subtle about it; take a big swipe to dry off your built-in beach ball, then wait for the wisecracks.

Hot peppers, hot food, and hot spices also discriminate against us. When a bald guy eats something hot, like a jalapeño pepper, not only do his mouth and stomach get hot, but the top of his head breaks out in a sweat, too. There you sit in a fancy restaurant, trying to look suave while you're wiping off your head and looking like you just finished catching the bottom of the ninth inning. It'll turn you into a closet jalapeño-eater.

Another bad thing about being bald is that you rarely win arguments. The American male is a strange animal. I don't care what topic is under discussion, from baseball to nuclear proliferation. If it looks like the bald guy is winning, the hairy guy gives him the line that always ends the discussion:

"Oh, yeah! Well, I've still got my hair." His "clincher" has nothing to do with what you're talking about, but "Hair" feels like he just beat "Bald" with a great argument. Sometimes I'll just agree and add, "Yeah, I shouldn't have stayed up until midnight pulling my hair out with a tweezer."

Men who use that strategy are living proof that lots of people are walking around bald on the inside. But if you think the "hair argument" uses weird logic, here's one even stranger that really takes advantage of us bald guys.

A friend's mother used to tell her that if she chewed gum in bed and fell asleep she'd go bald. Her mother actually told her the gum would fall out of her mouth, get in her hair, and she'd go completely bald. Not only did she believe her mother, but whenever she saw Yul Brynner or Telly Savalas, she thought they got that way because they chewed gum in bed.

Now, I agree chewing gum in bed can be bad for you. I don't blame a mother for trying to get her daughter to stop. But to use a bald guy as the bogeyman? That's just not fair.

Once you've made the BIG DECISION, your statement of "Here I am folks, this is me, this is the way I am," being bald is easy. It does have a positive side. In fact, I had what I thought was a great idea for the bald man, but it was turned down. I realize a grooming kit for a bald head is an unusual item, but maybe someday I'll be able to market it.

I'm going to call it simply the Joe Garagiola Grooming Kit. It contains a black pocket comb without any teeth, just ridges; you whip it out like the other guys and run it across the top without any damage. The kit also has a little jar of white flakes, very small and harmless, that you sprinkle on your shoulders when you're wearing a dark suit. At just the right time, your wife or friend flicks the specks off your shoulder and says loud enough for the people around you to hear, "Hmm, looks like you have dandruff." Another item is a fancy-looking tube with some harmless, greaseless salve called Stay-Bald; you tell people you use it only once a month to keep your hair from growing. Included in the deluxe model kit is a small portable hair dryer. It blows only cool air, though; we wouldn't want to risk blisters. Just think what a big help it would be after those "hot" meals.

I'm not the only person who sees the positive side of baldness. I have dozens of signs, T-shirts, pillow cases, and bumper stickers all proclaiming "Bald is Beautiful." If being bald depresses you, how about this guaranteed picker-upper? "God made only a few perfect heads. The rest he covered with hair." Or, as one of my many bald-headed fans once wrote, "Remember, they don't put marble tops on cheap furniture."

If that's not enough comfort, here's another which involves religious intervention: "The Lord is just, the Lord is fair. He gave some brains and others hair." Or "Grass doesn't grow on a busy street," and "If you're bald in front, you're a thinker; if bald in back, a lover; and if you're completely bald, you think you're a lover."

Even Shakespeare tried to be of some help (of course *he* was bald): "There's not time for a man to recover his hair that grows bald by nature." Hey, Will, no kidding. The French also tried to make us feel better with this proverb: "Long hair, little sense." And the Belgians added, "Experience is the comb that nature gives us when we are bald." I like the philosophical sound of that. I just don't know what it means. And it makes me wonder what the hairy guys get from nature. Even the British Association for the Advancement of Science announced, "Diminished hair growth liberates thyroid secretions to exert themselves elsewhere . . . we may view diminishing hair growth as an accessory factor in man's brain growth." Now that's what I like to hear.

The longer you're bald, the more you believe Carl Reiner. He's one of my heroes, not only because of his many talents but because he believes "anybody who has hair during the daytime is overdressed."

My hero St. Paul (you remember, the jock apostle) has been my favorite since I was in parochial school and had hair. As I got older and had somewhat less hair, I liked him even better, and here's why: St. Paul wrote to the Corinthians (and I really wish they'd written back on this), "Does not the very nature of things teach you that if a man has long hair, it is a disgrace to him?"

Most people, however, don't agree with my friend St. Paul. Hair is important. Watch a baseball player draw a walk. If he has a full head of hair, he'll take one step, take the batting helmet off, and prance like a Clydesdale horse down to first base, all the while trying to get his cap on. A bald guy wouldn't even dare take his helmet off. If he has to slide to break up a double play, he may be out, but he's capable of making a shoestring catch of his helmet if it starts to come off. Andy Seminick was the best. His hat never came off, and he was always in the dugout during the National Anthem. That's another unwritten rule for the baldies.

Whenever Dick Groat brought the lineup card to home plate, I'd try to get him into a conversation or an argument to make him forget about getting back to the dugout before the anthem. If *I* had to stand out there, I wanted company. Together we looked like two-thirds of a pawn shop, unless Augie Donatelli was the umpire. Then we did look like a pawn shop. Those times I was successful in keeping Groat out there, he'd moan and groan the whole time and guarantee me I wouldn't trap him again. I especially loved the part about the "red glare." "They're singing our song, Dick," I'd say.

On October 6, 1980 (dates always stick in your mind if one of your own is involved), during the Houston Astros–Los Angeles Dodgers one-game playoff, I understood the pain Art Howe was going through, lying on the ground after being picked off by Fernando Valenzuela. Only a man who has gone through it could know. Bad enough to get picked off in front of 56,000 people at the ballpark and a national TV audience of millions. But as he was stretching with both hands for the bag, his helmet fell off. Then everybody knew. Art Howe was bald! The bubble-gum card collectors must have been in a panic. What did this do to the value of an Art Howe card?

One night on the evening news I saw the Astros' Denny

Walling make a diving catch of a foul ball to stop a rally. The sportscaster, who had a full head of permed hair, said, "Watch this play closely. I never knew this about Walling. Never mind the play. . . . Denny Walling is bald!"

"I hope your hair dryer blows a fuse tomorrow," I yelled back at the TV. In the next story, I watched Buddy Bell dive to his left, then throw to first base sitting down to get Ozzie Smith on a close play. Bell's cap came off, but I sure didn't hear the sportscaster say, "Watch this play closely. I never knew this about Buddy Bell. Never mind the play; Buddy Bell is hairy!"

Have you ever noticed how many catchers are bald? My theory on this is based on the army helmet theory. When GIs came home from World War II, many with a lot less hair, their excuse was something like "Yeah, that helmet I had to wear, it was just bad for my scalp." Well, at least it sounded good.

The bald catchers theory is actually a variation on one of the world's oldest questions, baseball's version of "Which came first, the chicken or the egg?" Some people say catchers are bald because they're the only players who never take off their helmets. But I wonder. Are they bald because they never take off their helmets, or do they never take off their helmets because they're bald?

Actually, being bald isn't so bad. It has some definite advantages. In any room you're the first to know the location of the air-conditioning ducts. Outdoors, you're the first to know if it's starting to rain. Well, only if that really is a raindrop that hits you on the head. The worst feeling in the world is to think it's rain and reach up, only to realize our feathered friends have no class at all. I've been hit twice, and now I always root for the statues when I walk by.

When you're bald, forgetting a comb or a hair dryer doesn't cause any panic. Like the joke goes, and it's true, use a towel. Custer didn't show as much panic as the "styled hair" man who's forgotten his dryer when the stores are closed.

"I can't wear a headset; it'll make ridges in my hair." Sorry, pal. My problem is if somebody's used tape and the adhesive is still on the headset, I have to use a handkerchief, or the set sticks to my head.

The biggest advantage is that you're windproof. A man who wears a toupee actually has to walk leaning into a strong wind. I'm sure I'll get some arguments from the hairpiece makers, but every man I've ever been around who wears a piece needs to know which way the flags are blowing. He can't pass a mirror or a window without checking it, to see not only if it's on straight, but if it's still on at all. A man with styled hair or a transplant really has problems with the wind. I've seen men literally walk on an angle, looking deformed, to battle the wind. The bald head has the edge. What can the wind do to us? We couldn't get our hair messed up in a hurricane.

The "Today" show was in Chicago for a week, broadcasting from the roof of the Merchandise Mart. Chicago was really living up to its nickname, the "Windy city." It was like a NASA wind tunnel. Hugh Downs, Barbara Walters, and I were a funny sight, walking out on the roof that morning. Hugh, with those little divots in his scalp from his hair transplant, must have felt like his whole head was going to blow off, so he walked with his head bent into the wind. Barbara had a scarf tied very tightly to hold her hair in place, and she was using both hands to keep it secure. I walked out like Alfred E. Newman of *MAD* magazine: "What, me worry?"

In spite of the advantages of baldness, a lot of people still want hair. I'm convinced the people on Wall Street are all wrong when they look for economic indicators by studying graphs, trends, and charts. Check the hair. I think it's our leading industry.

Here's a list of some of the things you can do to your hair:

1. grow

2. thicken

3. curl

4. straighten

5. body wave or perm

6. color

7. highlight

8. shampoo

9. style

10. grease

11. bleach

12. cut

Stop doing any five and we have a recession. Stop doing more than five and we have a depression. And while the barber and the barbershop may be quickly becoming obsolete, the hairstylist and the salon are keeping the economy afloat. According to an article titled "Hairpower" in *The New York Times Magazine*, men's hairstyles now have names and make statements, just like the automobile.

Short sideburns and closely trimmed sides, made famous by Lieutenant Colonel Oliver North, is the popular Classic. (Some simply call it the Ollie.) The man who wears it says he's "in control."

Right behind the Classic in popularity is the Coiffed. I don't know what statement the coiffed makes except to say you have plenty of hair.

Next comes my category, the Boldly Bald. The statement we make? "Dominating and even sexy." (Every time I see words like "sexy" and "dominating" in the same sentence with the word "bald," I know the next thing I'll see are the names of Yul Brynner and Telly Savalas.)

Boldly Bald doesn't necessarily come cheap. Gio Hernandez, a well-known hairstylist with a salon in the Hotel Pierre in New York, supposedly charges $80 for the first cut. At those prices he ought to give you a 36-month warranty and have Dr. Michael DeBakey as his assistant.

Boldly Bald isn't necessarily easy for the barber though. Billy Consolo, a former American League infielder, went to work in his father's shop (salon) as a barber (stylist) when he left baseball. When I asked Billy which is his toughest haircut, he said without hesitating, "Guys like you." Hey, I thought I was a steal. There's nothing to cut.

Apparently that's the problem. "When you have more than three chairs," Billy says, "the haircuts have to last at least 20 minutes so all the barbers get a fair shot at the walk-ins. Do you know how hard it is to make *your* haircut last 20 minutes? After I'm done I stand behind the chair, with the scissors about four inches from your ear, so you hear it, snip, snip, snip, and think I'm still cutting. It's tough stretching a haircut for guys like you." So while we may be Boldly Bald to some, to others we're a tough 20 minutes.

"On a ball hit to right field, Vin wanted to say, 'There's a hot shot hit to right,' but it didn't quite come out that way. He quickly learned that you don't use *shot* and *hit* in the same sentence if you have to say it fast."

○

7

Broadcasting: It's Not High Mass, It's a Ballgame

I'LL ALWAYS WONDER about the year 1950 and what might have been. I had my best start ever. Everything was happening right for me. When I hit the ball hard, it shot between the fielders. I'd hit one off the handle, and the infielder would lose it in the sun or the lights. When I'd hit it on the ground, it would take a bad hop for a hit. It seemed like nothing could go wrong.

On June 1 I was hitting .356, my highest average ever. I had just finished a big series in Pittsburgh, hitting a three-run homer to help sweep the Pirates. We were just a game out of first place behind the Brooklyn Dodgers and getting ready to open a crucial home stand against them.

Left-hander Preacher Roe was pitching the first game for Brooklyn, so I assumed I'd be watching from the bullpen. I couldn't even use the word *left-hander* in a crossword puzzle. So when our manager, Eddie Dyer, read the starting lineup and I was in it, I almost fell off my stool in the

Will the real Joe Garagiola please stand up?

The 1952 Pirate protective helmet: If only they had found a way to protect us from ourselves.

On top of the world: We were on our way to a pennant and I was going to the barber every ten days.

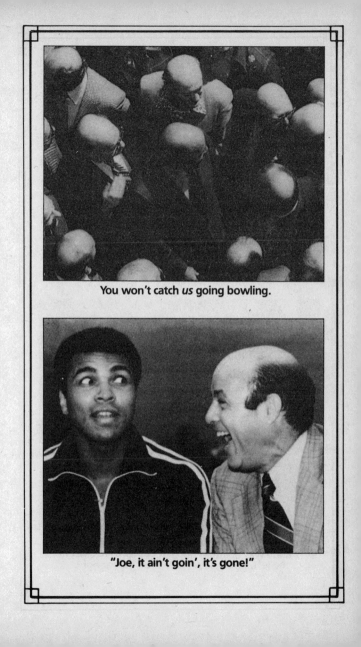

You won't catch *us* going bowling.

"Joe, it ain't goin', it's gone!"

Joe Garagiola Day, and Mama's only visit to the ballpark. She felt sorry for the boss who had to pay for all the lights.

Mama and Papa celebrate with friends (the turtle didn't get all the wine): My parents are second and third from the left, and Yogi's mama is on the far right.

My best man Yogi and good friend Stan Musial pour the "vino" for me and my new bride, Audrie.

UPI/Bettmann News Photo

We called this play "Get Me the Ladder."

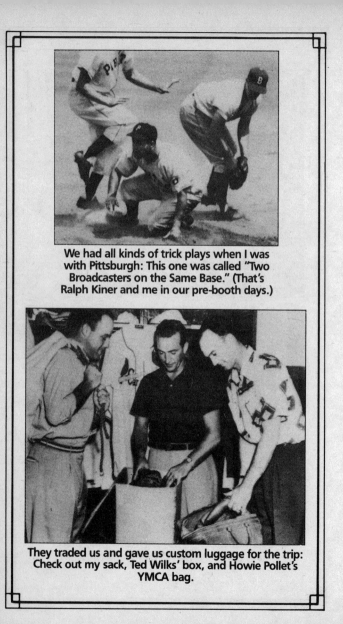

We had all kinds of trick plays when I was with Pittsburgh: This one was called "Two Broadcasters on the Same Base." (That's Ralph Kiner and me in our pre-booth days.)

They traded us and gave us custom luggage for the trip: Check out my sack, Ted Wilks' box, and Howie Pollet's YMCA bag.

I like Italian baseball, but eh, *mama mia*, shorts on a catcher?

"Joe," Casey used to say to me, "when they list all the great catchers, you'll be there listening."

My most recent Old-Timers game: proof that you *can* get jammed by a 54 mph fastball while bunting.

© 1976 United Feature Syndicate, Inc.

SIR! I THINK YOU'RE TAKING ADVANTAGE OF CHUCK...

DON'T BE SILLY, MARCIE!

CHUCK'S TEAM IS SO BAD ALREADY, YOU CAN'T POSSIBLY HURT IT, AND I REALLY NEED SNOOPY ON MY TEAM...

I NEVER THOUGHT I'D BE TRADED FOR A BEAGLE...

YOU SHOULD BE FLATTERED, MARCIE...

I COULD HAVE TRADED YOU FOR JOE GARAGIOLA!

Johnny Bench qualifies for another championship.

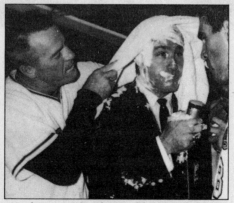

Hank Bauer wins the World Series and I get
a shaving cream shampoo.

Life in the booth.

Family and friends help me say a tough goodbye
on *Today*.

The *Today* show reunion in 1987: Front row: Gene Shalit,
Jane Pauley, Bryant Gumbel, Willard Scott, John Palmer.
Second row: Jack Lescoulie, Lee Merriweather, Tom
Brokaw, Barbara Walters, Hugh Downs, me. Third row:
Betty Furness, Edwin Newman, Frank Blair, Jim Hartz,
Pat Weaver, Betsy Palmer, John Chancellor,
Florence Henderson, Helen O'Conner.

Just sold another refrigerator for $10.

I substituted for Johnny Carson on *The Tonight Show,* and wound up interviewing the Beatles.

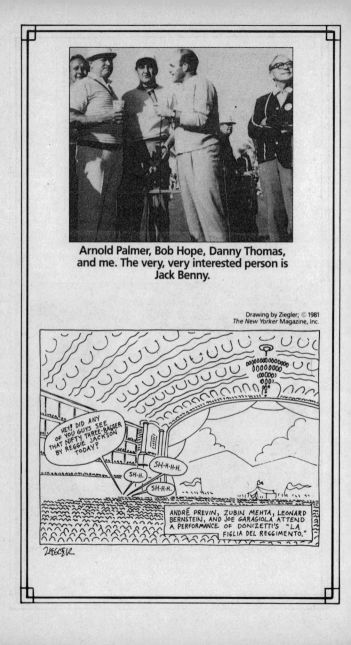

Arnold Palmer, Bob Hope, Danny Thomas,
and me. The very, very interested person is
Jack Benny.

The famous Stags team: That's Yogi and me on the bottom right (I'll let you figure out which is which).

"Yogi, first you make the *strike, then* I'll put it down." He did it, too.

We were fifteen years old before we knew
holy water was free.

This time we didn't have to meet under the lamppost: It
was even better—the Hall of Fame.

clubhouse meeting. "You're going good, kid," Dyer said (everybody is "kid" or "pardner" to a Texan), "and I'm gonna start you against the left-hander."

The day had been rainy, and the field was a little wet. When I came up in the fifth inning, we had runners at first and second. I was sure I saw the bunt sign; later Eddie Dyer said he never gave any sign. I bunted toward third and saw the Dodgers going for the double play, with shortstop Pee Wee Reese covering second and second baseman Jackie Robinson covering first.

Robinson was waiting for the throw as I neared the bag. The throw came in low, and he slipped on the wet ground trying to grab it and fell facedown toward second base. Sprawled on the ground, his legs across the bag, he reached out to smother the ball. As he reached, his legs rose up behind him. I tried to avoid stepping on him by stepping between his legs, but when his legs came up they clipped me across the shins, and I went tumbling, landing heavily on my left shoulder. As soon as I hit the ground I knew I was hurt badly; the pain was incredible. All I could think of was my wife, Audrie, sitting in the stands. We'd been married only a few months, she was pregnant, and I knew she'd hurry down to the clubhouse to see what had happened to me. As I lay on the ground I just kept thinking, "Please don't let her fall."

I was taken to the hospital for X rays, but even before a doctor looked at me, both Audrie and I knew my injury was serious. I ended up with cracked ribs and a shoulder separation.

The story of my collision with Jackie Robinson has since been told differently, depending on the particular need. As recently as 1987, Maury Allen, in his book *Jackie Robinson: A Life Remembered*, said I spiked Robinson. Maybe that reads better or makes a more controversial story. All I know is Jackie Robinson went back to the hotel after the game and I went to Deaconess Hospital.

One doctor suggested an interim operation, a "quick fix" to get me back into the lineup as soon as possible. But the Cardinals' owner Fred Saigh wouldn't have any part of it. He sent me to Dr. C. H. Crego, an orthopedic surgeon who was not a baseball fan and therefore had no interest in either the lineup or my .356 average, which was fast becoming a distant memory. Saigh and Dr. Crego's concern was to make me whole again, not to see how many games I could play in 1950. Two weeks later I had a serious operation to repair the damage in the shoulder and didn't play again until September.

Until all this happened, I thought I'd play forever. Maybe I'd stop off at the Hall of Fame—on an off day. But when Dr. Crego stopped by my hospital room after surgery, it wasn't to ask for tickets to my induction.

"Do you throw with that arm, son?" he asked.

"No, sir," I said.

"That's good, because if that were the arm you had to throw with, I don't think you could play baseball again."

It was that simple, that honest, and that scary. What would I do? What could I do if I couldn't play baseball? When you're only 24, with a new wife and a new family beginning, spending a week in a hospital bed and several more recuperating at home can make you do some deep thinking. I'd had some encouragement about a radio career, but I wanted to play baseball. I was a big leaguer and I didn't want to give it up.

I started the 1951 season with the Cardinals, hoping to put the injury behind me, but I didn't have a very good year. So I began to think a little more about broadcasting and to collect stories and observations just in case.

Then I was traded for the first time, away from my hometown Cardinals, the team I'd gone to the World Series with only a few years before. And it was tough. Regardless of what the general manager says or the sportswriters write, all you feel is "They didn't want me." I gave myself a pep talk about the Pirates wanting me more, but I still felt like damaged property.

Have you ever wondered how a player is told about a trade? Marty Marion was the Cardinal manager who sent me to Pittsburgh. Here's how he told me on the phone:

Marion: Joe?

Joe: Yeah

Marion: Joe. Marty.

Joe: Hi, Marty.

Marion: Joe, you've been traded.

Joe: Where?

Marion: Pittsburgh.

Joe: How soon do I have to be there? (After your first trade you learn there's no deadline, and you usually take a couple of days to take care of "personal business." At least that's the case if you're traded to a second-division team. If your new team has a chance to win the pennant, you can usually make it within the hour.)

Marion: As soon as you can get there.

Joe: Okay.

Marion: Okay.

Joe: Bye.

To borrow a phrase from Vin Scully, it was done "with all the warmth and verve of a meter reader."

In 1951, the Pirates finished. That says it all. In 1952 we lost 112 games out of 154. If you made 10 or 12 mistakes against us, we were the kind of team that could kill you.

In 1953, I started out with Pittsburgh and ended up with the Cubs, in that famous trade that involved such household names as Joe Garagiola, Toby Atwell, Preston Ward, Bob Addis, Bob Schultz, and Bill Howerton. The biggest names were Howard Pollet, George Metkovich, and Gene Hermanski. The biggest name was Ralph Kiner. I think only three players in the whole deal were even on bubble-gum cards. Mr. Rickey meant it when he said, "This trade could hurt both teams."

I'd spent eight years in the big leagues, and the Cubs were my third team. (Can you believe they *still* own me and will not release me?) The National League had only eight teams then, so I was beginning to think I wasn't playing baseball for a living but learning to be a travel agent. Where was the frequent-flyer program when I needed it?

No matter how I hit, hot streaks included, I knew I'd end up a .250 hitter, a part-time journeyman player, the player to be named later in any trade. Nobody wants to go through life as the player to be named later.

I was making $16,000 and had a wife, one child, and another on the way, plus two homes to maintain, one in Chicago and the other in St. Louis. This formula of one family, two houses, and $16,000 equals what economists call "negative cash flow," the government calls "deficit spending," and I called "going in the hole." I was definitely open to some new suggestion.

I'd just emceed a luncheon for all the politicians and influential people of St. Louis. I didn't know them, but sportswriter Bob Broeg filled me in on their backgrounds so I could build my introductions. After the luncheon, Al Fleishman, the man who handled Anheuser-Busch's public relations, told me how impressed he was with the job I'd done.

"You didn't know most of them," he said, "but you made it look like you did. When you're finished with baseball, come down to my office and talk to me."

So after taking stock of my financial empire (which took about 10 seconds), I decided to find out just how impressed Fleishman was. It turned out he didn't have a job for me, but he suggested I call Harry Renfro at D'arcy Advertising, which handled Anheuser-Busch's account.

So much was running through my mind. Anheuser-Busch owned the Cardinals, and their play-by-play announcer, Harry Caray, had once talked to me about a broadcasting career. Former catcher Gabby Street, Caray's color man, had also encouraged me about broadcasting in my Cardinal days. "Son, all you have to do is clean up a few of your bullpen stories and you'll be fine," he said. I was thinking about everything Fleishman, Caray, and Street had told me, and I had my own plan, too.

If D'arcy would pay me $1,000 a month, I'd make all the speeches the brewery wanted. My logic was simple: $1,000 a month for 12 months is $12,000, I could pick up enough $150 and $200 speaking jobs to get up to $14,000 and, if I were lucky, maybe $18,000 and someday maybe $20,000. And with just one house to maintain I might end up with some black ink.

D'arcy Advertising was interested in me, but their message was clear: come back to see us when you're finished playing baseball. So I decided I was finished that day and applied for the Voluntary Retired list of the Chicago Cubs, which brought Cubs general manager Wid Matthews down to St. Louis in a hurry. He asked me to play just one more season because he wouldn't have any other catchers until Harry Chiti returned from the army. I agreed, and Matthews promised the Cubs wouldn't sell me or trade me.

While I was in New Orleans for an exhibition game, I was served a subpoena to testify before the Senate Judiciary Committee's Monopoly Subcommittee in Washington. The process server said, "You don't seem too upset about getting this," and I thought, "Upset? I don't even know why they want me, unless some committee has finally made batting slumps illegal." I called Wid Matthews right away.

"Do you think I need a lawyer to go with me?" I asked. "No, just tell the truth and answer all their questions," he said, advice that later came back to haunt him. When the committee asked me how much money I made, I told them $16,000 a year. When I got back to Chicago, Matthews called me into his office, furious, wanting to know why I told the committee how much money I was making.

"You told me to tell the truth," I said.

"Well," he hollered back, "they printed your answer in the paper, and now four players want a raise!"

The Senate subcommittee wanted me to testify concerning a bill proposed by Senator Edwin C. Johnson of Colorado, suggesting that if a baseball team is owned by a big corporation like Anheuser-Busch, the ballclub should be subject to antitrust laws. Johnson felt the integrity of baseball would be in jeopardy if I were allowed to leave the Cubs to broadcast for the Cardinals. At first I couldn't believe he was serious, but as he continued to question me, I realized how serious he was.

Senator Johnson suggested perhaps tampering was involved, meaning the Cardinals were trying to lure me away from the Cubs. (Even in those days, who would tamper with a $16,000-a-year ballplayer?) I told him the Cardinals didn't come to me, I went to them. His next question helped me get my name in the newspapers: he asked whether the Cardinals might make an offer to Brooklyn's Roy Campanella to become a broadcaster if Campy would retire as a player.

"Senator, you can't compare me to Campanella," I said. "I'm a .250 hitter." I got a laugh, and plenty of newspaper coverage, but I wasn't trying to be funny. I could see my plans to get into the broadcast booth going down the drain, and I was scared.

An Associated Press story of April 8, 1954, had this to say:

> Garagiola didn't seem to grasp all the fine legal points expounded by Johnson and the other senators.
>
> "But I can quit baseball if I want to," Garagiola finally spoke up.
>
> "But you can't go to work for any other club, directly or indirectly," said Johnson.
>
> "Who can I work for?" Joe wanted to know.

"You can go to work for anyone not connected with another ballclub," Johnson replied.

Garagiola suggested his future as a broadcaster most certainly had to be connected with baseball.

"I can't sing," he explained.

Nothing ever came of those hearings, and that was the first and last time I was ever compared to Roy Campanella.

The 1954 season started, and to paraphrase Walter Cronkite, it was a season like any other season. I started by not hitting, then went into a slump, but at least I knew I'd never be sold or traded again. That is, until the month of September.

We were playing the New York Giants at the Polo Grounds when my manager, Stan Hack, said he wanted to see me.

"You've just been sold to the Giants," he told me.

"You can't do that," I said. "I'm quitting at the end of the year, and you guys promised you wouldn't trade me or sell me."

"That's all I know," Hack said. So I went straight to Wid Matthews before I had a chance to cool off.

"You can't sell me when I'm quitting," I told him.

"Look, Joe. The Giants are going to win the pennant, so go over there, don't say anything, and maybe you'll change your mind."

"Did you tell the Giants I'm quitting?" I asked, even though I was sure I knew the answer.

"No, just go over there and don't say anything. You'll get a World Series cut, and you'll hit a lot of home runs in that park."

I couldn't believe what I was hearing. I thought about the Senate committee's concern for the so-called "integrity" of our "national pastime" and thought, "So this is how they do things."

After the game, I told the whole story to my roommate,

Howard Pollet. I felt I also had to tell Giants owner Horace Stoneham, so through his friend, Toots Shor, we arranged to meet Stoneham at his apartment. When I finished telling him my story, he was fuming.

"I thought there was more to this deal when they let you go for the waiver price," he said. "We'll see about this."

After reassuring me that I wouldn't get hurt for telling him the truth, Stoneham called Commissioner Ford Frick and asked for a hearing the next day. The hearing didn't last too long, and I came out a winner. Here's what happened: Wid Matthews told his story, Stoneham told his version, and I told mine. Then the commissioner said:

"Gentlemen, we have three stories and three choices. One, I void the deal, and we'll have a lot of explaining to do. Two, Garagiola refuses to report, but that would make him look bad, as what player refuses to join a team about to win the pennant. Or three, Garagiola reports, and if he changes his mind and decides to continue playing, the problem is solved. If he decides to quit, the Giants will sell him back to the Cubs, and he will not be embarrassed because he was honest. We will abide by option three."

Matthews wasn't too happy because he lost a player. Stoneham was satisfied because he got a player but was also protected if I decided to quit. I loved the deal because the Cubs had to give me "moving money," and since I was going from a western club to an eastern club, I got the larger of the expenses, even though I was only moving from the Commodore Hotel on 42nd Street to the Henry Hudson on 57th.

The Giants won the pennant, and even though I wasn't eligible to play in the World Series because I joined them in September, I went to Cleveland with the club. I caught batting practice, watched the games, got a $1,000 World Series share, rode in New York's largest-ever ticker tape parade, and even appeared on "The Ed Sullivan Show" with the team. I felt like the grand prize winner in the Why I Love the Giants Sweepstakes.

While I didn't leave the game à la Mantle or Bench, with fanfare and a farewell celebration in every city, I did cause one problem. The Giants' general manager, Chub Feeney, had to find another catcher.

"I know you told us you're quitting, Joe, but unless you change your mind we'll have to make a decision. It's either you or I'll draft Mickey Grasso."

Think about my two great memories of 1954. Wid Matthews wanted me to fill in until Harry Chiti returned, and Chub Feeney had to make a tough decision between me and Mickey Grasso. To put it into perspective, here's the lifetime batting averages: Chiti, .238; Grasso, .226; Garagiola, .257. Those are lifetime averages, not area codes. How's that for a piece of baseball immortality?

The next season I started broadcasting for the Cardinals, and it's true, the fact that I was a player got me the job. Young, aspiring broadcasters who aren't former athletes are sometimes bitter and resentful because the job often goes to the guy who's fresh out of the clubhouse. Red Barber said many times, "Any of you young fellows who want to be broadcasters, just go out and buy a glove and spiked shoes. That's all it takes." Howard Cosell calls it "jockocracy." Skip Caray, who does Atlanta Braves baseball and Hawks basketball, says, "If a young guy asked me for advice on how to get into broadcasting, I'd say 'Hit .350 or win the Heisman.' " My answer to those criticisms: being a former athlete may get you there, but it won't keep you there.

I think the broadcast booth has room for both the announcer with playing experience and the announcer without it. What bugs me is the terminology. Calling one a "jock" and the other a "professional broadcaster" implies that a person can't be both.

Actually, everything about my baseball career prepared me to be a radio and television announcer (my year with the

Pirates alone gave me a lifetime worth of material). What helped me the most was having been a catcher and a "spear carrier." (A "spear carrier" is definitely not a star. You know you're a spear carrier when you're told not to use the game stuff to catch batting practice. Another way you know is when during a rain delay you're asked to get the resin bag on your way in from the bullpen so *it* doesn't get wet.)

A star doesn't know what it's like to come out to the ballpark not knowing whether he's going to play until he sees the lineup card. The star doesn't know what it's like to sit in the bullpen or on the bench, watching the game and talking about what's going right or wrong and why. The star hitter worries about stance, swing, and hitting .300. The star pitcher worries about keeping his curveball low and winning 20 games. The spear carrier worries about getting released. While the star is busy every day playing the game, the spear carrier is busy watching all the positions, as well as the manager.

The fact that former athletes served their apprenticeships on the field rather than behind a microphone simply means that they can bring a different viewpoint into a broadcast, especially if they work at it. Two announcers can look at the same situation and make observations each from his own perspective. Vin Scully once described a bunt as "dropping like a poached egg." To that colorful description I added that the bunt worked because the grass was high and the dirt in front of home plate was soft. Since the pitcher was a sinkerballer, they were expecting a lot of ground balls, so to slow down the first couple of bounces, the groundskeepers made the dirt soft. A "poached egg," or high grass and soft dirt—two different perspectives that give you a more complete picture.

A broadcaster who's never played the game probably knows about the dirt and the grass, too, but he's never been there, so he can't speak from personal experience. For example, when the pitcher motions to the catcher to come out to the mound, you don't need an "analyst" to tell you, "They're discussing some strategy." If your TV set is working, you can see that. So it's my job to do a little mental workout and try to guess what the meeting's about.

With a runner on second, I might say, "In a spot like this, the pitcher wants to be sure they're not stealing the signals." Then, thinking back to the many times I walked out to the mound as a catcher, I might add, "The signals can remain the same: one finger for a fastball, two fingers for the curveball, and three fingers for the change of pace. You decide with the pitcher which flash counts. Sometimes it's the second flash, sometimes the last, whatever." Now, the runner on second may be the kind of guy who could get lost in a car wash, but as a viewer, you get an idea of what could be happening.

Or maybe I'll say, "I had one pitcher call me out to the mound who wasn't worried about the runners at all. After a couple of line drives right back at him, he just wanted to know 'With the kind of stuff I've got today, do you think a guy could get killed out here?'" Whichever anecdote you use, if you've been there, it's a lot more believable.

Because former athletes do know what it's like to play, they can easily fall into the trap of leaning too much toward the players and not looking critically when a player doesn't make the play or makes a dumb play. You have to learn to be critical, but your experience as a player gives you the advantage of being able to understand the "why" of what happened, where a nonathlete broadcaster might criticize without understanding what the player is going through.

One of my pet gripes is the nonathlete announcer who says, "I don't mind the strikeout, but a called strike? You can't get called out in a spot like this. You have to go down swinging." Okay, that sounds logical and reasonable, but unless you've done it, you don't know the feeling. You see the ball, you want to swing, but you just can't pull the trigger, and you're called out. Why you didn't swing remains a mystery, even to you.

The difference is when you blow it in the broadcast booth, you can say, "Excuse me, what I meant to say was . . ." Only your coworkers know you made a mistake, and even if it's a live broadcast, the "Excuse me" takes care of everything. When you blow it on the field, try using "Excuse me" to explain to the manager why you took a third strike.

Based on everything I learned as a player, I try to be the fans' eyes and ears when I'm in the clubhouse and on the bench. Then in the telecast, I try to show things that can't be seen even by the people in the ballpark, to bring the viewers closer to the game and the players. That's when my experience as a catcher really becomes crucial.

How? Let's say a man's on first in a bunt situation. This is what you see on your TV: the pitcher comes to a set position with the runner on, then makes a lazy throw to first base. Now, you don't need somebody to tell you, "There's a throw to first base." The real game of baseball is the game you never see, and as a former catcher I'm going to tell you that the harmless throw to first was probably an attempt by the catcher to learn if there's a bunt play on.

I often asked pitchers to throw over to first base when I suspected a bunt. On the pitcher's first move, in this case to first, the batter would react. If he's up there to bunt, you'd see his hands start to slide up the bat handle. Everyone in the ballpark is watching the play at first, but the catcher is zeroed in on the batter's hands. And now, so are you, watching at home.

I guess I always knew I belonged behind home plate—I just didn't know how far. But because of similarities in perspective, the transition from player to broadcaster might be easier for a catcher. As a catcher, you're in on every pitch, and you're usually thinking two or three hitters ahead. The catcher is the only player who sees the game both close up and from a "wide-angle shot," similar to the view from the booth. And the pitched ball comes toward you and the batted ball goes away from you.

As a catcher, there were times I felt I should call a pitch-out. I still get that same feeling in the booth, and if I sense a pitch-out, I'll call it. Call it right and you're an instant genius. Call it wrong and you can bet the people watching turn to each other and say, "No wonder that dummy is up in the booth instead of on the field."

I can't always explain what I saw, but I just sense something is different. Roger Craig, former pitcher and coach and now manager, says, "A thief will do something different when he's going to steal, whether he's stealing second base or stealing from a bank." Sometimes you see something different; other times you just have a feeling. If a catcher calls for a pitch-out and breaks up the play, he's a hero. Even if he can't explain why he did it.

"Think like a catcher, not like a broadcaster," was great advice. I want viewers to get involved, to react to what I say, one way or the other, with either "I never thought of that" or "Joe, you're full of it." I want the broadcast to sound like two guys sitting at the ballpark, talking about the game, with the viewer eavesdropping. It's not High Mass, and it's not a seminar—it's a ballgame.

I've learned a lot in the broadcast booth, both from the people I've worked with and from the constantly improving technology. With advances like instant replays, slow motion, and multiple cameras, television now brings viewers a much more complete picture of the game. But the basics haven't changed, and that's why I rely on some tricks I've learned from people I've worked with over the years.

Tom Gallery, then head of NBC Sports, brought me to New York and introduced me to NBC. His philosophy of baseball broadcasting is still with me. Concentrate on the "Big Five": the score, the batter, the count, the outs, and the inning. "Follow the ball and remember the game is the reason you're there."

I've worked with many different broadcasters, from Harry Caray, who gave me my start, and Lindsey Nelson, who introduced me to working for a network, to the Hall of Fame roster of broadcasters I've sat next to during All-Star games and World Series. But the most practical advice I ever got came from Red Barber, who always said, "Never start a broadcast on an empty stomach or a full bladder."

Red also passed on to me a very simple solution to a baseball announcer's most basic problem. He used a three-minute egg timer to remind him to give the score. No doubt, an egg timer looks strange sitting among scorebooks and notes, but you always know that when the sand from the top falls to the bottom of the glass, it's time to give the score. Every baseball play-by-play announcer could help himself with that little trick.

One habit of a fellow broadcaster that I *don't* think would work for everyone was Phil Rizzuto's way of scoring a game. Instead of using the numbers that correspond to each position, like 4–3 for a ground ball to the second baseman, Phil had his own system. His scorecard was full of things like "GO" for ground out, "FO" for fly out and "PO" for pop out. During one game he took a break, and when he came back he asked me what the "WL" meant that I'd written on his scorecard. "Wasn't looking," I said.

When it comes to broadcasting baseball, I'm like Will Rogers: I've never seen a game I didn't like. I started as a "color man" with Harry Caray in St. Louis, and now I'm an "analyst" with Vin Scully on "NBC's Game of the Week." What's the difference? Only the years and the money.

I've always liked the teamwork of the booth. Just like any situation in which you learn to work closely with another person, a play-by-play and color broadcaster have to get used to each other and discover how the other works. A good team will learn to work together instinctively, just like a shortstop and second baseman or a pitcher and catcher. With Vin and me, it happened at the 1983 All-Star game in Chicago.

By the third inning the American League was leading 9–0—it was like a Sunday afternoon game in the park between the Fats and the Leans. This was a real "Roto-Rooter" game: to keep people watching, we'd have to do some digging. Since the play-by-play man controls the flow and sets the pace of the broadcast, I was wondering which way Vin would go: I wanted to take a light approach, but would he want to stick with the game and play it straight? If he starts the conversation in one direction, I can't say anything that takes the conversation another way.

He answered my question when he said, "Do you get the feeling there ought to be a keg of beer at every base and the winner takes all?"

That's what it means to work together instinctively. It's not something you can plan; it just has to happen.

I like a two-person team best, and I don't think it matters whether one is a former athlete or both are. Their experience is secondary to their personalities and how well they work together. Tony Kubek and I each brought a different perspective to the booth, he as a former shortstop and I as a former catcher. We saw things from different angles. We weren't afraid to disagree, and almost every argument we had centered around second base or home plate. On a stolen base, for example, I'd say something like "Take a good look at the way he took the throw—he's behind the bag. If he catches it in front of the bag, all he has to do is drop his hand, and the runner's out. Forget that the baserunner stole on the pitcher; blame that on the infielder."

After that, the catcher had to pass a Kubek X-ray exam. "Look at how the catcher caught the ball and the extra step he gave the runner. And the throw was to the shortstop side of the bag. Even with the extra step, if the throw had been on the first-base side, it's an easy out."

We both won some and lost some, but it was all part of being ourselves. You can't fake arguments about things like that, or the fans will sense you're not being genuine. The relationship between the announcers in the booth has to be real.

The booth is like any other working situation—you need the time and the opportunity to develop a working relationship with your partner. That's why it's difficult to have a good broadcast when the booth gets crowded, with either too many visitors or too many announcers.

We had six in the booth for the 1980 World Series between the Philadelphia Phillies and the Kansas City Royals. Tony Kubek and I did play-by-play, Bryant Gumbel did the pregame show and a commentary from the booth, Tom Seaver analyzed pitching strategy, former umpire Ron Luciano commented on controversial calls, and Merle Harmon interviewed people in the stands during the game. Three more guys, and we could have played an Old-Timers Game. The play-by-play man ends up being a traffic cop, spending all his time introducing announcers in the booth, bringing somebody in with an interview, going back to somebody in the studio. He's more maître d' than announcer. Soon you're giving replays of the station breaks. You can't develop a relationship with anybody you're working with because all you really do is pass the mike around. With so much individual input, the broadcast can't develop any continuity. It's not fair to the game or the announcers. Like Phil Rizzuto said about the old Yankees' five-man radio team, "We've got so many announcers, I got spiked the other day."

The play-by-play announcer has to be concerned with the technical nuts and bolts of the broadcast, everything from commercial breaks and promos to switching to other broadcasts. (That can get out of hand, too. During one World Series, we had to stuff so many promos into each broadcast, Johnny Carson opened his "Tonight Show" monologue with this spoof of our play-by-play: "Dusty Baker hits a fly ball to deep lift center. Roy White goes back, back, back to the wall—which reminds me that 'Quincy' will have *his* back to the wall tomorrow night at 9:00, 8:00 central time. . . .")

The analyst has just one main concern: think about the game. That's why I enjoy doing color, because it allows me to concentrate on what the players are doing and forget about the technical things. As an analyst, I can watch the whole field, not just the play-by-play on the monitor. I can look beyond what the TV viewer is seeing to the "why" and the "how" of a play, and bring some extra information to the game.

That's where preparation plays a crucial role. I never could have kept my job by only telling baseball stories about Joe Garagiola. I'd have had about three games to talk about: the World Series game when I had four hits, the time I played both ends of a doubleheader in Pittsburgh, and a playground game that I won by walking with the bases loaded. Athletes-turned-broadcasters need to use their experience for a frame of reference, but it's today's players the fans want to know about.

Since I have to prepare for all 26 teams for the "Game of the Week," I rely on newspaper accounts, team news releases, telephone calls, and cable TV, but there's some homework I can only do when I get to the ballpark on Saturday morning. One of the first things I do is check in front of home plate. Is it hard or soft? How high is the grass? Are the foul lines tilted? Then I do a ballplayer's weather report. Is the wind blowing out? Will clouds make it easier to see high fly balls? I watch infield practice. Does the ball die when it hits the grass? Who's throwing well? Who's joking around? I try to learn as much as I can just by watching.

Then I go to a set list of questions that I ask each team every week. Who's hurt? Who's hot? Who's playing hit and run? Are the baserunners on their own? Then I use three questions I picked up from Ray Miller when he was a pitching coach for the Baltimore Orioles. He always wanted to know three things about the opposing team from his starting pitcher:

1. If you have to throw a fastball in a game situation to a particular hitter (say Don Mattingly or Dave Winfield), where will you throw it?

2. Who are the three hitters in the lineup you really have to do a good job on to win the game?

3. With men on base, who are the batters who will try to hit you to the opposite field or go the other way?

Besides these questions, I also verify stories and quotes I've gathered from the papers and news releases. Mostly, though, I just talk with the players and the coaches—you never know when something you talk about might be useful in a broadcast—and to do that, you need to get out of the booth and go down to the clubhouse, sit on the bench, and hang around the batting cage.

At the All-Star game in 1987, I saw home run hitter Mark McGwire of the Oakland Athletics for the first time. During batting practice, I couldn't help noticing how he looked at the pitcher and how similar his head position was to Stan Musial's. Stan always had both eyes focused on the pitcher, straight on. He didn't want a side view. Where did the rookie McGwire learn this? Had he studied Musial or any other hitter? His answers, that he just wanted to see the ball the best he could and that he never studied any hitters, gave me a chance to talk about him as more than just a statistic.

The Yankees' Don Mattingly is another good one to talk to about hitting. The first time I saw him hit, I wondered about a few things he did in the batter's box. Like all good hitters, he has his own theories and his own ideas.

First, I asked him why he points the toes of his front foot in. "To remind me to keep that front shoulder in and not open up too soon," he told me.

"Why do you seem to take the first pitch all the time?" I followed up.

"I like to gauge a pitcher," he said. "I want to take him deep in the count, and if he's nibbler, he'll miss with the first pitch for ball one, and now I'm ahead. Late in the game, if the situation calls for it, I might swing at the first pitch." You're almost hoping for a rain delay so you can use all the good information Mattingly gives you.

Only by asking a lot of questions before a game can I get this kind of information. For example, while talking with the San Francisco Giants' batting coach Jose Morales during the 1987 National League Championship Series, I got an insight into what some coaches do between innings. "Watch the opposing pitcher warm up," Morales said. "Some pitchers will show you what pitch they have the most confidence in by throwing mostly that pitch. He might throw a couple curveballs, but if his slider's working, he'll probably throw five sliders, two curveballs, and one fastball. Pretty apparent what's working for him."

During the same series, standing around the batting cage, young Will Clark was talking about a conversation he'd had with Keith Hernandez. When I asked Will about the adjustments he had to make in hitting his second year, he said, "The more hits you get, the fewer fastballs you see." Then he added, "Hernandez told me, 'Study the catchers, not just the pitchers. Learn the catchers' habits. You'll learn that most catchers, when they know their pitcher's in trouble, will call for the pitch that they [the catchers] can't hit.'"

Preparation involves constant checking. You can't take anything for granted, because things change from one game to the next. Once when I was doing a Kansas City Royals game, I checked my notes and saw that Frank White was the team's best hit-and-run man. So before the game I asked manager Dick Howser if that was still accurate. "No, he can't seem to pull the trigger," Howser told me. Based on previous games, my scouting report on White said "a good hit-and-run man." But this day, that wasn't the case, and I was glad I asked.

What you hear sitting on the bench or around the cage isn't always inside baseball talk, and it can really help show a player's human side. I remember sitting on the bench in Fenway Park next to Angels' manager Gene Mauch, when his young starting pitcher, Willie Fraser, walked by. Fraser's from upstate New York, and Mauch knew he'd have lots of friends and family at the game.

"How many passes today?" Mauch asked him.

"I ain't walking anybody!" young Fraser answered.

That story tells more about Willie Fraser than any statistic I could have read. And since I was the only nonplayer on the bench, I also had an original story, the kind a broadcaster is happy to get, because you always have to have new and more information. You can make a point, but you can't overuse it. If you have something good, it won't be good anymore if you keep repeating it.

Although it's necessary to come into a game prepared, you can't just rely on what you've planned; you have to watch what's going on and try to anticipate what the viewers might be curious about. Also, prepared anecdotes really help out in a 10–1 ballgame, but in a close game you have to be ready to put all that aside and let the game take over the broadcast.

Nowadays, you have to be ready to comment on anything and everything, since television's technology has improved and our crews are able to get just about any shot you could possibly want. In 1947, the first World Series telecast used 3 cameras. In 1986, NBC used 10 stationary cameras around the ballpark, one minicam, one blimp camera, and one camera in each locker room. We use five for every regular Saturday "Game of the Week."

With that kind of coverage, you get reaction shots, slow motion, and instant replay isolation from several angles. The pictures now tell the story so much better and more completely that it's changed the announcer's job. Today, all you have to do is remind people a pitcher has a no-hitter going and let the picture and the crowd do the rest. Silence can sometimes be the announcer's greatest tool.

During the Mets' 10th-inning comeback win in the sixth game of the 1986 World Series, NBC executive producer Mike Weisman clocked the silence in the booth at three and a half minutes. Just pictures: the run scoring, the crowd, the players, the replay. The crowd supplied the sound. It's one of the hardest things for an announcer to learn, but it really brings the viewer into the ballpark.

When I go to the ballpark on Saturday, I'm not the only one asking questions. The players have a few of their own. In fact, there are four questions players are guaranteed to ask me when I walk into a ballpark as the "Game of the Week" announcer.

Question 1: "Is this the 'Game of the Week'?" If the player is an old friend with a sense of humor, I usually say, "No, this isn't the 'Game of the Week.' I was just sitting at home thinking, 'Why don't I get on a plane and fly over to see you?' You're a good guy, so here I am." I get either a big laugh or a nick on the shins with the bat.

Question 2: "Will this game be seen in [the player's hometown or where his folks live]?"

Question 3: "Could you say hello to so-and-so?" This varies from the player's family or a friend who's a great fan to the "guys." The "guys" might be at the country club or the saloon. When we have a game close to Mother's Day or Father's Day, the messages get even more personalized.

Question 4: "What did you mean when you said _____?" Before I can answer I usually hear, "My wife/

brother/dad/coach told me you said _____ ." This report obviously came from someone close to the player, so I'm wrong no matter what I say. That is, if I even said what he claims I said. I've been accused of saying things that someone else has said on another broadcast, and I'm sure other broadcasters have experienced the same thing.

Basically people hear only what they want to hear or only the way they want to hear it. Every year we're accused of being biased at the League Championship Series or the World Series. Those charges are as much a part of the big, postseason games as the "John 3:16" sign. If you say somebody made a great play, people say you're rooting for that team. If your opinion on a controversial play doesn't favor their team, they say you're rooting for the other team.

People look for any connection. During the 1982 World Series, some Milwaukee Brewer fans accused me of rooting for the Cardinals because I'm from St. Louis and I used to play for the Cardinals. Of course, it had been more than 30 years since I'd played there, but they weren't counting. In the same series, some Cardinals fans said Tony Kubek was pro Brewers because he's from Milwaukee.

Sometimes the fans really stretch. During the 1980 World Series between Philadelphia and Kansas City, Phillies fans said I was rooting for the Royals because I'm from Missouri. In Kansas City they said I was rooting for the Phillies because I'm a National Leaguer! What does that mean?

Two blistering letters, both dated October 15, 1978: "We know now that you are for the Dodgers." The other: "You and Tony are so obviously rooting for the Yankees in this series that it's becoming nauseating!!" That year, NBC executive producer Don Ohlmeyer kept track of the letters: 287 letters from Dodger fans wanting to know why Tony and I were so biased toward the Yankees and 294 letters from Yankee fans wondering why we were so biased toward the Dodgers. Were these people even watching the same telecast?

During the 1975 World Series between Cincinnati and Boston, I got the usual phone calls from fans, but this one topped them all. A woman called me at the hotel in Cincinnati, really upset that I "favored" the Red Sox. I asked her what made her think I was so pro Boston, and she said "because you kept saying Carlton Fisk is a good catcher." As soon as I said "Red Sox," the Cincinnati fans wanted equal time and vice versa. You just can't do a broadcast that way.

The reason for all this is the strong allegiance fans feel toward their team, and since we're the bearers of bad news when they lose, the fans get mad at us for it. And everything is magnified in the League Championship Series and the World Series.

People say we're rooting, but often we're just trying to be heard. For example, if the Cardinals hit a home run in, say, San Francisco, you can bet the crowd isn't going to react. So you can say in a normal tone of voice, "There she goes, home run." But then if the Giants hit one, and the whole ballpark goes wild, you have to "punch" it a little bit to get over the crowd noise. So the people in St. Louis say you're rooting for San Francisco. And then, of course, the Giants' fans do the same thing when you go to St. Louis.

The problem is that the fans just aren't used to listening to a network broadcast. All season, fans are used to hearing their local announcer, and in many cases he *is* cheering for the home team. People always say to me, "I thought announcers were supposed to be impartial." But that's not really what they want: they want us to root, but only for their team. When we're impartial, they hear it as rooting for the other team. Well, maybe we are rooting, but only for a good game. So, I just figured if we hear the criticism from both sides, we must be doing a good job.

I'm really troubled, though, by how angry and violent the

fans have become at World Series time. Winning the pennant or the world championship can be the best thing to happen to a city, the glue that holds it together for months. Everybody's a fan, and they forget about their problems. People who never speak to each other are saying, "Hey, did you see what happened last night?" People should be having fun.

Yet in Philadelphia in 1980, Tony Kubek and I needed police protection to go from the ballpark to our hotel. We sat in the back seat of an unmarked car, between two plainclothes police officers. We had to use the kitchen entrance to get into our hotel. And this was after the Phillies had just become World Champions. It made me sad.

In Milwaukee in 1982, I remember trying to convince Pee Wee Reese that I had a bodyguard. He couldn't believe it when I pointed out the big guy who was assigned to me for protection. "You don't believe it, Pee Wee? Watch where he goes when I walk over to the Brewers' bench." Watching this guy follow me wherever I went, all Pee Wee could do was shake his head.

And what about when the Tigers won the World Series in Detroit in 1984? The fans swarmed all over the field, and a few of them began ripping up pieces of turf and throwing them into the stands. Soon everybody was doing it—sod was flying all over the place. It was scary. Vin had to crawl underneath the desk and do the sign-off on the floor of the booth.

So the job does have a downside. But one of the biggest rewards of being a baseball broadcaster is having the opportunity to develop positive relationships with the players. I've had the chance to get to know some interesting men who've amazed me with more than just their baseball talent.

Like Reggie Jackson. He handles television cameras better than any player I've ever known. He knows what televised baseball means to the game, to the networks, the sponsors, and the fans.

Right after one of the weekly Steinbrenner-Jackson "disagreements" in the newspapers, we were in New York for the "Game of the Week." I asked Reggie if he'd come on and talk about it, and he agreed. We taped the interview, and as always, Reggie told the complete story. In this case, it was too complete; word came back from the director that it was too long and we needed to do it again.

"I can't do it again, and I can't tell the whole story if you ask me to be shorter," Reggie said. "Don't worry about it; it'll work." He had it all figured out. "When I come to bat the second time, regardless of the situation, you start the tape and stand up in the booth. I'll walk up to the plate, then call time and go back for another bat. I'll look for you up in the booth, and if you're still standing, I can go for the resin bag, the pine tar, the dirt, whatever I need until the tape gets to the end. When it's over just sit down."

As if we were choreographed by Bob Fosse, the second time Reggie walked up to home plate, I stood up in the booth, and he did his entire routine until I sat down. Interview over, the game goes on, and Reggie doubles.

Another player I've had the opportunity to know taught me a lesson I've never forgotten. In the strange way people's lives cross, I was able to pass that lesson on; of all people, I ended up giving advice to one of baseball's greatest hitters.

Bobby Bonds, a good ballplayer who went into coaching after his playing career, taught me a lot at the funeral of Yankee catcher Thurman Munson. Thurman was the kind of guy who got mixed reviews from writers and broadcasters. If you asked him a question he thought was stupid, that's exactly what he'd tell you. Many people, in delivering their eulogies, seemed to feel they had to explain Thurman, saying things like "Those of us who knew him knew he was a good guy, not the guy you read or heard about."

But Bobby Bonds paraphrased a well-known thought as he remembered Thurman Munson: "For those who love him, no explanation is necessary, and for those who don't, none is possible." I thought about that a lot and realized that if you change the word *love* to the word *know*, the thought works just the same. I put that thought on a card and literally carry it with me every day.

Soon after, we were in Detroit for an Angels-Tigers game. Rod Carew was having a tough time. From Opening Day he kept hearing that ridiculous criticism, "But he doesn't drive in any runs." How could a man possibly hit for as high an average as he did and not help his club? The criticism got so tough he was talking about quitting baseball.

Talking with Reggie Jackson, I said, "Rod can't quit this year; baseball needs him. He shouldn't pay attention to any of that stuff. I know that's easy for me to say, but those of us who know him know better." Then I showed Reggie the card with the Bobby Bonds lesson on it.

"Go over and tell that to Rod," Reggie said. "He needs it."

So I talked to Rod and told him the story. He asked me to write down the line for him, which I did.

On our next trip into Anaheim, he pulled me aside and said, "I want to show you something." He took a small brass plaque from his pocket, and on it was engraved, "For those who know me, no explanation is necessary, and for those who don't, none is possible." He made my day complete when he said his wife Marilyn had embroidered that message and hung it in their home.

I'm a collector: autographed balls, bubble-gum cards, everything. But one autographed ball is right in front. When Rod Carew got his 3,000th hit, he sent me one of the game balls, which he'd signed. On it he'd also written what we now call "our saying." It means a lot to me.

Those moments are among the many reasons I wouldn't

trade my job for any other. It's always different. Whether it's the World Series with its added glitter or a local broadcast, a baseball game means at least two hours and 30 minutes of having to react to what's happening in front of you, with no clue to what might happen next.

Hawk Harrelson says, "Baseball is the only game where the team with the ball is on defense." Once the pitcher throws the ball, who knows what will happen? If the batter misses it, will the catcher catch it? If the batter hits it, will it be caught? If it is caught, will the fielder make a good throw? Will the runner miss a base and be declared out? The possibilities go on and on. Few guaranteed plays exist in baseball (like the fourth-and-long-yardage sure punt in football). A baseball broadcaster has to have a certain amount of spontaneity, and that's what can cause problems. Problems? Spell that b-l-o-o-p-e-r-s.

I redefined the Brooklyn Dodgers' fans with one of my bloopers. Ebbets Field had a short right-field fence, the scoreboard in right center, a high screen, and padded walls. The outfield fence had all kinds of angles. Carl Furillo, the Dodgers' rightfielder, played the caroms as if he'd designed and built the wall; he knew every nook and cranny in right field. Unfortunately, it came out that he knew "every crook and nanny in right field."

Vin Scully gets a good needling because he always looks like he just stepped out of an air-conditioned room. When people ask me what Vin is like, I simply say he doesn't sweat, get his hair messed, or go to the bathroom. But he is real, and he doesn't wear a sign saying "Batteries not included."

On a ball hit to right field, Vin wanted to say, "There's a hot shot hit to right," but it didn't quite come out that way. He quickly learned that you don't use *shot* and *hit* in the same sentence if you have to say it fast.

Some of our fellow blooper club members include the New York Mets' announcer Ralph Kiner, who once had a broadcast that experienced "audio technicalities." San Diego Padres' announcer Jerry Coleman had this unique station break: "We now pause 10 stations for a minute identification." Broadcasting a game from Royals Stadium in Kansas City, Coleman said, "The sky is so clear today you can see all the way to Missouri."

The Cardinals' Mike Shannon fondly remembered Jack Clark's home run that beat the Dodgers in the 1985 National League Championship Series, recalling "the concussion of the ball hitting the bat." When a San Francisco batter lined out hard to first base, Shannon said, "Well, the Giants just got a taste of the medicine they've been enjoying all day."

Jim Hart, the football player-turned-broadcaster, joined the blooper club early with "They must give the offense better field condition." Larry King, while doing color for the Miami Dolphins, once reported the Colts' "drug and bugle corps" was on the field. And football's John Madden made this observation about Earl Campbell: "From the waist down, he has the biggest legs I've ever seen on a running back."

Tony Kubek gave viewers some inside information during a College World Series broadcast when he said, "One of the ways to get extra time so your bullpen can get ready is to fake a legitimate injury."

Phil Rizzuto told his listeners about a letter he received from a woman who listened faithfully to every Yankee game on her Walkman each night before going to bed. I don't think it came out the way Phil wanted it to, though, when he said, "I can't think of a better way to go to sleep than listening to Yankee baseball."

Byrum Saam, a baseball broadcaster for 50 years, called this unusual play, involving Philadelphia Athletic outfielder Bob Johnson: "There goes a long fly to left. He's going back, back . . . his head hits the wall. It bounces off. He reaches down, picks it up, and throws it to second base."

Broadcasters aren't the only one affected by "word

demons." Paul Owens, the Phillies' former manager, general manager, and super scout, once asked a cabdriver who was playing his radio very loud, "Hey, cabbie, could you turn that thing down about a hundred disciples?"

When managing the Phillies, Frank Lucchesi wanted to make sure he wasn't blamed for a tough loss: "Nobody can make me the scrapgoat," he said. Former Minnesota Twins owner Calvin Griffith must have had a very unique knee operation: "They took out the cartridge," he said. Public address announcer Bob Casey told the fans the penalty on the Vikings was for an "illegitimate receiver downfield."

Sometime it's possible to edit in midsentence, but that usually confuses things even more. During a Cardinals-Mets game, Ralph Kiner said, "Tommy Herr has had three knee operations." Now, we all know Tommy Herr doesn't have three knees, but Ralph wanted to make sure, so he added, "Not on three knees, but two on one and one on the other."

Often you don't realize how something will sound until you've said it, and by then it's too late, as Olympic cyclist Eric Heiden found out when he was doing color commentary on a cycling event. Pointing out that the front man cuts air friction for the man immediately behind him, Heiden said whoever leads "will be breaking a lot of wind for whoever's second."

All these "occupational hazards" can help make a live broadcast a little more lively and unpredictable. Some of those broadcasts I wish I could forget, and I hope some of the people I worked with get a busy signal should they ever call me again. Or better yet, I hope they lose my number. But many of the broadcasts and events bring back great memories and make me wish I'd get a call from some of the people I worked with, saying, "Let's do it again sometime."

"Even his wife calls him Yogi. Carmen still laughs about how, after more than 30 years of marriage, she got an anniversary card signed 'Yogi Berra.' She asked him if he thought he had to sign his last name so she wouldn't think it came from some other Yogi."

○

8

I'll Take Lawdie: Yogi & Me

ALL SPORTS-MINDED KIDS have their own variation of the free-agent draft. In the St. Louis neighborhood where I grew up, called "The Hill," the draft began when one kid tossed the bat to another. You know the game: you alternate hands up the bat, one on top of another, until there's no more room. If your hand is on top, you get the first draft choice. What came next was never a surprise, because no matter what the sport was, the first pick was always "I'll take Lawdie."

"Lawdie" was a nickname for Lawrence, but nobody called him that. They still don't, except on formal occasions like his induction into the Hall of Fame. They call him Yogi.

I never saw a nickname catch on faster than "Yogi." Bobby Hofman, who later played for the New York Giants, hung it on him. One day at a movie, Hofman watched a scene about an Indian yogi, who made a snake curl up from a basket. When the yogi got up and walked away from the camera, Bobby said, "That yogi walks like Lawdie Berra."

Even as a youngster, Yogi Berra had a distinctive walk. If you've ever watched him walk out to the mound to talk to a pitcher, you know what I mean. The second time you see him you don't need to check the number on his back to know it's him. He's the only guy I've ever known who scuffs his shoes on the inside.

From the moment that yogi on the movie screen started to walk, Lawdie Berra had a new name. He became "Yogi" to everyone, and I mean everyone. The name became so much a part of him that even his mother, who spoke very little English, started calling him Yogi after a while. Lawrence Peter Berra made that nickname one of the best known anywhere. You don't ever hear anyone ask, "Yogi who?", do you?

Even his wife calls him Yogi. Carmen still laughs about how, after more than 30 years of marriage, she got an anniversary card signed "Yogi Berra." She asked him if he thought he had to sign his last name so she wouldn't think it came from some other Yogi.

Lawdie Berra grew up to be a legend, and like most legends, like Paul Bunyan or Pecos Bill, he doesn't really exist. It's as if there are two Yogis, the one I've known all my life and, as Yogi himself once said, "the one you read about in the papers, who's a kind of a comic-strip character, like Li'l Abner or Joe Palooka." The legendary Yogi Berra is a funny-looking guy who's always making jokes and getting his words mixed up, is not too bright and not at all sensitive. And he has caused the real Yogi to be one of the most misunderstood people I've ever known.

Before I go to work on the legend, let me present my credentials for the job. How long have I known Yogi? I don't ever remember not knowing him. We grew up across the street from each other—Yogi lived at 5447 Elizabeth Avenue and I lived at 5446. Our fathers worked together and our brothers worked together. We were together just about every day, playing one sport or another, and every night, sitting under the lamppost talking about our favorite players, Joe Medwick of the Cardinals and Harlond Clift of the Browns.

When a guy makes it to the big leagues as I did, he's usually the best player in his town, or in his school, or at least in his neighborhood. I wasn't even the best player on my block. Yogi was the best anywhere. But Yogi and I never felt we were competing against each other. I always knew Yogi was the better player. We all did. Regardless of the sport, when it really meant something, Yogi was the guy who would get us out of the hole. If it was short yardage, give the ball to Yogi. If we needed a long punt, let Yogi kick it.

He had an instinct for doing the right thing at the right time, no matter what the sport. He'd suggest a play— sometimes so simple we wouldn't think of it, sometimes so complicated we wouldn't understand it—and if we gave him an argument, he'd say, "Just do it and see." And he'd be right. Yogi wasn't loud, just sure of himself. He led by doing and by being himself. How can you be jealous of a guy like that?

Yogi made our neighborhood games possible. He was the great organizer. He engineered the whole project of turning an abandoned clay mine, which was really the neighborhood dump, into our baseball field. Yogi was the project foreman, and had us hauling in rusty, wrecked cars along the foul lines to be our dugouts.

He'd get the equipment together for street hockey—the sticks and the stacks of magazines we used as shin guards. We'd show up to play, and Yogi would have everything waiting. He laid out the football field in the street for us, playing hooky from school one day to paint the stripes. He ruined Papa Berra's best paintbrush, but we had a first and 10 like the big guys.

Yogi even figured out a way to get us good footballs, and in those days that was as valuable as being able to run long yardage. St. Louis University played its football games within a mile of our houses, and when the team would practice, we'd all line up in the street about 30 yards apart, outside the stadium fence. When a football flew over the fence, whoever caught it would throw it to Yogi, since he could throw the straightest and the farthest. He'd throw it to me, and I'd throw it to the next guy, and the line would keep going until we'd relayed it safely back to our neighborhood. The student equipment managers didn't have a chance.

Yogi could have been anything he wanted to be. Can you imagine him as a boxer? He could have been a good one. When we were about 12 or 13, a guy in our neighborhood was training some kids for the Golden Gloves. He needed a sparring partner, so he persuaded Yogi, who was just standing around watching, to help out. Yogi knew only one thing about boxing—he hits me, I hit him back. Never mind this thing called "sparring." Yogi hit back so well that they stopped the sparring, and he was the new neighborhood boxer with the best chance to win. He won eight out of nine fights before his older brother found out about his new career and made him quit.

When we played touch football in the street, one of our strict rules was that Yogi did all the punting on fourth down—for *both* teams. Not only did he kick farther than anybody else, but he also kicked the straightest—and we didn't have a budget for broken windows.

One day we were playing soccer in Tower Grove Park, while the Southwest High School football team was scrimmaging on another field. We really envied those guys in their *real* uniforms; they had shoulder pads, helmets, and shoes with cleats. One of their guys shanked a punt over to our field. Yogi picked it up and, with his old hand-me-down sneakers, kicked it back. The flight was so long they could have shown a movie. Before the ball even hit the ground, Lou Kittlaus, the Southwest coach, was over on our field on bended knee, begging Yogi, "Look kid, just come to school three days a week, take some books home, whatever you want—just play for Southwest!"

In a close game, Yogi's effort and ability went into overdrive. He gave that "extra." That's why he was such a great clutch hitter.

For our team, the Stags, the biggest game was always against the Edmonds. We might be short a couple of players against other teams, but not against the Edmonds. Everybody showed up, and everybody wanted to play. We always wanted to beat them because they were the only team in the league with real baseball uniforms. We had uniforms too—our older brothers' overalls.

The game was close and Yogi was the batter. We needed a home run, and he was swinging for the short right-field fence.

The Edmonds' manager was trying to rattle Yogi. "You'll never hit it over that wall," he yelled. "You'll never do it."

Yogi stepped out of the batter's box, looked at him, and said, "For 10 bucks?" Yogi didn't have 10 bucks. Our whole team didn't have 10 bucks, counting our First Communion money. But it was a bet. Never mind Babe Ruth calling his home run in the World Series; this was real pressure. Yogi swung at the next pitch, and we knew by the sound that Yogi had won his bet.

Sports was our whole life. After school, we'd run home as fast as we could, because if you piddled around, the other kids would choose up sides and start without you, and you'd have to just sit and watch. They didn't know we'd go to the major leagues and Yogi would end up in the Hall of Fame. If you weren't there when they were choosing up sides, you didn't play.

Sometimes, though, we couldn't run right home. To make a little money, we'd sell papers after school, three cents apiece. One night, sitting under the lamppost as usual, Yogi said, "You know who one of my paper customers is?"

"No, who?"

"Joe Medwick, that's who. He's buyin' the paper from me and givin' me a tip."

The next day looked like a scene from *Boys Town*. We all went to watch Yogi sell a paper to Joe Medwick.

"Did you hear that?" we hollered. "He called him Lawdie. Joe Medwick called him Lawdie; he knows him." Of course, everybody knew Lawdie, but Joe Medwick? After that, you could have charged admission to stand at Yogi's corner.

By the time we were teenagers, Yogi and I were pretty good ballplayers, good enough to be working out at Sportsman's Park, the major-league park in St. Louis in the 1940s. Even then, Yogi was popping balls off the screen in right field.

We were part of the "donkey brigade," a nickname for the tryout kids. We were treated a little better than the others, though, thanks to Yogi. We'd bring Butch Yatke-man, the clubhouse man, a bottle of homemade wine that Yogi would smuggle out of his pop's wine cellar.

When I was 15, the Cardinals were interested enough in me to give me a job, not as a player, but as the assistant groundskeeper for their Springfield, Missouri, farm club. For $60 a month I caught batting practice, helped cut the grass, and washed the sanitary stockings of the players, including those of a young outfielder named Stan Musial. Though it might be hard to believe, the Cardinals were "hiding" me so other clubs wouldn't sign me.

The following winter I received a $500 bonus for signing a contract to play in Springfield. General Manager Branch Rickey made it sound like all the money in the world, which to me it was. Today when you talk about bonuses, it takes a lawyer, an accountant, a banker, and two actuaries to assess the "intangible considerations" and arrive at a figure. In my case, it wasn't quite so involved. I asked for $500 because that's how much money my father owed on our house.

Mr. Rickey told me not to say anything about my contract, since I hadn't yet reached my 16th birthday when I signed. Twenty minutes later I told Yogi. He was happy for me, but neither of us could figure out why he didn't get a contract. He was already 16 and easily the best player of the donkey brigade.

The next summer, I went off to Springfield and Yogi stayed in St. Louis to play with the Stockham Post American Legion team. A former sandlot umpire, Leo Browne, who was doing some "bird-dogging" for the Yankees (a bird dog is a guy who keeps his eye out for promising young prospects, then tips off the scout who actually has the authority to sign players), told the Yankees about Yogi. And before long, they signed him to a contract with their Norfolk, Virginia, farm club, also for a $500 bonus.

Two things about Yogi's signing have rarely been mentioned. The Yankees have been given a lot of credit for their foresight in signing this "unpolished" young player, yet they were so sure of their "foresight" that they wouldn't commit to the $500 until he stayed all season and made the Norfolk team.

The other thing is the criticism directed at Branch Rickey for overlooking Yogi and letting this hometown boy get away. Sure, he let Yogi get away, but I don't think he overlooked him. The truth was, Mr. Rickey was leaving the Cardinals at the time to take over the Brooklyn Dodgers. Almost as soon as he got to Brooklyn, he sent Yogi a telegram asking him to report to the Dodgers' spring training camp in Bear Mountain, New York (this was during World War II, when the clubs had to train close to home because of travel restrictions). But Mr. Rickey's telegram came too late—Yogi had already signed with the Yankees. I've often thought if Yogi had spent his career in Ebbets Field, that short right-field fence would have made him the first player voted into the Hall of Fame while he was still playing.

We weren't in the minor leagues long before we both went into the service. I went to the Pacific in the army and Yogi went to Europe in the navy. When the war ended I joined the Cardinals, and before long Yogi was with the Yankees. Since we played in different leagues, we didn't see each other often, but we remained close. I was the best man at his wedding, and he was the best man at mine.

Who, or what, is Yogi Berra? Well, if you really want to find out, don't make the mistake of judging him by his manner and appearance. As a rookie he was the target of a lot of bench jockeying because of his looks, but he took the abuse, saying, "I never saw anybody hit with his face."

I have to admit, though, while he had all the necessary "tools" to be a great catcher, he never sounded or looked the part of a baseball player. Bill Dickey, the Hall of Famer who preceded Yogi as the Yankees' catcher, was the exact opposite. Tall and lean, he was a blueprint for building a catcher. He even sounded like a big-league catcher. Despite these differences, the Yankees assigned Dickey to help convert Yogi Berra from an outfielder to a catcher.

Both men deserve a lot of credit for the result. Many superstars fail as teachers because they insist that young players do things their way. Dickey didn't do that. Instead of trying to create another Bill Dickey, he concentrated on making a better Yogi Berra.

"Yogi already had talent and desire when he came to me," Dickey says today. "All I did was polish a diamond in the rough by showing him a few things." What he doesn't say is that when he got through polishing, this diamond in the rough was on his way to Cooperstown.

Like his hero, Joe Medwick, Yogi was known as a "bad ball hitter," a guy who'd swing at and hit a pitch most batters would let go by for a ball. Good hitters usually subscribe to the theory that you "hit the ball where it's pitched"; Yogi's philosophy was to hit the ball *if* it's pitched. In his words, "A bad pitch ain't a bad pitch anymore when you hit it into the seats." He probably violated all the rules of good hitting except one: he hit the ball where nobody could catch it.

Many things came easily to Yogi, but not everything. After watching the Yankees experiment with Yogi in the infield, the great Red Smith wrote, "Watching Yogi Berra play third base is like watching a man trying to put up a tent in a windstorm."

Watching Yogi try to catch a pop foul also could be an adventure, as former Yankee pitcher Allie Reynolds found out. Reynolds had only Ted Williams between himself and a no-hitter. Williams hit a pop foul, Yogi danced a tarantella under it, and dropped it. On the next pitch, Williams hit another pop foul. Yogi caught this one.

"There was no way I wasn't going to catch the second one," he said later. "Reynolds wanted to choke me after the first one. If I'd done it again, he would have."

Ballplayers often say, "I'd rather be lucky than good." Yogi is both. If your neighborhood was like mine, it had a candy store that sold chances on a punch board. When all the chances were sold, they lifted the big seal on the board to find out who was the grand prize winner. When we bought our chance, nobody dared punch out anything. Yogi always did it. Yogi usually won.

The Berra luck is real. And it's still as strong as ever. Just ask Joe Pignatano, the former Mets coach. "We all took our laundry to the same place in spring training. One day we go in to pick up our laundry, and when it's Yogi's turn to pay, a star comes up on the cash register, and the girl says, 'There's no charge, sir. Every thousandth customer gets his laundry free. That's what the star means.' That kind of thing could only happen to Yogi."

Billy Martin once said, "My luck is so bad, if Mickey Mantle and I bought a cemetery, people would stop dying." If Yogi were a partner, they'd strike oil the very first time he turned a shovelful of dirt.

But let's face it: despite the fact that he played in 14 World Series, more than anybody else in baseball history, won the American League's MVP Award three times, won pennants in both leagues as a manager, and is in the Hall of Fame, the most famous part of Yogi's legendary image is not the way he played. It's the way he talks.

People have labeled him "Mr. Malaprop," but that's not accurate because he doesn't use the wrong words. What he does do is put words together in ways nobody ever thought possible. Such as, "It ain't over 'til it's over." Now you may laugh and shake your head, but be honest: you've repeated it at least once, and you've heard it repeated at least two dozen times more. It makes sense, and we all know it.

In fact, that's the key to "Berraisms"—Yogi's simple logic. His funny way of talking is actually full of common sense, just succinct, plain-people talk. It's his way of looking at things. He may take a different road to get where he's going, but you'll see that his route is usually the fastest and the most honest.

Managers are always talking about how they've trained: they've studied players and studied the game, they played for this manager and played for that one, then took a little from each and learned to be managers themselves. So when Yogi became the Yankees' manager in 1963, he was asked how he'd prepared for the job. "I observed a lot by watching," he said. Can you argue with that?

Yogi could always take a complex problem and crumble it with his simple logic. We were once playing soccer on a snowy, bitter-cold day, and Yogi, who was rarely sick, felt lousy. His condition made sense to him, though. "If a guy can't get sick on a day like today, you ain't healthy."

Yogi's way with words has often been compared to "Stengelese," the mysterious language spoken by his old boss, Casey Stengel. A conversation between Casey and Yogi would have been the ultimate challenge for Berlitz.

However, where Casey's sentences contained no punctu-
ation, and frequently no subject, verb, or end, with Yogi
you're lucky to get even a sentence. If you say it in a
sentence, he says it in a word. If it takes a word, he nods.
Yogi's conversation is normal dialogue after taxes.

Casey was a funny man who said funny things. Yogi
doesn't say funny things; he says things funny. But he says
what he means, and if you laugh because of the way he says
it, he'll laugh about it, too. He's always been that way.
There was no fancy stuff in Yogi then and there's none now.
If you like him, you like him forever. He's exactly what you
see.

When Yogi makes a statement, especially about baseball,
he gets right to the point and makes sense. He says things
easy; we just have to listen hard. When Kansas City was
having attendance problems, Yogi pointed out: "If the
people don't want to come out to the park, nobody's gonna
stop 'em." When everybody was giving dissertations on the
shadows at Yankee Stadium, Yogi had the definitive answer: "It gets late early out there."

His now-famous theory about a popular restaurant might
make the most sense of all. "No wonder nobody goes there;
it's too crowded." That makes perfect sense to me, and
probably to you, too. Now you're beginning to understand
the Yogi logic.

I've heard that restaurant story dozens of times. I've read
it happened in Minneapolis, Boston, Kansas City, New
York, and Sarasota, Florida. That's one of the reasons Yogi
is so misunderstood—the stories about him are more legendary than he is.

I hear a lot of stories and lines attributed to Yogi that I
know he never said. A story will make him out to be a
clown or a comedian, then back it up with some made-up
line. You can always tell the real ones because they make
sense. They're not clever or witty, not plays on words—just
his unique way of looking at things.

Catfish Hunter tells a story about when he was with the Yankees and Yogi was a coach. One morning they were eating breakfast together in the hotel coffee shop, and Yogi said, "Don't look now, but there's somebody famous at the table behind you."

"Yeah? Who is it?"

"Well, I'm not sure," Yogi whispered. "See, he's one of two brothers, but one of them is dead. I can't remember which one died, so I can't figure out which one this is—the one that's alive or the one that's dead." You might not say it that way, but you know what he means.

I've been accused of putting words in Yogi's mouth with some of my stories, creating a comic character who doesn't exist. But how could I make him up? How can you improve on Yogi?

I once got lost going to his house in New Jersey, so I called him for directions. I certainly didn't make up his response: "I know where you are, Joey; you're not too far. But don't go the other way; come this way." (Incidentally, once a man passes 50 it seems about time for the boyhood *y* to be dropped from his name. But I'm resigned to the fact that to Yogi I'll always be "Joey.")

I didn't make him stand up in front of the crowd honoring him in St. Louis and thank "everyone who made this night necessary." He really said it, and he's been able to laugh over it since. In fact, he's never lived it down.

It's part of the Yogi Berra legend that disappoints a lot of people. They think they're going to meet Henny Youngman, and when he doesn't rattle off one-liners, they resent him for holding back. He likes to laugh, but telling jokes is not his style. What's funny about Yogi is his natural way of looking at the world. My advice to people who make up bad Yogi stories: "If you can't imitate him, don't copy him."

Another part of the legend that grew out of Yogi's interesting way with words is the idea that he isn't too bright. Another myth. Yogi is plenty bright when he needs to be. For example, in school, math was never one of his favorite subjects. In fact, school was never one of his favorite subjects. The rules of arithmetic say 2 and 2 makes 4, but Yogi doesn't care. If it makes you happy if 2 and 2 makes 90, that's okay with him.

But if you're playing gin rummy with him, and he catches you with a lot of cards when he goes out, you'll hear something like "Gin. Twenty-five, 10, 7, 3, Jack, 6—that's 61." You haven't even laid your cards down and he's figured out the total. Correctly.

True, Yogi doesn't have a lot of formal education—he never went to high school. He started working after the eighth grade, partly because his family needed the money, but mainly because he just couldn't keep his mind on it. In fact, after he started working he lost one job after another because he'd cut out around 3:00—when we all got out of school—to play ball.

Baseball was all he wanted, and the result is a plaque in the Hall of Fame. Yet all his professional life people have been misunderstanding him and finding out later they'd made a big mistake. When a bright young catching prospect named Hank Foiles had to choose between signing with the Dodgers or signing with the Yankees, he didn't hesistate. He signed with the Yankees and later explained, "Bruce Edwards was the Dodgers' catcher and he impressed me. I figured I'd never get to play with him ahead of me. But Yogi didn't look so tough to beat out, so I said 'no' to the Dodgers and signed with the Yankees. You think I misjudged Yogi a little?"

As for being bright, I know a lot of politicians who should have listened when Yogi warned a radio interviewer, "If you ask me something I don't know, I'm not gonna answer." And can you think of a better way to get along with the boss than Yogi's formula for working with George Steinbrenner? "It ain't hard. We agree different."

Probably the most mistaken notion about the legendary

Yogi is that he's not sensitive. His sensitivity might not be very obvious, but it's there, and it's deep. He has always been sensitive in his own quiet, sometimes funny way.

Yogi was already with the Yankees when he started dating Carmen, and soon word got around St. Louis that he was going to marry her. During the winter, Yogi and I went to a sports banquet, where Harry Caray did an interview with Yogi.

"This girl, Yogi, is she Italian?" Caray asked. Yogi said she wasn't. In our neighborhood it was almost a sin not to marry an Italian.

"Well, Yogi, what will the girls in the neighborhood think?"

"I dunno," Yogi said, as he kind of bowed his head. "They all had their chance."

In all the times I've known Yogi, I've never seen him hurt anyone's feelings. He's more likely to give himself an ulcer worrying about someone *else's* feelings. For example, he found out in spring training of 1963 that the wheels were in motion for Ralph Houk to move up to the position of Yankee general manager and for him to become manager in 1964. Several years later he was telling the story of how he found out, when Carmen insisted that no, he didn't know he'd be managing until spring training of '64, because that's when he told her the news. Yogi corrected her, saying, "I would have told you sooner, but I know how you worry about those things, and I didn't want you to worry an extra year."

Perhaps nothing shows the real Yogi better than his relationship with his mother. Most ballplayers talk about the influence their fathers have had on their careers, but Yogi's mother had the greatest impact on his life. An unusually strong bond existed between them.

When the Yankees sent Yogi to Norfolk, his mother knew nothing of farm systems, baseball, or Norfolk. She was a simple Italian immigrant lady, and all she knew was that her boy was barely making enough money to eat. So she somehow found a way to stretch an already-tight household budget to help him out. She'd send him $10 or $15 with a note in Italian, saying, "Don't let Papa know you're hungry, or he'll make you come home." She always understood how much baseball meant to him.

During the 1956 season, Yogi began to suffer from a mysterious skin rash. One diagnosis said he was allergic to leather, so he started wearing white cotton gloves to protect his hands from his catcher's mitt. Another diagnosis blamed something in his diet for causing him to break out. Or it was caused by a virus. Or something he had touched. Everybody except the Amazing Kreskin came up with a reason for Yogi's skin rash. I felt it was caused by something else, some kind of battle going on inside him.

I was living in St. Louis at the time, broadcasting the Cardinals' games. Yogi knew whenever I'd visit my mother, I'd go across the street to see his mother, too. She had been in a wheelchair since having a leg amputated, and she was very sick, although not willing to admit it to anyone. For many Italian immigrant ladies, including my mother, the time comes when they know their "job on earth" is over. And though it saddened everyone around her, Yogi's mother was looking forward to the trip. She had raised her family, and now it was time to move on.

Yogi knew she was very sick, but he couldn't be with her. Because I'd known him so long, I could easily see how heavy his heart was.

"How's my mother, Joey?" he'd ask me.

"She's better, Yogi." And I'd see the same look he'd get as a kid, the one that gave away what he was feeling, and I'm sure my look gave me away, too. His eyes would well up—quite a contrast to those tough Yankee pinstripes he wore—and he'd say, "She ain't doin' so good, is she?"

Although he was in the spotlight of Yankee Stadium, and she was sitting in the shade of her front porch on The Hill, each was worrying about the other. But then she knew a lot more about baseball than she let on.

I remember one day I stopped by to see her. Yogi had been in a slump, and she asked me what was the matter with him. I told her I thought he'd been hurt lately. "But even when he's not hurt, he don't do nothing," she said.

"Mama Berra, you sound like a manager," I said laughing. It was one of the rare happy moments I could report to Yogi.

And when the end finally came for her, Yogi's skin rash disappeared.

I've often been asked if I'm surprised by what Yogi has accomplished, and I always say "no," because he's always been successful at what interests him. He works hard and is one of the most positive thinkers I've ever known. When ballplayers get into a slump, they almost always start experimenting. Not Yogi. If a pitcher got him to swing at a high pitch for a third strike, it wouldn't faze him. All he'd say was, "How can a pitcher that wild stay in the big leagues?"

I do have to admit, though, Yogi's success as a manager did surprise me a little. Not that he couldn't make out a lineup, or changer pitchers, or make any of the other so-called strategy moves, because I knew he could do that. But a lot of other things make up a manager's job. The constant news conferences, radio and television interviews, and public appearances didn't come easily to Yogi, and I'm sure they were his least favorite part of the job. But he learned them, worked at them, and didn't slough them off. Playing ball was easy and natural for him. Managing brought some tough challenges. You might say God made Yogi a ballplayer, but he made himself a manager.

Yet all of the accomplishments are not the measure of our friendship. What's important is everything we've shared along the way.

In 1964, I was broadcasting the World Series between the Cardinals and the Yankees. During the second game in St. Louis, I remember looking down at the dugout, and it really hit me; Yogi was managing the Yankees in the World Series, and I was broadcasting it for NBC. That we could be the same two kids who spent so many nights sitting under the lamppost barely seemed possible.

Yogi . . . eating a banana and mustard sandwich . . . the night our whole club walked down Magnolia Avenue, wearing the shoes Uncle Joe Causino gave us, army shoes we turned into soccer shoes . . . how Yogi could go down the sewer after the ball better than anybody else. I thought about the time we stuck a Campbell's Soup label on Kenny Yost's jalopy because it was red just like a real city license . . . and listening for the Blackmer Post's 4:30 whistle, which meant Pop would be home in half an hour, so get the "tuleen," the beer bucket, and head for Fassi's Tavern . . . playing football on the grass at Shaw School until the lights went out as our five-minute warning to leave the playground and Yogi running right into an iron pole in the dark . . . trailing the vegetable man, Gene Baleen, and his horse, who'd always leave "souvenirs," and whether it was Papa Berra or Papa Garagiola, our orders were the same: "Get those 'mecats'—they're good for the garden."

I thought about the winter we both worked at Sears, and Yogi always wanted to go to Musial and Biggie's for lunch. I couldn't figure it out. We couldn't afford to eat there, so we never ate; we just sat. Finally I figured out that he just wanted to look at this girl Carmen, who was working there. He kept saying, "She won't go out with me." I'd say, "Ask her, Yogi." He did. She married him.

We began by sharing dreams, and how they turned out wasn't nearly as important as the fact that we are still sharing them.

Trying to sum up a lifetime in a few pages is tough, but this I can say: if the yardstick is talent, or knowing one's business, or honesty or sensitivity or friendship—above all, friendship—I'll still take Lawdie.

"Casey Stengel gave Whitey Herzog this advice: 'There are three ways to do anything: the right way, the wrong way, and my way. If my way turns out to be the wrong way, nobody's ever gonna know because my way is the only way we're ever gonna do it anyway."

O

9

Let's Talk Some Ball

EVERY TIME I see Dodger great Pee Wee Reese, he says hello with a great "country hardball" expression.

"Hey, Joe, you wanna talk some ball?" Pee Wee asks, and we start with the language of baseball.

Actually, all sports have their own language. As soon as you hear *blitz*, you know it's football, *dogleg* is golf, *top of the key* says basketball, *double play* tells you baseball. Use the right term at the right time with the right amount of confidence, and you can sound like you wrote the rule book. A few key words and phrases and the guy next to you will be asking for your autograph.

For example, as soon as the pitcher throws the ball, you have all kinds of options. If the ball is hit into the air, and you turn and say, "He got under that one," the average fan will probably be impressed. If the next batter hits one on the ground, and you immediately say, "He got on top of that one," your new friend will be sure you know what you're talking about and won't be able to wait for your next goodie. On a big swing and miss, the magic words are "What a cut! Look at that follow-through." Now he's hooked—he'll want to sit next to you at every game.

Your analysis can vary with each swing, with your observations ranging from a "great follow-through" to the pitcher's "good velocity." If the batter misses a low pitch, then the pitcher's either throwing a "cut fastball" or he's "sinking it."

Of course, the most important factor in all of this is confidence. You don't want to overplay your hand, but once you're completely confident, the whole field is yours.

On a successfully stolen base, just say the runner had "a good jump," and [name the pitcher] "can't keep lifting his foot and expect to hold the runner on." No fan would dare question that dazzler.

If the runner's thrown out stealing, it's even simpler. "Give [name the catcher] a chance and he gets 'em. And see how [name the pitcher] drags his foot instead of lifting it. That freezes the runner." Use those two at the right time and people will think *your* face should be on a bubble-gum card.

You can also use lots of simple throwaway lines, but the key there is knowing when to drop them in. When an outfielder catches a fly ball, it's because he "got a good jump." Of course, if he doesn't catch it, or if it drops in front of or behind him, he "got a bad jump and broke the wrong way" (by then it's too late for your friend to figure out which is the right way).

You can say plenty about the infield too, although that gets a little tricky. Whether it's a tough ground ball or an easy out, the infielder makes the play because "he's got good hands." However, if he has to run more than four steps to make the play, then "he's got good range."

Once you've built up your confidence, you can move on to tougher terms, and these can bring you into the elder statesman division if you look the part. In the right spot, these sound almost profound. Can't you just hear Connie

Mack saying, "Baseball is a defensive game. Ninety-nine percent of the games aren't won, they're lost. Somebody makes a mistake, and the other team scores and wins."

Offer these at the right time and your friends will be coming back for more during the seventh-inning stretch: "Good pitching stops good hitting and vice versa." If that goes over well, try "A half pitcher never gets a whole hitter." You'll have even the best baseball fan saying, "I never thought about it that way." Or borrow from pitcher Tom Candiotti: "You gotta take two steps back before you can take one forward."

The fans aren't the only ones who've helped make baseball a game of phrases and labels. The "official family" has played just as big a part: the owners, managers, coaches, scouts, and the writers and broadcasters who follow the team.

Every manager I played for—and that means at least 10—said the same thing when a player tried to stretch a base hit. If he's safe, he "knows how to run the bases"; if he's out, he "has no idea on the bases."

The little guy hits a home run in a tryout, and the scout, manager, or director of player development says, "Sure, he hit a couple out of the park, but I'd like to see him do it again." If he's a big guy, though, they say, "Sure, he popped it up, but if he ever gets a hold of one, look out."

A young player who shows his temper is a "hothead," but the veteran player is a "competitor" or a "take-charge guy." The yardstick is either the birth certificate or the batting average. The guy who's hitting .300 and popping off is a "leader," but the one hitting .200 and popping off is a "clubhouse lawyer" and a "troublemaker." If a player is hitting but doesn't say much, he's "quiet," but if he's not hitting, he's "moody." I'm sure you've heard about the winning pitcher who's "unflappable, loose, and nothing bothers him." If he's losing, he's "lackadaisical and not serious."

The birth certificate helps the younger player when he's not hitting, because he's just "in a slump." When the guy who's been in the league a couple of years stops hitting, it's the "law of averages." But when a guy over 35 stops hitting, he's "getting old." And their averages can be identical.

Baseball people have labels for other problems too, like weight. If you weigh more than you did last year and you're hitting, it's because you've been working with weights; you're "bigger" and "stronger." If you weigh more than last year and you're *not* hitting, it's because of all the banquets—you're "fat."

League standings have a lot to do with the labels you hear. I've seen fights in both winning and losing club-houses. When the league leaders fight, they're "a real bunch of competitors." But a fight on a last-place team is "a sure sign of dissension." And how many times have you heard about a veteran team winning because "they know how to play?" Of course, if they're losing, they're "old and over the hill." If the young team is winning, they're "aggressive," but if they're losing, they're "inexperienced."

The winning manager who changes the lineup daily is "using the whole roster to keep sharp." The losing manager has to learn that "you just can't play like that. You have to have a set lineup. There's too much confusion." Of course, the winning manager is a great communicator, and the losing manager's problem is that "he just can't communicate" (and it's possible to be both in the same year).

A slump is a slump is a slump. Well, maybe. It actually depends on when it happens. Lose five in a row in April or May, and it's just a "slow start." Lose five in a row in July or August, and it's a "slump." Lose five in a row in September, and you're "choking."

Pitching and hitting coaches have their way of labeling players, too. If you're not hitting and you're moving your bat, you have a "hitch." But if you're moving your bat and you're hitting, then you have a "trigger mechanism." If you're hitting, it's a "home run swing." If you're not hitting, it's an "uppercut."

You can bet the Mets' Ron Darling, who went to Yale, has heard this one plenty of times: when he's winning, it's because he's "studious"; when he's losing, "he thinks too much."

The pitching coach will tell you that if the control pitcher, the guy whose fastball doesn't register on the radar gun, has a winning year, it's because he "knows how to pitch." If he has a losing year, it's because "his fastball isn't good enough and he needs another pitch."

The hitting coach knows that the big bonus prospect who's not hitting is just "making some mistakes. Let him play awhile and he'll relax and start to play within himself." If he *is* hitting, the coach says, "If you think he can hit now, wait until he learns how to hit."

Often, picking the right label for a player comes down to one question: which team is he on, yours or the opposition's? For example, if a first-year winning pitcher is on your team, it's simple: "If you think he's good now, wait until he learns the hitters." If he's on another team, "He's off to a good start, but wait until the hitters see him the second time around."

If your guy hits a home run, he "hit it a mile." If the other guy hits one, "the ball hung; he hit a mistake." If your player slides hard, he's "aggressive," but if *their* guy does it, he's "a dirty player."

The catcher falls into a special category. If he can hit, he can rarely do anything wrong. Any stolen base against him happens because "they're stealing on the pitcher." He can have a rubber hose for an arm, because if he can hit, "he knows how to run the game." Even if he can't hit but he's the best catcher available, then he's "a great handler of pitchers." Mamas, Willie Nelson may not want your babies to grow up to be cowboys, but you shouldn't mind if they grow up to be catchers.

Once you've mastered the language of labels, you're ready to "relearn" some baseball terms. This can be complicated. Sometimes you think you know what a word means, but there's actually a lot more to it. Players, managers, coaches, and fans are constantly refining the language and coming up with new words as well as new meanings for the old words.

The word *slump*, for example, has about as many definitions as there are players in the big leagues. But for the Yankees' Dave Winfield, the word doesn't even exist: he calls it a "statistically acceptable variation." Roy Campanella defines it as something that "begins with your swing, goes to your head, and ends up in your stomach."

Some other definitions that are different from Mr. Webster's:

○ *Utility player:* like going to a restaurant to watch other people eat, says former big leaguer Carmen Fanzone.

○ *Umpire:* like a pickpocket—notice either one too much and his career is over.

○ *Career savers:* infielders who throw you out by so far you don't have to run the last 20 feet.

○ *Piranha pitch:* a biting fastball, says Tommy John.

○ *Bad runner:* his baserunning keeps both teams in the game.

○ *Statistics:* can be used to support anything, including statisticians, according to Bill Lyon of the *Philadelphia Inquirer.*

○ *Third-stepper:* a pitcher who always has the manager
   out on the third step of the dugout, says scout Eddie
   Lyons. Also called a *top-stepper* by former Dodger
   manager Walter Alston.

○ *Potential:* a French word that means you aren't
   worth a damn yet, says Atlanta Falcons center Jeff
   Van Note. It's not baseball, but it fits.

○ *Middle relievers:* "They aren't born," former pitcher
   Steve Stone says. "They're starters who have been
   reassigned."

○ *Home run:* a rally killer. Former pitcher Jim Kaat
   says that when a team has momentum and everybody is hitting, all it takes is someone to hit a three-
   run or a grand-slam homer, and the rally slows
   down. Catcher Bob Brenly says the same about the
   solo home run: "The bases are empty, and the
   pitcher can bear down against the next hitter."

Some words have so many definitions you can guarantee
you'll start an argument just by saying them. Like *choke*, or
gutless, or *afraid*. You hear them all the time, and almost
everybody has a different theory about them.

I'm with the group who says we all have a choke point.
I've seen it on the baseball field, on the banquet circuit
when the words just don't come, and at golf pro-ams on the
first tee. Golfer Lee Trevino describes it best: "We all leak
oil, but the good ones control the flow."

Guts is a matter of confidence. One player feels he can do
it while another player isn't too sure. Some players just
react better in tough situations. You can't measure it by a
base hit; too many times I've seen a player hit the ball hard
in a clutch situation but make an out, only to hear somebody

say "He didn't come through." Then a lesser hitter will break his bat, bloop one in, and hear "He's a clutch hitter."

Reggie Jackson put it this way: "One player feels fear and fights it; another player feels fear and gives in to it." Former player and manager Joe Torre says it happens when "a player wants too bad to be good." And a man who should know, General Omar Bradley, said, "Courage is controlled fear."

When the topic of guts used to come up in the bullpen, you'd always hear two stories that would put an end to the argument.

Rocky Marciano was the heavyweight boxing champion at the time, and nobody questioned *his* courage. So the question was posed that if Marciano batted against a sidearm right-hander and bailed out, would you say he was gutless because he didn't stay with the pitch? On the other hand, Stan Musial stood in against all types of pitching; he wouldn't give ground to a sidearm left-hander. Yet if he refused to fight Marciano, would you call him gutless?

The other story that always broke up the discussion involved two boxers. The challenge was to identify the difference between fear and gutlessness. Joe Louis was a great boxer, a devastating puncher who'd been heavyweight champion. Max Baer, a good heavyweight, defined fear after he fought Louis. Baer certainly had guts, because he was in the ring with Joe Louis. But did he know fear? "Fear," he said, "is to be seated in the opposite corner from Joe Louis, look across the ring, and realize that he wants to go home early."

Maybe the best way to sound like a baseball expert is to listen to the experts themselves—the players, coaches, and managers. You might start with the bench jockeys, because it's always good to go to the ballpark with a few zingers to show that you know what's going on. Like "He has to take a full swing to bunt," or one they used to say about my old

1952 Pirates, "They score runs in bunches of one and none."

I guarantee that when the singles hitter (whose greatest strength is getting a base on balls) takes a couple pitches in the batting cage, he'll hear "That's the first time I ever saw a guy take batting practice and draw a walk. What are you doing, getting some 'taking' practice?"

Or try Rollie Fingers's line to Reggie Jackson: "When you field a ball, it sounds like Big Ben at one o'clock—bong!" Or broadcaster Richie Ashburn's comment when the TV camera showed the equipment man mending the glove of Dave Kingman, who was a poor fielder: "They should've called a welder."

And don't leave out the umpires. Someone starts a rumor that one of them is going to quit, and the next thing you hear is:

"I hear so-and-so is going to call it quits."

"If he does, that's the only call he's gotten right yet."

But to really "talk some ball," your best source is the manager. Managers have a collection of stock phrases for every situation. They used these when I was playing, and they're probably still using them:

○ Hold 'em and we'll get you some runs.

○ Stay close and you'll beat him.

○ You never know.

○ They're a good team, but they can be beaten.

○ Don't let him get a walking lead. (Applies to any base stealer.)

○ Throw over there.

○ Throw strikes. You can't catch a walk.

○ Hold 'em on.

○ Be alive.

○ Bear down.

○ He ain't got that kind of stuff. (When the pitcher's shutting you out.)

○ Don't give in.

○ Get on top.

○ Stay within yourself. (A lot of 0-for-4 days I would have liked to have left.)

○ Make 'em hit the ball.

○ Let him walk you if he wants, but don't strike out.

○ Go in on a ground ball— watch the line drive.

○ Don't give up a run until you get a run.

○ Get a good lead—tag up on a fly ball.

○ Don't give him a good ball to hit, but don't walk him.

○ Get a good lead—don't get picked off.

Even when they stray from these standards, they still have a unique way with words, their own kind of language. Start with Casey Stengel, well known for having his own language, who gave Whitey Herzog this advice: "There are three ways to do anything: the right way, the wrong way, and my way. If my way turns out to be the wrong way, nobody's ever gonna know because my way is the only way we're ever gonna do it anyway."

Casey also helped Whitey deal with the media, saying, "Let 'em ask you one question, then you keep talking so they won't ask you another one."

Another lesson you can learn from managers is how to make anything sound like it makes sense, just by using the right amount of authority. Like Davey Johnson, who calls Dwight Gooden "the one pitcher who can make the wrong pitch right." Huh?

When the manager goes to the mound to make a pitching change, you have a great chance to sound like you were born between the pages of the *Spalding Guide*. Most managers say the same thing, but not Sparky Anderson: "Put the ball in my hand gently like an egg and remove yourself," he tells pitchers. "I don't want them talking to me unless I ask them something."

Earl Weaver also liked to do the talking, but his advice didn't exactly come from Ann Landers. Ross Grimsley was getting hit all over the place, and when Weaver had finally seen enough, he walked out to the mound and said, "If you know how to cheat, start now."

When you're sitting at the ballpark, you can also try out on your friends some theories on a manager's importance to his team. According to Sparky, "A manager doesn't win games; he avoids losing them." It's a thankless job, says Birdie Tebbetts: "A manager gets paid half his salary for winning, half for worrying, and nothing for losing." And Whitey Herzog is both practical and realistic: "If you don't die on the job or own the ballclub, you're gonna get fired."

But getting fired isn't so bad if you're Billy Martin or Harvey Kuenn. Martin just has to wait for George Steinbrenner to rehire him, and Kuenn relies on this fatalistic approach to get him through: after losing the third game of the 1982 World Series, he said, "The world is not coming to an end. If it does, you're not gonna be here anyway."

Kuenn even knows how to put into perspective the insecure position of interim mangers: "Being an interim manager doesn't bother me. When you look at it, every manager in the major leagues is an interim manager."

So by now, if you're casually dropping these into your conversation in the right places, you either have an interested, captive audience or you've cleared out your section. But if they're still around, end the discussion with the ultimate philosophy on how to play baseball; this "gem" from Charlie Dressen: "Go up to home plate, hit the ball, and get back to home plate as fast as you can."

Since you want to avoid the trap of sounding too technical, just forget about "point of release" or "weight shift at impact" and stick with the simple observations. Here's where baseball's many theories are a big help. Everybody in the game has a theory on everything, and there's no reason you can't borrow them so you can sound good at the ballpark.

After all, who wouldn't listen to what Reggie Jackson has to say about his first series slump? "When you're young, a slump creates doubt. You start thinking, 'Have they found me out?' I remember Charlie Finley called me and said, 'Keep the windshield wipers on going through the storm.' He was telling me to just keep driving the car, don't pull off the road, just keep driving, and I'd be all right sooner or later."

It's a good bet you'll see a pop foul during the game, and whether the catcher makes the play or not, here's your chance to use a real down-home description from Roy Campanella: "It ain't gonna stay up there. It goes up one chute and comes down another chute. Just guess the right chute. And take your time. You can't reach up to get 'em. You can't catch 'em until they come down."

Or you can quote Whitey Herzog on the Cardinals' speed and give your whole row something to smile about: "I'm waiting for the day we get a sacrifice fly on a pop up to the catcher."

You're practically guaranteed to see an outfielder make a one-handed catch on a routine fly ball, so you can either wait for someone to ask why no one uses two hands anymore or you can jump in and explain what the outfielder might be thinking, using the words of Leon Wagner, one of the first players to make a one-handed catch: "I want the kids to know that one hand is better than two. It's the bare hand that makes the errors."

Certain ballparks, like New York's Shea Stadium, will help you prove your statements and really make you sound like you have some inside information. You often see players look at the flags and maybe toss a handful of grass into the air to check which way the wind is blowing. Now, wouldn't your friends be ready to send you to Cooperstown if you turned and said, "Never mind the flags—the wind swirls here at Shea. Keith Hernandez uses the planes over at La Guardia Airport, nearby. He says that when the landing pattern has the planes coming in right over your head, it means the wind is blowing out to the left field."

One topic you often hear at the ballpark is the difference between the majors and the minors. Kerry Dineen put all discussion to rest when he was a rookie with the Yankees, by saying, "The conditions up here are so much better. The lighting is better at some of the night games up here than at some of the day games in the minors."

Another thing people like to argue about is the size of players, especially what the little guy is capable of doing. Whitey Herzog has his own way of measuring: "A player's never little if he can run."

A lot of people use statistics to "talk some ball," but I think former Yankee pitcher Jim Bouton is right when he says that statistics are about as interesting as a first-base coach. Besides, you can't be worrying about numbers when you're trying to convince everybody that *The Sporting News* calls *you* when they need an answer. So if you really want to get their attention, say something like "I heard that the strikeouts-to-base-on-balls ratio doesn't tell you that much. You have to consider some pitchers wild even though they give up a low number of walks. The 2-and-2 count is really important, because that's when the consistent winner will throw a strike with something on it." You should have them wondering here, so take a breath and continue. "The 'nibbler' throws a ball, now it's 3 and 2, and he has to come in with it. He never walks anybody, but he has a lot of 3-and-1 and 3-and-2 counts. He lets the hitter get a good swing on a deep count."

After that, be prepared for the guy next to you to say, "Hey, Abner Doubleday, so then what makes a good pitcher? I can't use wins and losses, earned run average, strikeouts, or base on balls, so how can I measure it?"

Great! Now you have him set up perfectly for this one from Cal State–L.A. coach John Herbold: "A good pitcher is one who throws *what* he wants, *where* he wants, *when* he wants, and to *whom* he wants . . . and probably to a catcher who knows *why!*"

Or maybe you could answer his question with some help from golfing great Ben Hogan. That sounds strange, but Tommy John says he once got a pitching lesson while listening to Hogan talk about golf.

"He says he always knew which side of the fairway to miss a shot on," John says. "I realized that also applies to pitching. I always know which side of the plate to miss on. If I'm throwing my sinker to a right-handed fastball hitter, the side for me to miss on is away from him. If I miss toward him and inside, I'm asking for trouble."

Another thing you might tell the crowd that's now gathered around you is that great pitchers never lack confidence. And to make your point, just quote some great pitchers.

Nolan Ryan: "You are one dimension of a two-dimensional game. Whatever happens offensively is out of your hands. My objective is to shut out the other team and give us a chance to win."

Whitey Ford always made pitching look so easy, maybe because he felt like "I've always got the batter's front foot on a string."

And when Sandy Koufax was asked after one of his no-hitters when he first started thinking about it, he said, "Just after I finished my warm-up pitches."

Pitchers have made it even easier for you to "talk some ball," because they're loaded with theories, strategies, and philosophies.

Warren Spahn: "A pitcher needs only two pitches: the one the batter is looking for and one to cross him up."

My old teammate, Howard Pollet: "Throw strikes, but in the sixth, seventh, eighth, and ninth, throw low strikes."

Bob Gibson had an equally simple theory on location: "Pitch outside, it's a single. Pitch inside, it's a home run." (Be careful with this one, or they might think you're talking about pitching in the Astrodome.)

And I wonder how much greater Cy Young or Walter Johnson would have been if they'd known about these:

Curt Simmons, on why you pitch most hitters low in the strike zone: "If the arms were on the knees instead of the shoulders, you would pitch everybody high. Where the arms are is where the action is."

Former White Sox pitcher Saul Rogovin: "Throw the ball right down the middle. The high-ball hitters swing over it, and the low-ball hitters swing under it."

And Tug McGraw's "Frozen Snowball Theory": "Scientists have predicted that 50 billion years from now, the sun will burn out and the earth will orbit like a frozen snowball.

When that day comes, who will care what the batter I'm looking at did to one of my pitches?"

Key words and phrases about pitchers can really turn loose the expert in you and maybe get a laugh along the way. Think of it as a word association game:

Scuff ball—Houston's Mike Scott: "If they're worried about what the ball's going to do instead of about hitting, it's another pitch that I've got that I don't have."

Location—Boston's Mike Brown, on a foggy night: "It hurt my location, because I wasn't sure just where the location was."

Forkball—Former Red Sox coach Eddie Popowski, when the opposing pitcher suddenly came from nowhere with a great "forkball" to win a lot of games: "He ought to call it a 'spoonball', because you can't hold spit with a fork."

When you watch a game, all you can really do is guess whether a pitch is a slider, a forkball, or even a spitball, but there's one pitch you can be sure about. When the catcher's glove is the size of a truck tire and he's just taken his 30th trip back to the screen, you can guarantee it's a knuckleball.

Scientists try to explain the knuckleball by talking about everything from aerodynamics and wind currents to high cholesterol and body fat. I can't explain it, just like I couldn't hit it and I couldn't catch it. Some pitchers use their knuckles, but the good ones throw it by gripping the ball with their fingertips. So even though it sounds strange, a hangnail to a knuckleball pitcher is a serious injury. You don't know how many times I rooted for the hangnail.

The pitch is ugly. Even the name is ugly. Maybe if the knuckleball had a better-sounding name, it would be easier to accept. I never seem to feel as hostile toward the knuckleball when I listened to the French-speaking broadcasters in Montreal, who call it *le papillon*, the butterfly. You can't feel as bad about a passed ball knowing it was caused by *le papillon*. Striking out because you didn't hit *le papillon* almost makes you feel like you should get an award from some environmental group. But the word *knuckleball* should have a health warning attached to it.

A knuckleball pitcher usually has several different knuckleballs. The basic one just spins toward the plate. He can throw it for strikes, and he uses it to get ahead of the hitter, who's usually thinking, "I'll just take his knuckleball and swing at anything else." Except for slugger Harmon Killebrew, whose theory on the knuckleball was to just "hit it between the seams." Sure, Harm.

The second kind of knuckleball breaks a little more. He throws it early in the count, and your chances of catching it are about 70–30. Your chances of hitting it are about the same as with the first one—not good.

The true personality of the pitcher comes out with his third kind of knuckleball, his best one. He usually throws it with a count of no balls and two strikes, and it's practically skywriting "The Star-Spangled Banner" on its way to the plate. As soon as he releases the ball, you can almost hear him laughing, and you can tell by the look on his face he's wishing the hitter and the catcher "Good luck." It's the kind of look that would make a perfect Halloween mask.

I finally found out why I couldn't hit or catch the knuckleball. I don't really understand the explanation, but I feel better just knowing there *is* an explanation. From *The New York Times*: "Scientists are focusing on the role of the baseball's stitches in creating turbulence in the airflow, and they calculate that, under certain conditions, the knuckleball undergoes an aerodynamic 'crisis' that warps its trajectory in midflight." It must be the same warping crisis that happens to the catcher.

But a catcher's *real* problems don't really begin with the knuckleball. They actually start with the street games as a kid. In my neighborhood, nobody *ever* wanted to be the catcher. Even the kid who couldn't play, the one you tried to hide, didn't want to play badly enough that he'd volunteer to catch. Lack of equipment was an important factor, because who'd want to catch without a mask or a chest protector? We *did* use *National Geographic* magazines for shin guards, but it was still hard to get a catcher, even for a softball game.

I think if the position had a better name you'd have more applicants for the job. Like Italian baseball has the *racevitore* (pronounced rah-chay-vee-TORE-ay). The sound alone makes you feel like Luciano Pavarotti is your lockermate. *Catcher* sounds like something left over from a yard sale.

After you're in the major leagues for a while, you hear about the "veteran infielder," the "much-traveled outfielder," and the "crafty pitcher," but it's always the "old catcher." This, after he's spent his whole career without a glamorous label, like "first-sacker," or "he plays the hot corner." No, the catcher wears the "tools of ignorance." That's never been one of my favorite expressions, but in trying to find its origin, I ran across a description for catchers that makes the "tools of ignornace" sound beautiful.

"Catcher. In the good old days when Grandpa was ace baritone of the corner barbershop quartet, the catcher was commonly known as 'the behind.'"

So take your pick. Would you like to be known for wearing "the tools of ignorance" or as "the behind"? Now that's a tough decision.

Catchers are baseball's most underappreciated players. First of all, every other position has an eraser. The pitcher makes a bad pitch, but the outfielder can make a great catch. The ball goes through the infielder's legs and the outfielder backs him up. The ball goes through the outfielder's legs and the wall backs him up. The catcher misses the ball and the run scores and the manager is waiting for him.

Usually, though, the catcher just goes unnoticed, unless there's a way to blame him when something goes wrong. Because he's the catcher, he doesn't even have to touch the ball to get the blame. The key hit, the home run, the base on balls—the manager gives equal opportunity to every excuse for why things went wrong and how it's the catcher's fault. They may have different ways of saying it, but in the end, it comes out of the grinder as a second guess.

"What the hell was that he hit? How in the hell can you give him a pitch like that? Why do we waste time in meetings if you ain't gonna listen? He's hitting .190 and you give him a pitch he can handle." The list is long, and the catcher has to stand there and listen to it, even though he hasn't even touched the ball.

Believe me, catchers get no respect, and I should know. When I joined the Giants near the end of the 1954 season, Leo Durocher started me against the Phillies. It was one of those games that didn't mean anything because the Giants had already clinched the pennant. Leo read the lineup, then looked right at me, and with all his charm and warmth said, "You catch. I don't want to get Westrum hurt."

My first time up I struck out against Murry Dickson on a rising submarine roundhouse curveball, and I came back to the bench saying, "He's gonna throw me that American Legion curve again and I'm gonna nail it." Two innings later, with the bases loaded and one out, I get my chance. I'm looking for the roundhouse curve, and here it comes. I'm waiting and I really nail it—right back to Dickson, who catches it and fires to first for the double play to end the inning. When I get back to the bench and start to put on my shin guards, Durocher comes over and says, "Next time, why don't you just strike out and keep the inning going?"

When something good happens, rarely does the catcher get any of the credit. Too many times when a pitcher wins a close game it's because he had "good stuff." Let him get knocked out early and the whispers say the dummy behind the plate called a bad game. The catcher puts himself on the line even before the game starts when he decides what the pitcher's best pitch is that day. Take too long to find out and the pitcher's gone. Bad pitch selection has sent more pitchers to the showers than the opposition's bats.

Catching involves one particular action in a personal, one-on-one, battle of egos like no other in baseball. I'm talking about the stolen base. It's your arm against his speed. The pitcher throws a home run ball and it's just part of the game—so is an error. But not a stolen base. People might use the cliché "He stole on the pitcher," but the next day the coach is talking to the catcher about a quicker release. Don't talk to the 15-game winner about holding runners on; it might take away from his concentration. And you have to make an appointment to talk to the 20-game winner. So you talk to the catcher. What's the difference if he was stapled to the wall with a slide or hit with a few foul tips? He has to work on his release.

Catchers like Yogi, Campy, Johnny Bench, Bob Boone, and Gary Carter amaze me because they've played so many games. Keeping the bare hand behind the back has helped minimize hand injuries, but a catcher still has plenty of nicks taken out of his body by foul tips. Very few games do you feel even 70 percent. It's almost like some part of your body is missing or, at the very least, isn't working right. Like former catcher Jerry Grote said, "When you can put the cap back on your toothpaste tube, then you know your hands are okay."

Yet everybody takes a catcher's injuries for granted. Next time you're at a game, pay close attention to a minor injury. A runner might limp a little when he passes first base and then call time, but the number of people responding is determined solely by his batting average. If he's a .300-plus hitter, out comes the trainer, the manager, the Red Cross, and a bishop, while the owner is poised in the stands ready to join them. But when the catcher goes down after a nasty crack from a foul tip, he better stay down if he needs attention, because the only person near him is the umpire. And what's he doing? He's checking the ball.

Most of the important things catchers do never even show up in the box score. When you go in to talk contract, all you hear is "What did you hit? How many runs did you drive in?" Nobody ever says anything about how many balls you blocked to keep runs from scoring. Isn't that at least as important as the big hitter getting an RBI by tapping a ball to the shortstop with nobody out and a man on third and the other team giving up the run?

Aside from the times when he acts as a human dead end and blocks the plate, when was the last time you heard a catcher get applause? When a player at any *other* position makes a key play, you hear lots of cheering, right? Even if it's bad baseball, when an outfielder makes a throw all the way to the catcher on the fly to hold the runner at third, you hear the "oohs" and "ahs." The catcher blocks the ball and there's silence. Vin Scully's theory is that the fans are more relieved than anything else that the ball didn't get past the catcher for an extra base, or even worse, for a run. As a former catcher though, I can tell you it would be great just once to hear even a sigh of relief.

While the catcher may be underappreciated by many, he *is* appreciated by the bench jockeys. The catcher is an easy target. Go out to talk to your pitcher and immediately you hear, "The only thing you know about pitching is that it's hard to hit," or "If you had any brains you wouldn't be catching." Bench jockeys have been hollering those gems for a hundred years.

Fortunately, not everyone underestimates what the catcher does. Dr. Ernest Dichter, at the Institute for Motivational Research sees the importance of the catcher as going beyond even what happens on the field. He says baseball is actually "a tribal feast, laden with ceremonious ritual." In this feast, "The pitcher is the symbolic father and the catcher is the symbolic mother. Everyone is there for one purpose: to overthrow and destroy the primal father. The diamond is symbolic of the four-cornered area in which the infant took his first tentative steps: the crib or the playpen," Dichter says.

The catcher as a "symbolic mother" might be hard to visualize, but try these analogies, from guys who know. Catcher Carlton Fisk calls it the "Dorian Gray position: you can look young on the outside while turning to dust on the inside."

Bob Brenly adds, "When the season is over, I feel like a used car." He might have added that it's one with a lot of miles, a few dents, could use a paint job, and won't ever win Best in Show. But come next season, you can bet it'll start with the first turn of the key.

You can't "talk some ball" without talking about hitting. Lucky for you, there are probably more theories and philosophies about hitting than about any other part of the game, so you'll be well prepared.

For starters, how about this poem by Joe Morgan scribbled in one of my old scorebooks:

> See the ball before you stride
> Let it go if it's outside
> If it's a curve it should break down
> So jack up and hit it downtown.

Morgan may not have been Pulitzer Prize material, but he definitely was MVP material.

Sam Rice has a theory for hitters who always take the first pitch: "Why worry about the first pitch? If it's no good, you're ahead of him. If he gets a good pitch over, you can be sure he'll come back with it again, and then you're laying for it."

Japanese home run hitter Sadaharu Oh had an almost religious approach to the game: "The ideal state is a cool mind and a hot, fighting spirit." Of course, when *he* needed to get psyched up, he'd stand on his head in the dugout and hold his breath.

Ted Williams's theory on the strike zone still makes sense. He says the batter has three strike zones: his own, the opposing pitcher's, and the umpire's:

"The umpire's zone is defined by the rule book, but it's also more importantly defined by the way the umpire works. A good umpire is consistent so you can learn his strike zone. The batter has a strike zone in which he considers the pitch the right one to hit. The pitchers have zones where they are most effective. Once you know the pitcher and his zone you can get set for a particular pitch."

Mike Schmidt places extra importance on his first time at bat in a game, even if he doesn't get a hit.

"If I just hit the fastball hard, it tells me I can handle his velocity that night. It also gives the pitcher the same thought."

George Sisler used to stand behind the batting cage when I was with the Pirates to try to help us with our hitting (what a challenge). I wish I'd gotten a hit for each time I heard him say, "Some hitters are prepared to take every pitch unless it's good. Be positive—think the other way. Be prepared to hit every pitch and lay off if it's bad."

All you have to do is throw these thoughts into your ballpark conversation, sit back, and wait for the reviews.

Dave Winfield: "Good hitting is the result of relaxed concentration."

Hank Aaron: "For the first two strikes, I just guess. After that, all I'm looking for is the ball. I guess that he's gonna throw it."

Rod Carew had a little trick he'd use on himself late in the season, when he'd get tired and go to a shorter bat. "I turn the trademark away from my face, and I see nothing but blank bat, which makes it look longer."

Everybody likes to be in on a secret. Stan Musial's secret

to hitting the spitball was as simple as you can get: "Don't worry about it; just hit the dry side."

When Wade Boggs talks about one facet of his hitting technique, it sounds like an old dance we used to do. He calls it "cheek-to-cheek hitting." He says, "It's a timing mechanism. When the pitcher turns, I turn."

Now, if you really want to knock people out and sound like a real deep thinker, you might try some of these questions on them. Or if you're sitting at the ballpark near a know-it-all you want to keep quiet, just ask one of these and head for the hot dog stand:

When there's nobody on and the pitcher is in the stretch position because he feels more comfortable, whom does he check? What base does he check?

Why does a left-handed pitcher work from the stretch when there's only a runner at third base? I'd think he could watch him better if he took a full windup.

Why don't catchers take infield practice with their equipment on? The only time you ever throw without gear on is during infield practice.

Why doesn't the catcher ever step on home plate after coming back from a conference on the mound?

Why does a manager holler to his batter to "Get your pitch"? You have to figure the opposition knows what his pitch is, too.

On defense, the same manager hollers, "Don't give in, don't give him his pitch." The question is, how do you get your batter to wait for the pitch that you keep telling your pitcher not to throw?

When it came to talking baseball—or just talking—nobody could say it like former general manager Branch Rickey. Quote him a few times and I guarantee you'll impress people at the ballpark—even if they don't know what you're saying.

I first knew Mr. Rickey (I don't know why, but that's the

way everybody I know has always referred to him) when I was with the Cardinals and then again with the Pittsburgh Pirates. During his Cardinals days he had some good teams, although he was gone by the time we won the pennant in 1946. In Pittsburgh he had some bad teams—we lost 112 games in 1952, and that's all you need to know.

Mr. Rickey had a great way with words, both the words he used and the way he put them together "Baserunning isn't a lost art. It's a lost necessity," he'd say. He also had some unique ideas about the game: "A dumb player can hit, but a dumb player can't pitch. Throw, yes; pitch, no."

Sometimes I'd agree with him, then realize I really didn't know what he'd said. Like "There is temptation in the inertia of defeat." Think that one over. Yet no mater what he talked about, I almost always walked away saying, "Only Mr. Rickey could say it like that."

One of my favorite examples concerns a batter's hitch: Is it good or bad? Can it be corrected? I don't know if Mr. Rickey answers those questions, but I wouldn't argue with his logic.

"The hitch is correctable but very seldom is corrected. It is a habit, a bad habit, acquired probably from the earliest playing days of the individual. It is not a brain lesion in the field of timing such as overstriding, but is an obstinate habit and can be broken only by acquiring a correct substitute *in form* which in itself must become habit and therefore needs many pitches and long practice. The suggestion of that change in form can be followed instantly but can be abandoned instantly also." (I had a hitch in my swing that helped me become a broadcaster, but I was at least relieved to learn I didn't have "a brain lesion in the field of timing.")

On the pitching machine: "It tends to give confidence to batters who have no confidence. Pitchers, for example, are subconsciously afraid of a pitched ball—some consciously. The curve coming at them makes boys who have no experience in the hitting of curves fearful. They sag, they buckle, the 'tail goes out,' or they 'water bucket.' Now, pitchers have just as good mothers and fathers from the standpoint of intelligence and courage as do other players, but pitchers from boyhood days have had to pitch to batters and have never had the chance of batting. To stand up at the plate and learn actually where the plate is and to come to know that it is not 18 inches wide but only 17 and to know where his knees and armpits are as related to the pitch, and to become unafraid as he watches the ball go by—these things are worthwhile."

Mention Branch Rickey and luck in the same sentence and chances are you'll hear, "Luck is the residue of design." But that wasn't the only thing he said about luck:

"I do not at all enjoy the emotions of continuous defeat and as a lifetime experience I am by no means accustomed to it. I am unable to be restful simply waiting for the break of chance to make a great club. Luck is a by-product of effort, and if I don't work hard, and if everybody else doesn't work hard, I am to expect bad luck, but if I do everything I can and try to get everyone else to do what he can to produce a pennant-winning team at the earliest possible minute, then I am entitled to good luck and I expect it. Bad luck will feature any club which is satisfied with mediocrity."

On speed: Hitting is of value only on offense.

Fielding is of value only on defense.

Running is of value on both defense and offense.

Branch Rickey's sense of humor was well known to those of us around him. One of his favorite practice drills for catchers was to have a pitcher bounce curveballs in front of us so we could practice blocking them. This was one of my least favorite workouts since I knew when it was over I'd be admiring my black and blue marks. During one of these sessions, he walked by me and asked our manager, Fred Haney, how I was doing. "Better, I got a new glove for him," Haney replied. "I think you made a great deal," Mr. Rickey said.

He could make you laugh and he could make you think. One of my favorite trips through the English language with Mr. Rickey is his thoughtful description of the game of baseball:

"It is a game of great charm in the adaptation of mathematical measurements to the timing of human movements. For example, the stolen base is the artistic achievement of a skilled lead and break—a victory, perchance, over the pitcher's move and a catcher's $30,000 arm. He catches and throws at a distance of 126 feet to a game chap who has mastered the art of the tag, while the runner negotiates, say 80 feet. Now the slide—deceptive, elusive, abandoned.

"The umpire, with thumbs up or hands down—and his decision seldom has universal approval. 'I beat the play,' or 'He never touched me,' sincerely said, meets his ears. Such are the exactitudes and adjustments of physical ability to hazardous chance. The speed of the legs, the dexterity of the body, the grace of the swing, the elusiveness of the slide, these are the features that make Americans everywhere forget the last syllable of a man's name or the pigmentation of his skin."

Whether it's Branch Rickey's poetic description of the game or the guy next to you at the ballpark simply saying the outfielder got a bad jump, it's still the same. The theories will get fancier and the philosophies deeper, but it will always be the answer to Pee Wee Reese's favorite question: "You wanna talk some ball?"

"When I walked in the door my wife called to my three-year-old daughter, 'It's Daddy!' My little girl answered, 'What channel?' When your kids only recognize you when you're on TV, it's time to do some thinking."

○

10

"Today," "Tonight," and Times in Between

"HEY, JOE, IS Johnny Carson funny in real life?"

"You remember when you cursed on TV, Joe?"

"My mom won a car on 'Sale of the Century'—you remember her?"

I've heard all those questions and lots more like them. I usually hear them when I'm walking through an airport. People are surprised to see me, and it's like multiple choice when they start a conversation. They talk baseball, "The Tonight Show," game shows, some even remember my acting debut on "Lucas Tanner" and my appearance on "Police Story," commercials, parades, and the "Today" show.

When people ask me about "Today," they always ask these two questions, and not necessarily in this order: "What time did you have to get up to do that show?" and "What is Barbara Walters really like?"

I was living in the New York suburb of Scarsdale when I

was a regular on "Today." When I first started, I had to take the 5:26 A.M. train, so I'd get up at 4:00. On those mornings when I just couldn't get the body to react, I'd "sleep in" until 4:15. I felt like a permanent altar boy for the early Mass with the grumpy priest as the celebrant.

Plenty of people have to get up that early to go to work, and I'm sure they'll agree: you adjust, you accept it, but you never get used to it. When the evening news is late-night television, how can you get used to it?

My first experience with "Today" was as a guest in 1960. Producer Shad Northshield put me on when my book *Baseball Is a Funny Game* was published. He introduced me to host Dave Garroway, and I stood there, in a new suit and plenty scared, and heard Garroway say as if I wasn't even there, "I don't know anything about baseball. Let [Jack] Lescoulie interview him. I don't want to do it." All I wanted to do at that point was go back home.

When Garroway walked away, Northshield said to me, "Look, there's only time for two questions: what does a catcher say to a pitcher and what do players say to umpires when they get thrown out of games. You just keep going, keep going, don't let him back in." Garroway did the interview just as Northshield had planned, and it went fine.

I didn't give any "yes" or "no" answers. In fact, every answer was an audition, because soon after, I began doing a regular sports segment every Monday. I was living in St. Louis, doing the Cardinal games during the week, the "NBC Game of the Week" on the weekend, then flying to New York every Sunday night to do the Monday morning "Today" show. If it sounds hectic, it was. This story tells it best. I came home from another long road trip, and when I walked in the door my wife called to my three-year-old daughter, "It's Daddy!" My little girl answered, "What channel?" When your own kids only recognize you when you're on TV, it's time to do some thinking.

My next role on "Today" came when producer Al

Morgan made me a sort of semiregular, easing me into nonsports interviews and features several times a week. He gave me my first chance to say something besides "runs," "hits," "errors," "touchdown," or "puck" on a network broadcast. At this point, since I was practically a regular on "Today," my wife and I decided to move our family to New York.

Then in the late 1960s, I became a regular host of "Today," along with Hugh Downs and Barbara Walters. Al Morgan left the show shortly after, and Stuart Schulberg became producer. Stuart was one of the most versatile men I've ever met. He could talk sports with me and in the next breath discuss opera, Shakespeare, or foreign policy with a guest. He could go from an MVP to a Nobel Prize winner without any difficulty.

Stuart's style was completely different from Al Morgan's. Al would watch the show at home in Bronxville every day so he could see it from the same perspective as the viewers. He'd make notes, and then when he'd get to the office, we'd discuss what he liked and didn't like. Stuart, on the other hand, was in the studio every morning. He was there in the control room, making suggestions, getting involved in everything, all the while watching what ABC and CBS were doing.

One morning I was in the studio at about 6:00, when Stuart came hustling up to me. He asked if I knew Angelo Dundee, Muhammad Ali's manager. When I said "yes," he asked if I'd call him in Chicago. "It's five o'clock in the morning there," I told him. "I don't know anybody well enough to call that early. I'm not sure I know my wife well enough to call her at five in the morning." But Stuart always felt that if he was up, the rest of the world was up, too.

Stuart also had some definite ideas about what the mood of the show should be. He banned the use of the words *interview* and *guest*, for example, because of the attitude they implied. "We do not 'interview,'" a memo read. "We talk to . . . we question . . . we discuss . . . sometimes we even chat with." He felt we had to be involved, not just ask prepared questions and get prepared answers.

" 'Today' is not a parlor where 'guests' drop in to pass the time of day," the memo continued. Since everybody who came on the show had something to sell, whether it was a book or an idea, he felt the atmosphere should be "more a marketplace than a living room. On a bad day we're out traded, but most of the time we get the best of the bargain."

Stuart Schulberg completely turned me loose on "Today." Al Morgan got me started, but Stuart threw me into deep water. Reviewing the musical *Hair*, covering Lynda Bird Johnson's wedding, talking with the Indian guru Maharishi Mehesh Yogi, I never knew what to expect.

I can't tell you how many times I went into Stuart's office saying, "What are you doing to me? I can't do this interview."

"You'll be all right," he'd tell me. "Read the book and you'll be okay."

Being on the "Today" show is like playing handball with a golf ball on a closed four-wall tile court. It's going all the time. I'd read the paper on the train into the city, get to the studio, and there were all those people I'd been reading about in the headlines. We took the show to Japan, Scotland, Ireland, and Romania and made an especially memorable trip to Chicago to cover the Democratic convention in 1968. I went from Mantle, Maris, and Berra to Abbie Hoffman, Jerry Rubin, and Tom Hayden, with several stops in between.

One of my favorite interviews was with Pulitzer prize-winning poet Marianne Moore. I was a little nervous about talking with a poet, since outside of "Roses are red, violets are blue" and the little verse umpire Bill Byron used to recite after a third strike ("You'll learn before you get much older, you can't hit the ball with the bat on your shoulder") I didn't know too much about poetry.

Miss Moore was 81 when I met her, and she was a big baseball fan who'd lived and died with the Brooklyn Dodgers. We talked a lot of baseball, and I asked her to show me how she'd hold the ball to throw a curve.

"You have long fingers," I told her, as I handed her the ball. "Your fingers are longer than mine."

"You have bullpen hands," she replied, breaking up the crew and winning me over for good.

I learned a lot on "Today." It was like what Connie Mack said when somebody asked him why, at the age of 88, he still managed the Philadelphia Athletics. "Because every day I go to the ballpark I learn something," he said. "Today" was like that for me.

I remember very well a lesson I learned from Harry Edwards, who's now a special assistant to baseball commissioner Peter Ueberroth in the area of minority hiring. At the time, Edwards was a professor at the University of California–Berkeley, a renowned expert on racism in sports, and an outspoken critic of the way many colleges exploited athletes, especially black athletes. He happened to be on the show the same day we were doing a segment with several of the New York Mets' wives. Edwards and I were talking during a break when he pointed toward the Mets' wives and said, "I see you have only white women in this spot."

I told him we'd invited Mrs. Cleon Jones, but she hadn't shown up.

"Be sure to mention that when you do the spot," he said. I told him I didn't want to embarrass her, that she's a nice lady, and I'm sure she had a good excuse.

"Did she call?" he asked. I told him no. "Then you have to say something. She has a responsibility here. People all over America are going to be saying, 'Look at Joe. Look at "Today." They have players' wives on, but they're all white.' You owe it to yourself and to the show to point out that she was invited and didn't come." I took his advice.

The most important lesson I learned from "Today" was discipline. Not the discipline to get up at four in the morning, but the discipline to read an entire book for a three-minute interview, then get right to the most important information in that short period of time.

Many people think of "Today" as a two-hour show, but it's really a two-hour show broken down into very short segments of news, interviews, and commercials. If I wanted to expand on something in an interview, and the clock said I couldn't, I just couldn't. I learned that you don't live or die by what you don't get to say. I still use those lessons in interviews.

The most important element of "Today," though, is that it's live. Television editors might have a chance to fix any major disasters for the West Coast airing, but for most of the country it's live. And the TV gremlins can get you good when a show is live.

In a way, playing baseball helped me with the live aspect of television. You take your best shot, and if you fail, you just keep trying. I remember a conversation I had with Chuck Connors when his series, "The Rifleman," was very popular. We'd played in the National League at the same time, and I asked him which he thought was tougher, baseball or television.

"Baseball's tougher," he said. "The difference is in one word—retake. If they had retakes in baseball, I'd have wound up in the Hall of Fame." And as I found out over the years, he was right.

First I learned that you don't say certain words early in the morning when most people's ears aren't wide awake yet. For example, in conversation you might refer to your "old pastor," but at seven in the morning you'd better call him your "former pastor." Say it fast, too early in the morning, and "old pastor" sounds like his parents never married.

I once did an interview with the Grand Knight of the

American Knights of Columbus. I was the resident conservative church man for "Today," and I usually got the religious assignments. So I felt I was pretty much on my turf.

I thought the interview would be simple. I'd ask him four or five innocuous questions, he'd answer them, we'd wrap the whole thing in a blue ribbon, and when the FCC asked what we were doing for the community, we could whip out this interview.

My first question was "I'm a Catholic. Why should I join the Knights of Columbus?" If ever there was a puff question and a chance to deliver a commercial, this was it. Well, my guest turned away from me slightly, looked right into the camera, and gave a long-winded answer that didn't seem to have anything to do with the question and that I couldn't understand. But more puzzling was the fact that we were seated side by side and he had turned his back to me.

When he finished talking, I thought maybe I just wasn't listening hard enough, so I tossed him another lollipop: "What is the need for the Knights, and what is its purpose?"

He went off on his own again, and I couldn't figure it out. Since I was sitting right next to him and couldn't understand him, I knew the guy at home shaving didn't have a chance. So I interrupted him, trying once more with "Tell me the reason for having an organization like the Knights of Columbus."

Finally he turned to face me. "Well, Joseph," he said, and then he turned away *again* and started talking.

I hadn't been called Joseph since the seventh grade at St. Ambrose School. And when he turned his back on me that last time, it really ticked me off. I leaned around him so I could look over his shoulder and suddenly saw something I hadn't seen before. He was reading his answers from a script. He was making a speech. I didn't even know what I was going to ask him, and he had prepared answers. I reached around him, on camera, grabbed his speech, and said, "Now let's talk, you and me."

He was upset, but so was I. Many television people can stay cool in a situation like that, answer everything with a "That's interesting," and get the guest off in a hurry. I was on the show when Edwin Newman thought George Jessel's jokes were tasteless (and they were). "Why don't you leave?" Newman suggested. Jessel did, and the interview was over.

But I'm not like that. When I get upset, it shows in a lot of ways, the most obvious being that I start to talk faster. Again I went to my powder puff question to try to get an answer.

"What do the Knights of Columbus do?"

"We give food baskets at Christmas and do other charitable works."

"Do you get more involved than that?"

"We give food baskets at Christmas and do other charitable works."

My cork blew, and my next question must have come in at about 100 miles an hour. "With all the members you have, and with the church torn apart with birth control, priests getting married, divorce, abortion, people leaving the church . . . and all you people are doing is giving away baskets of food? Right now there's a synod of bishops in Rome, and you're telling me all the most powerful organization in the church wants to do is give away food baskets?"

As he started into his answer, I saw Stuart Schulberg come flying into the studio, holding up a sign that read "Commercial." You don't fool around when that happens. I figured the Russians had invaded Nebraska and we were going to a news bulletin, so I interrupted my guest and went to a break.

Stuart ran up to the desk with a panicked look on his face

and said, "What did you just say, what did you call the pope? The switchboard is all lit up."

"What are you talking about? I didn't call the pope anything. I don't even know him. He never comes around the neighborhood."

"The callers are saying you called the pope a dirty name."

"What? I didn't say anything—" and then it hit me. When you say "synod of bishops" fast, it doesn't sound like that at all. Try it. I had to come back on the air to explain what I said and apologize for the misunderstanding. That interview certainly didn't win any awards, but if there were a Blooper Hall of Fame, I'd be in it.

Doing a live show, you find out fast that the blooper shark gets everybody eventually. Hugh Downs did a certain commercial live just once. Tape, maybe, but live, never again. It was for Sealtest Strawberry Fudge Tarts. You just don't play around with that one.

The blooper shark got Barbara Walters too when she interviewed fashion designer Yves St. Laurent. She'd covered most of his new designs and was getting to the end of the interview when she fell victim. "Everything looks so good," Barbara said, "but we all know your best ideas are in your pants. Tell us about it."

The famous Alpo dogs put each of us in the blooper history books at least once. When it was time for a live Alpo commercial, it was always an adventure to see whether the dog would eat the food put in front of him. You never knew.

One morning Barbara was trying everything to get the dog to eat, and nothing worked. There she was, talking about how much dogs love Alpo, and the dog just sat there, refusing to eat. But as soon as the camera turned away, the dog, as if on cue, ate everything. He gulped down the food, then started in on the nearest chair, and finished with Barbara's shoe. Of course, while he was on camera for the whole country to see, he had lockjaw.

The "Today" host I worked with the longest was Hugh Downs. Barbara and I always agreed Hugh was the "glue" that held the show together. He moved it along and smoothed over the rough spots. On those mornings when everything seemed to be happening at once and our producer was determined to cover all of it, I'd start an interview and wonder if I'd actually get to finish it. Some days were so hectic, I'd start a *sentence* and wonder if I'd get to finish it. On those days, only one word could describe Hugh Downs: unflappable.

Hugh is the kind of guy who, if the studio were on fire, would sit calmly while the rest of us were scrambling around screaming "Fire!" and say very matter-of-factly, "The studio is on fire. The fire was caused by spontaneous combustion due to a combination of hydrogen gases trapped in the ozone, causing the nitrogen to dissipate. In due time it will be brought under control, and we will be right back after these messages from your local station. This is 'Today' on NBC." He'll get the job done no matter what.

I don't know of any subject in which Hugh isn't interested, and I know of very few subjects he doesn't know something about. By his own definition, he's a generalist. He says: "The joke about generalists and specialists is that a specialist is somebody who comes to know more and more about less and less until he knows everything about nothing. A generalist is just the opposite. He knows less and less about more and more until he knows nothing about everything."

Barbara used to joke, "Ask Hugh what time it is, and he'll tell you how the watch is made." When we traveled with the "Today" show, we'd rely on Hugh to fill us in on anything we didn't know. If he didn't have the answer, he'd revert to what I call the "Downs Doctrine": make them think you know the answer until you have a chance to find out.

When the show went to Montreal for a week, Hugh had

an appointment to interview Prime Minister Pierre Trudeau, and since I had nothing scheduled, I went out for some sight-seeing with my wife, Audrie, and Hugh's wife, Ruth. We set a time to meet Hugh for lunch.

One of the stops on our tour was the church of Notre Dame, a beautiful and impressive structure. We were admiring its beauty when I noticed a lot of scaffolding. "You know," I said, "I've never been in a cathedral that didn't have scaffolding. I wonder if there's a cathedral anywhere in the world that's finished." Both Ruth and Audrie said they really didn't know.

"I bet Hugh will know," I said. "We'll ask him at lunch."

When we met him, I told him what we'd seen and asked, "Is there one that's finished?"

"Don't any of you know?" he asked. We all shook our heads, and Hugh said, "Well, in that case, the answer is no." The Downs Doctrine in action.

One of Hugh's greatest talents was one the television audience never got to see. While we were on "Today," Hugh was commuting from his home in Carefree, Arizona; he'd finished the show on Friday morning, go right to the airport, and fly to Arizona. Then on Sunday night, he'd take the "red-eye" back to New York and come to the studio right from the airport. During those Monday shows, he would literally sleep through a commercial. And I don't mean he'd just close his eyes. He'd actually sleep. We'd go to a commercial, he'd put his head down on the desk, sleep for 58 seconds, then wake up and continue the show. It was amazing. (I couldn't sleep during commercials, but thanks to my 4:00 A.M. wake-up call, I was able to do something equally amazing: I used to fall asleep in the dentist's chair—with the drill in my mouth.)

Perhaps the most well-known side of Hugh's personality is his daring, his love of frightening and even dangerous challenges. His philosophy is "There's only one way to handle fear: go out and scare yourself!" So he's willing to try anything, from conducting a symphony orchestra and sailing across the Pacific to taking part in an expedition to the South Pole.

One year we did the show from Indianapolis during the week of the Indy 500. For one of our openings, Hugh was supposed to drive around the oval track with the cameras following him. He was going to make one full circle, then stop at a designated mark, get out of the car, and open the show. But driving a race car is a little different from taking the family car out for a spin.

Hugh got into the car dressed as if he'd won the pole position—the fireproof suit, the helmet, the whole outfit. I was standing next to two of the drivers who would be in the race on Memorial Day, Cale Yarborough and the late Art Pollard.

Cale said, "Bet he doesn't get it out of the pits. He'll kill the engine before he gets it rolling. It ain't easy."

"Don't bet on it," I said. "Knowing him, I'll bet he gets out with no problem."

Well, Hugh not only came out of the pits like he'd been doing it all his life, he really started to zoom. He'd already gone around a couple times, and we weren't even close to going on the air. He just kept going around, and I knew he was enjoying every minute.

Then we went on the air. He knew the cameras would follow him around the track, and he knew exactly where to stop. So he went around once, got to the spot—and kept driving. Then he zipped around again, just flying by everybody.

All we could do was stand and watch him go by a couple more times. At one point, when he got to the far turn, Art Pollard said, "He's got it well over a hundred miles an hour. There's no way he's gonna stop when he gets here."

Art was right, of course. Hugh was enjoying the ride so much that he missed the opening and took some extra spins.

"You sure come to those turns in a hurry," he said when he finally stepped out of the car.

"Where did you learn to drive a car like that?" I asked, somewhat amazed.

"Oh, I went to Bill Bondurant's Driving School when I found out we were coming to Indianapolis for the race." Not only did he get the job done; he got it done at 175 miles per hour.

Hugh was good to work with, especially in those first days when I was still learning what "Today" was all about. Television is an incredibly competitive business, and when the cameras start to run, you can't always be sure the person sitting next to you is secure enough to let you look good. Some people will happily put the banana peel in front of you and tell you to run. Not Hugh. I could always be sure that if I got into trouble, he'd throw me a rope, not an anchor. On a baseball team, Hugh Downs would bat third. He'd always find a way to get on base and keep the rally going.

What's Barbara Walters like? I always knew I was really making a big impression when that was the first question everybody asked me.

When I first started coming on the show, Barbara was a staff writer, doing periodic features. When Maureen O'Sullivan left the program, someone wisely decided the fluffy "Today Girl" idea was out of date, that a professional female broadcaster was needed to fill the vacancy. Barbara was given a shot.

Barbara recently said that one of her philosophies about having a career is to "forget titles and perks. Make sure you get your foot in the door and then work your fanny off." And that's exactly what she did. She proved herself by working harder than anybody else, no matter what the assignment was. She was always prepared and took nothing for granted. She often went out and got her own interviews. She didn't wait for somebody else to do it for her. She was, and still is, a good reporter.

From the beginning, Barbara was very aware of her role

as a groundbreaker for female television journalists. She always felt she was on the spot. In a sense she was always auditioning, never satisfied with her work. I don't think Barbara ever did an interview after which she didn't come back to the desk and say, "I should've asked him this." She did at least three interviews with every guest: the one she prepared for, the one on camera, and the one in her mind after the interview was over.

She wasn't insecure, just hard on herself. Barbara was the toughest critic of her work; you couldn't convince her that no one else knew the questions she didn't ask. Barbara led the league in "should've" and "could've."

She was also torn between doing what she knew was right and what other people saw as the "woman's role." On one hand, she made no secret of the fact that she didn't want to do just "women's spots," such as "how to get catsup stains out of the carpet," or "20 ways to make your kitchen more efficient." I was on her side for three reasons. One, she was good. Two, she was my friend. Three, I'd been given nonjock assignments, so why shouldn't she get the same opportunity?

Yet when she did the serious interviews, she took a lot of criticism for going right to the penetrating questions without any opening niceties. But that's what we all had to do. When you have three minutes, you don't have the luxury of asking, "How've you been doing? How's the family?" You go right to the meat of the subject, right to the jugular. Barbara did that. She knew why the guest was there and that she had three minutes to get him or her to tell the audience why. If people came on with the idea of being evasive, they were in trouble. Sometimes Barbara's questions were tough, but that was part of the job. As Barbara herself once said, "If a man says something pointed, it's authoritative. But if a woman says it, it's aggressive." She was often criticized for being abrasive, but to her credit, she didn't let the criticism stop her.

She was once interviewing Peter Townsend, the former fiancé of Princess Margaret, about his new book. When she asked about his broken engagement, he became flustered and annoyed, saying something about how those kinds of subjects seem to be interesting only "to you ladies" and that he was sick of talking about it.

"Well, if you're sick of talking about it," Barbara quickly said, "why is it in all your publicity releases?"

Barbara never complained about cameras breaking down or other technical failures. She didn't complain about working conditions on remotes either, whether she had to go into a coal mine or stand in the cold Scotland rain. But when people made her wait because they were goofing off, or when they were doing something that didn't pertain to the show and they weren't ready when they were supposed to be, she'd let them know about it. She demanded professionalism from the people she worked with, because she knew it was demanded of her.

Barbara's a complete professional. That's the reason she's able to get so many famous people, from Katharine Hepburn to Fidel Castro, to talk to her when they won't talk to anyone else.

I passed on to Barbara a lesson that Lindsey Nelson taught me during our baseball broadcasting days. Lindsey used to say you can't have a good Amos and a bad Andy; it's either a good "Amos and Andy Show" or a bad one.

What he meant was that the success or failure of a program doesn't rest on one person; the entire program is judged. Viewers often attribute questions and statements to the wrong person. It happens even now on the "Game of the Week" to Vin and me, even though we're the ultimate sweatshirt odd couple and we sound so different.

I told Barbara that if you make your partner look good, you'll look good, too. You can't have a good Hugh Downs and a bad Barbara Walters or a good Barbara and a bad Joe. We're all good or we're all bad because it's either a good

"Today" show or a bad one. I've never forgotten that and neither has Barbara; in fact, she often reminds me of it when we see each other. In sports it's called "picking the other guy up." Hugh, Barbara, and I had that on "Today."

On a baseball team, Barbara Walters would be your leadoff hitter, your catalyst. She could show strength, get the rally started, and upset the other team in the process. I'd want her on my team. Just put her in the lineup and she'll know what to do.

If I had to draw a blueprint of the ideal "Today" host, I'd take Hugh's unflappability, Barbara's dedication, and Frank McGee's approach.

When Frank McGee became the host, my life certainly got easier. He lived near me in Scarsdale, and since NBC was sending a limousine for him, I was hitching a ride. We had an agreement not to talk if either one of us woke up in a bad mood, but I don't think we ever had to fall back on it.

In a way, I missed the train ride, because I didn't see my group anymore. Five of us "regulars" got on in Scarsdale, and we became friends without ever knowing each other's names, just faces and where each got off.

If one of the "regulars" was missing, somebody would always ask about him. "Oh, he's on vacation," or "He just got transferred." Somebody always knew. Yet I don't think one of us knew what any other did for a living. They certainly didn't know me, because they were going to work at the same time I was, so they weren't watching the show.

One morning the routine changed drastically. I had done the telecast of the Macy's Thanksgiving Day Parade, and the next morning, one of our group, whom I knew only as "the guy who rarely made small talk and always got off at 125th Street," was waiting for me at the station. He was all excited. "Hey, I saw you on TV. I watched the parade, and I told my wife, 'That's my friend. We go to work together.' Why didn't you tell me? Can I bring my wife down tomorrow morning to meet you?"

The next morning at 5:05, my usual time, they were there. "Hey, honey, I want you to meet my friend, Joe." Not only did we meet; we also had coffee and rolls. That's when the difficult part of the television business pays off.

The train was okay, but I must admit riding to work with door-to-door limo service was a bit better, especially in the winter. More important, though, it gave me a chance to get to know Frank, and we became good friends.

I quickly learned he had no tolerance for lack of preparation. He didn't teach it or preach it, but he got the message across in the stories he told.

In the early days of television coverage of the space program, people thought of Frank as *the* space expert. But according to him, "I was no space expert, but I knew if there was a delay we had to stay on the air, so I learned about space."

When we did the show from Dublin, Ireland, Frank insisted on going to war-torn Belfast to see what was going on. If he was going to *talk* about the violence there, he had to *see* it firsthand, despite the danger.

Frank was a tough interviewer. We each reacted differently to uncooperative guests: Hugh would start to call them "Sir;" the more polite he'd get, the lower would go the temperature in the studio. Barbara would start to talk faster and her voice would get higher. Me, I'd lean in closer to the guest, like he was an umpire, and talk a little louder and faster. But Frank always knew how to put subtle pressure on his guest. It was like he'd take a gun out of his pocket, point it at the guest, and say in his calmest voice, "Okay, now answer the question."

Yet Frank also had a good sense of humor. I can still hear him laughing about the morning we pulled up in the limousine at the traffic light at 49th and 6th. Two hookers were standing on the corner, and they perked up a little when they saw the limo. So I rolled down the window, stuck my head out, and said, "No thank you ladies." They both looked, then one of them yelled, "Hey, it's that bald-headed Joe from the 'Today' show!" Frank fell off the seat laughing. We both wondered later if the network's demographics (showing the ages, occupations, and educational levels of viewers) included those ladies on the corner of 49th and 6th.

Frank McGee left us too soon when he died of cancer in 1974. I remember the day he told me how sick he was. He wasn't dramatic; that wasn't his style, and he wasn't a complainer. He just tipped me off so I could put the pieces together.

We were riding to work as usual, and somehow the conversation got around to being bald. I guess I'm kind of an expert on that subject.

"You never have worn a hairpiece, have you?" he asked me. "You don't have to; you've got a nice round head."

"Sure, it's always the guy with hair who says that. Now you're gonna tell me you have a pointed head and you'd look awful if you were bald."

"Hey, let me tell you something," he said. "I've seen myself bald. I've been taking this therapy, and I've lost most of my hair. When I put my 'piece' on this morning— I'm wearing a 'piece' now, you know—I looked in the mirror and saw a shriveled up old man. The hairpiece helps."

I know we finished the conversation, but I can't remember it. I got the message. Suddenly I understood his slow pace and why he sometimes rested his head on the desk during commercials. Soon after, he went into the hospital. He came back and did his job, but you could see he was in trouble. Still, he carried that trouble with a very special kind of class. Gene Mauch said it about baseball manager Fred Hutchinson, but it fit Frank as well: he showed us how to live, and now he would show us how to die.

If Barbara led off on my team, and Hugh batted third, Frank would be my number 4 hitter. You knew you could count on him to do what had to be done, whether he had to drive in a man from first or hit a home run. Everybody should be lucky enough to have a number 4 hitter for a friend.

"Today" is structured so that a station break always comes at 25 minutes past the hour. The cue is, "This is 'Today' on NBC." Most of the local stations use that five minutes to do early-morning news. But a number of stations don't program that time, so "Today" fills it. It's called the "co-op."

Some of the funniest moments came out of the co-op. The audience was smaller, and everybody was a bit looser and more candid. The spots got so good that Stuart Schulberg considered keeping the tapes and running a "Best of the Co-Op" segment once a week.

We didn't prepare much for it because no one thought the time was that important. So our preparation would go one of two ways. As we neared the time, Frank would ask, "What'll we talk about?" or maybe "Ask me about [something interesting he'd think of]."

One morning he asked his usual "What'll we talk about?" and I said, "Ask me about my turtle, the one I had as a kid."

"Is it self-serving?" he asked. Frank hated anything that was self-serving.

"Hey, Frank, how can a turtle be self-serving? Just ask me, will you?"

So he began. "Everybody has a pet when they're growing up," Frank said. "Did you have a pet as a kid, Joe?"

"Well," I said, "he really wasn't a pet; he was more of a necessity. We had a turtle we kept in the basement. In my neighborhood, almost everybody had a turtle in the basement to eat the bugs; he was more like our Orkin man than our pet. Actually, I hardly ever saw him with his head out of his shell. He was just this little blob in the corner.

"Once a year, though, we'd get a real good look at him. My father made his own wine, and it was a major project:

the grapes would be delivered, and a couple of the men would come over to the house and help squeeze them, then the juice would ferment in big barrels.

"There'd always be a leak by the bung, that big plug used as a cork, and that's when we'd see the turtle. When that thing would start to leak, out he'd come and put his head under the cork for about five minutes. Then for two days he'd walk around with his head sticking way out of his shell looking for the cat."

A lot of people wrote in to say how impossible it was for a turtle and a cat to have a romance. All I know is, the happiest days of that turtle's life were when Papa made his wine.

I shouldn't have been surprised to get so many letters about that poor turtle. We never knew how our viewers might react to something—only that they would definitely react.

We got thousands of letters every week, about absolutely everything. I got a lot about religion (including pamphlets about saving my soul), remedies for baldness (including a few hair oils and "magic formulas"), complaints about either too many liberals on the show or too many conservatives, suggestions about my grammar, jokes for me to use on the air (I still get those for the "Game of the Week"), complaints about my commercials or game shows, and lots of advice about everything from my wardrobe to my politics. Our audience was made up of experts on every subject.

The viewers worried about us, criticized us, laughed with us, and shared our sorrow. We were part of the family. Maybe it's because we came into their homes so early, before they'd had their morning coffee. They'd be getting ready for work or getting the kids off to school, shaving or putting on makeup. If they can take you at that time of day, they're doing more than tuning you in—they're adopting you.

I felt that very strongly during my years on "Today." I was in Miami with the show when my mother died, and I had to leave suddenly for St. Louis. The avalanche of cards and letters from viewers was unbelievable. They just wouldn't let me go through such a tough time alone.

I also found out that not only were our viewers concerned; they were also observant. As in any profession, occasional slumps are part of the job. I'd go through periods when I'd forget things, not call people, get my days mixed up, or read a book for an interview someone else was scheduled to do. In the middle of one of these slumps, I kept forgetting to put on my rings in the morning. I wear only two rings: my wedding ring on my left hand and my World Series ring on my right hand. Soon I started getting letters and calls from people wondering if I was having trouble at home because I wasn't wearing my wedding ring. At 7:00 in the morning, most people are lucky if they can see the bathroom door, yet a lot of folks out there noticed my missing rings.

Viewers can be critical too. I once made the mistake of getting flippant with a priest as I thanked him off the show, and I heard about it for days.

I thought the tone of the interview was too heavy, especially at the end when he turned to me as if he were going to give me two more Commandments and said, "My thanks to you. Please pray for me."

Okay, I probably shouldn't have said anything, but that was a little too much for me. So I said, "Pray for you? Hey, Father, with the year I'm having, you should pray for *me*. After all, you're in management, I'm labor."

Well, if people actually lit all the candles for me they said they did, the flames would have equaled the Chicago fire. I heard "And you, a Catholic—how could you be so disrespectful?" Some told me to go to church and to confession. A few others just eliminated the in-between stops and told me to go straight to hell.

No matter what you say on TV, somebody's always going to have a comment about it. Somebody wrote to me about a shaving cream commercial, "We can't understand why you would want to lose so much dignity in the eyes of the public by trying to infer that all lather wouldn't stay moist on a hot, wet, sweaty face." One of my favorite letters was from a viewer with a question about one of my Dodge car commercials: "Your script says if you want to know how good a car Dodge is, just 'ask the million who own one.' I wonder why a million people would own one car."

Besides all the letters, I tried to take as many phone calls as possible. It was the best way to find out what the viewers were thinking (although you had to draw the line somewhere, or you'd be on the phone all day). We had viewers who called every day. Usually my secretary could get an idea of what they wanted to talk about so she could prepare me for the call.

One lady was calling every day, but she wouldn't give a hint of what she was calling about. She finally won over my secretary, who started saying things like "Oh, she's so nice, so soft-spoken. I know she just wants to talk to you." So after about a week I decided to see what she had to say.

She started out by telling me she was a former English teacher. I thought to myself, "Here it comes, the 30-minute lecture on my bad grammar."

"I really enjoy the 'Today' program, and you are my favorite person." (She can't be all bad, I thought.) "You do such interesting things." (Hey, she's a bright lady.) "I never know what to expect when you're on, and I like that." (Why didn't I talk to her sooner?) "But I want to talk to you about something you do." (Uh-oh, here comes the torpedo. She set me up, and now she's got me.)

"Your elocution is terrible, Joe. You always drop your i-n-g's. You say runnin', kickin', throwin', and pitchin'. I wish you would try to change that."

"You're right," I told her. "But you know, if I start saying runn*ing*, kick*ing*, and throw*ing*, I ain't gonna be work*ing*."

Another lady helped me out with a list of almost 100 words I could use to say one team "beat" another. Describing herself only as a "lil' ol' grey-haired lady who teaches little fingers to play piano," she sent me a carefully handwritten list that included *defeated, downed, nosed out, dropped, clobbered, shaded, topped, slipped by, walloped, blasted, subdued, tripped, demolished, rocked, dumped, buried, squeaked by, walked away from, nipped, bowed, trampled, got by, ripped, stripped, whitewashed, scored, led, tamed, out front, bombed, rolled over, upset, swamped, clawed, manhandled, shocked, stunned, breezed by, mauled, whipped, nicked, in front, chilled, pounded, smashed, overtook, smothered, took, outclassed, outplayed, knocked off, clipped, toppled, nudged, edged, tromped, outslugged, cut down, stopped, grounded, KOed, routed, romped past, fell, humiliated, sunk, outgunned, clubbed, shackled, drubbed, blanked, trimmed, pinned, swept, triumphed, shelled, crushed, hacked, rooted out, victorious over, smeared, overruled, outlasted, held off*. . . . Hey, can you beat that?

Viewers scolded and tried to help because they really cared. How else can you explain almost 2,000 letters at one time on the subject of my bald head? I was scheduled to interview Ray Nitschke, the former Green Bay Packers' star, who's as bald as I am.

We usually had a couple of minutes to visit with the guests before the show went on the air, but that morning I didn't see Nitschke. All I could find was a scholarly-looking man, with a full head of hair and horn-rimmed glasses. I thought he was either a visitor or a writer.

Finally he grabbed me and said, "Hey, Joe, Ray Nitschke." I couldn't believe it. He was representing a company that manufactured toupees.

"You can't come on the air like that. Nobody will know you. Take the piece off, we'll talk a little football, break for a commercial, and then they can put the piece back on you and put one on me too."

So we started the interview *au naturel*, a bald baseball player talking to a bald football player. When we got the commercial cue, I said, "Friends, when we come back, both Ray and I will be wearing toupees, so call your friends, because right after these messages you're going to see two beauties."

The makeup people and hairdressers moved in like a SWAT team. If it's true that a professional likes a challenge, these makeup artists were probably still talking about Nitschke and me at their next convention. I could see what they were doing to him—Andre the Giant was turning into Tom Selleck right before my eyes—but I couldn't see what they were doing to me.

When we came back on, I took one look at the monitor, and I couldn't believe it was me. "Hey, I look pretty good."

"You do, Joe," Ray said.

"You do, too, Ray," and for two minutes, two "gorillas" told each other how good they looked.

Of course, I wasn't considering wearing a hairpiece, nor did I ask for any opinion. But we got more than 1,400 letters telling me I should wear it and about 500 against it. Some of the comments:

"I like your head with the shine."

"You look 20 years younger; keep it on."

"Take it off, circle it with chalk, and call it 'ground under repair.'"

"Don't change a hair for me."

"Keep it on. Now I don't need sunglasses to watch the show."

"Get out from under that doily."

"Your honest shiny head is one of the few real things on TV."

"Piece at any price!"

The mail not only told me something about the loyalty of America's bald-headed men; it also told me something about the priorities of our viewers. General James Gavin was on that show, outlining his policy on the ongoing war in Vietnam. He received about 20 pieces of mail. I got almost 2,000. The general was a great guy; he just had too much hair.

With all the energy it takes, and the weird hours you keep, "Today" is really a 24-hour-a-day job. By 1:00 in the afternoon, you're like a rubber band: you're stretched to the limit, and then you reach back and stretch some more. And then you do it again. It takes a lot out of you.

My life was suddenly spinning very fast, and everything revolved around my work. Besides "Today," I was doing game shows, a daily radio show, everything I could. One week I filled in for Johnny Carson as host of "The Tonight Show," and a few days later I got a letter from a regular viewer of "Today." He'd gone to bed about 10:30 one night and dozed off with the television on. He woke up about an hour later, saw me on the screen, and go up to get ready for work. I knew just how he felt. I felt like I was locking up the RCA Building at night and opening it in the morning.

Finally, I decided to leave "Today." The choice was either the show or my family. It's tough to get up at 4:00 and go to bed at 9:00 when your kids are growing up. When most people were enjoying the evening, I'd be trying to sleep, and my wife would be trying to keep the kids quiet. In the morning, my alarm would go off, and of course she'd wake up too, with little hope of ever getting back to sleep.

The easiest thing about the job was actually doing the show itself. No matter how tired I was, when the red light went on, the adrenaline was there. My problems came when the red light *wasn't* on. The show was over at 9:00, but I'd work on the next day's show until 2:30 or 3:00 in the afternoon. When I'd get home, I'd try to enjoy dinner with my family around 5:30 or 6:00, but having been up since 4:00, I'd be about as animated as a foul pole.

A social life? Mine was comparable to a party in a Trappist monastery. I'd tell Audrie, "We'll go out Friday night because I can sleep late Saturday." By Friday I'd be too tired to do anything, and I'd say, "How about tomorrow night? I can sleep late Sunday and go to 5:00 Mass." Then on Saturday when we'd go out, I'd be thinking about the book I had to finish for the interview on Monday. So dinner was a bunch of "uh-huhs" followed by "What did you say?" separated by a meal. I started to feel my wife and I were drifting apart, as if I were going down one road and she were going down another.

It's easy to become preoccupied like that when something really takes hold of you. I remember comedian Phil Silvers telling about a time in his life when he was gambling big on sports. He was appearing on Broadway, and he took advantage of his one day off to visit his mother in Brooklyn. He spent the whole afternoon with the radio turned down low, listening to a ball game he'd bet on. That evening on the subway ride back into Manhattan, he realized he'd spent the whole day with his mother and couldn't remember one thing she'd said. I knew how he felt. I wasn't paying attention to anyone around me.

My family was paying a big price for my being on the show. And it wasn't just the time and the fatigue. When I did what I thought was a good interview, it would make my whole day. Unfortunately, the reverse was also true. If I did a bad interview, I'd fight a bad mood all day; I felt like going up to strangers to explain why the interview wasn't better.

I also went through a phase when I thought everything I did was the most important thing in the world. *I* interviewed so-and-so. Guess who called *me* today? Did you see the story about *me* in *The New York Times*? Never mind what

Audrie and the kids did. Tell me about it, but make it quick so I can get back to talking about *my* day.

For a long time, I couldn't understand why everybody didn't feel the way I did about the "Today" show. Weren't we the reason the network was running? We were *the* show on television. After I left, however, I found out a whole lot of people didn't even know the show was on the air.

Being on a show like "Today" is very heady wine. You get invited to state dinners. You're invited to opening nights. A TV writer once called "Today" "the best inter-office memo in Washington. The quickest way to get a point across to someone is to get on that show." So it wasn't unusual to say something and get a call from a senator or a member of Congress, or maybe even the White House. Movie and television actors are on the phone looking to get a plug, and you're convinced all these things happen because you're such a "warm and wonderful person." The thing to keep in mind, and this is what I told both Gene Shalit and Bryant Gumbel when they asked me about the pitfalls of being on the show, is that it's not you, it's the show. When I left, I was still just as "warm and wonderful," but the invitations stopped, and the politicians and celebrities suddenly lost my phone number.

I should have known better, because I'd been through a similar thing as a ballplayer. After we won the 1946 World Series, I was everybody's friend. The phone just about jumped off the wall. A year and a half later when I was back in the minor leagues, was I still popular? I kept looking for my name in the obituaries.

My decision to leave "Today" surprised a lot of people in the television business. They didn't exactly jump off bridges or circulate petitions to get me to stay, but they just couldn't believe I could walk away. You see, people in television, especially in news, sometimes look upon the business as Holy Orders, some kind of special calling. To me it was a job. Glamorous, exciting, rewarding in many ways, but still a job. I was hired, not ordained.

The "Today" show was a great experience for me, and so were the game shows. I started as a guest on "Match Game." Then, Bob Noah, a producer at Goodson-Todman, asked me to audition as host for a show called "He Said, She Said," which was revived a few years later as "Tattletales." After hosting that show, I went on to "Sale of the Century," "The Memory Game," "To Tell the Truth," and a new version of "Strike it Rich."

Some viewers thought I shouldn't have been doing "Today" and a game show at the same time. People would tell me I was betraying them by doing a "hokey" game show. But my feeling has always been that television is a medium for entertainment, just as much as it is one for social commentary, public information, or news. Television has a place for all these things, and as long as each TV set has control dials, the people working those dials can decide how to use them.

I've enjoyed every game show I've done, and the reason is simple: everybody feels good before, during, and after a game show. For the contestants, it's probably the first time they've ever been on TV, so it's exciting as they become instant celebrities to their friends. As the emcee, I benefit from all the excitement, too; I get a kick out of watching people enjoy their big television moment. More than once a contestant has said to me, "I don't care if I don't take anything home; this has been the greatest." And of course, they think I'm the greatest guy in the world for giving them the trip, the refrigerator, or the fur coat. I make a lot of friends. If you want people to like you, be a game show host. You can't lose.

Game shows are full of surprises, so you always have to be ready for anything. The contestants are usually nervous, and they soon find out the game was a lot easier when they were playing at home. They're told, "Have fun and be yourself," but with the bright lights, the audience, and what seems like a hundred different instructions, stage fright can cause anybody to forget who's buried in Grant's Tomb.

Since you never know whether a question will seem easy or hard to a contestant, you never know what you might hear. What's especially funny is the nervous, unpredictable answer that isn't always wrong.

"Name something you don't have to go to the doctor to cure." That seems like a simple enough question, with any number of answers. A headache, a nosebleed, a splinter. How about this answer, though, which broke me up completely:

"A ham."

Or when asked to "name something with horns," a contestant said, "A car."

The "Memory Game" wasn't on the air very long, but the contestants made for some funny moments. In this game, we gave each contestant 10 questions and answers, and they had to try to remember them and match them correctly. When people concentrated too hard on just the questions *or* the answers, they made some very memorable matches.

Q: "According to legend, who peeped at Lady Godiva?"

The right answer was Peeping Tom. The contestant said, "Her horse."

Q: "What did Hyman Littman invent in 1932?"

The right answer was the pencil with an eraser. What came to the contestant's mind was "The Sistine Chapel."

Q: "The Lazy S, Mashed O, and Running W are all examples of what?"

The answer is cattle brands. The contestant's answer was "speech problems."

Q: "According to their titles, King Alfred was Great and Czar Ivan was Terrible. What was King Pepin?"

The correct answer is bald. The contestant's first answer was "happy-go-lucky." "That's wrong," I said. "He's a lot like me." "Oh, he was Italian?" she said.

• • •

"To Tell the Truth" was always a lot of fun because of the people involved—host Garry Moore, and panelists Bill Cullen, Kitty Carlisle, and Peggy Cass. The panel would hear a story about a guest, then three people, all claiming to be that guest, would answer the panel's questions. The two impostors were always so well informed about the subject they were hard to detect. (In fact, a fan once asked me, "Do the impostors know the real one?")

On one show, the impostors needed not only intense preparation, but several hours of makeup as well. My son, Joe, Jr., and Kitty's son, Chris Hart, were impostors of a decoy police officer who walked the New York City streets in various disguises to attract muggers. The NBC makeup department did a fantastic job of turning three young, good-looking guys into a blind old woman, a frail old man on crutches, and a seedy-looking bum.

But Kitty and I had no idea our sons were going to be on the show. So after the questioning, when the real detective identified himself, and Chris Hart revealed *his* identity, I laughed louder than anybody else at the joke played on Kitty. She just couldn't believe her son was behind the disguise. I thought it was great. How could she not recognize her own kid? Then, when contestant number three (the dirty bum with a few front teeth missing who looked like he'd been sleeping on the sidewalk in his suit for two weeks) announced that he was Joe Garagiola, Jr., I was flabbergasted.

"Take it off! I don't believe it," I shouted, still not able to recognize my son beneath the makeup. I was completely fooled. "Joe, say something to me." He pulled out the wads of cotton stuffed in his mouth and a few fake broken teeth and said, "Hi." I haven't trusted that kid since.

On "To Tell the Truth," you never knew who would ask the question that would send everybody, including the studio audience, into a laughing fit. The show was funny, informative, and most of all unpredictable. One of the rules of the show was that if you recognized or knew any of the three contestants you had to disqualify yourself.

The subject was the owner of a talking bird. The three contestants came out, we heard the story about the real subject, and the questioning began. When it was Bill Cullen's turn he said, "I have to disqualify myself because I recognize one of the people."

"A friend of yours, Bill?" Garry Moore asked.

"No, but when I went into the men's room, I saw him there with his bird in his hand."

Try to continue a show after that.

Thanks to "Sale of the Century," I had people across the country offering prayers for my soul. This also marked the first time in television history that a tape reel jumped from the storage rack to the tape machine without being touched by human hands.

I was asked to do a 30-second commercial during the break between taping two shows. The ad agency hadn't delivered the script yet, but our production people told me they'd get it to me as soon as it arrived.

During the break, I got the script for a product called Nonesuch Mincemeat. I assumed the copy would be on the teleprompter, and I'd just have to familiarize myself with it, then read it. Teleprompters are great. The copy you're reading is right on the lens of the camera, so eye contact is no problem.

I read the copy once and didn't see any words or phrases that would be booby traps, so I was ready. I asked to read it once off the prompter.

That's when I was told, "There is no prompter." That should have been my first warning sign. I should have known this just wasn't going to work.

"I don't have it memorized. I just got it," I told them.

"We'll put it on cue cards."

Unfortunately, the guy writing out the cue cards was a

newcomer, so reading them was going to be a real adventure. Since we had to get it done before the second taping, everybody was in a hurry. The writing on the cue cards was so small that I needed binoculars to read it.

We decided to try it anyway. The commercial wasn't complicated; all I had to do was stand in one spot, read the copy, hold up a can of mincemeat, then hold up a recipe book.

On the first take, the ad agency's account executive (at least that's what I started out calling him) was holding the cue card on the floor instead of off to the side of the camera lens. When I finished, the adman said, "Can we do it again? Your eye contact with the camera wasn't very good."

I told him that if he kept holding the card on the floor, it wasn't going to get any better. He said he'd try to remember to hold it next to the lens. But the second take wasn't much better, and I got the same message about eye contact.

"Look," I said, "I just got the copy for the first time this morning, we don't have a teleprompter, and everybody's waiting for me to get through this so we can do the next show. Can't we do this when we're finished taping?"

His answer was "no," and he was uptight about it; this was his agency's first national ad and his first account, and he wanted to get it done. I knew such pressure conditions weren't right for making a good commercial, but I thought I'd give it one more shot.

"Look, I can't read the cue card," I told him. "Trust me to put it into my own words, and I promise you I won't change the nuts and bolts of the commercial. The company's name and the address will be right."

So we went for number three. I was really sailing along and looking right into the lens. Pick up the can—perfect. Put down the can and hold up the recipe book—perfect. I had it nailed. All I had left to do was remind people to send for the booklet: "Nonesuch Mincemeat, Post Office Box 1000Z, Newark . . ." and I stumbled. I started to say

"Newark, New Jersey" instead of "Newark, New York," and knowing we'd have to do another take, I said, "Jesus Christ, I'm sorry, goddammit. We gotta do it again."

So we cranked it up and we did it again, sailing right through it. My little ad guy took off with his cue cards to live happily ever after.

This was Tuesday. On Thursday, the day the commercial aired, I was in a meeting when I got a frantic call from my secretary. "What did you say on TV? Everybody is calling, and they say you cursed on TV. They want you fired. What did you do? And Larry White [the head of daytime programming] wants to see you right away."

When she told me I had supposedly cursed on "Sale of the Century," I couldn't figure out what she was talking about. But when I got to Larry White's office, the tape was cued and there it was, as clear as Pavarotti's best note.

The first thing I had to do was go on the air and apologize. Then we had to figure out what happened.

We went to the control room to ask some questions. Nobody should have saved a bad take except maybe for a private Christmas party showing. This happened long before bloopers became so popular on television, so to have a "real" blooper was great.

We checked the log, but naturally, nobody was officially listed as "on duty" at the time the commercial aired. We talked to a few of the technicians, but everybody was either on a break, at lunch, or taking the day off. We finally concluded that for the first time ever, a tape reel went from the rack to the machine and played right on cue without ever having been touched by human hands.

The viewer reaction covered every emotion. People said prayers to save my soul. One practical-minded priest said Mass for me to save my job. A few people called NBC and wanted me fired. A lady from West Virginia wrote, "I failed to hear the slipup that caused so much uproar. Do you suppose you might get NBC to run the tape again?"

Most people understood what happened and had fun with it. I even made *Newsweek*, not on the cover but as sort of an "oops." The newspapers had a great time with it, coming up with headlines like "And Now, &%$X#, Here's Joe!," "Joe 'Blue' the Commercial," and "Catcher Foul on TV." A Catholic church bulletin from Ontario, Canada, said, "Joe, you have the consolation of knowing that many of the crudities of TV make your lapse appear almost angelic." And Wade Mosby, the TV editor of *The Milwaukee Journal*, sent me a note that put the whole thing in perspective: "I don't know what all the hollering is about. In this Christmas season, you acknowledged the birth of the Savior, expressed repentance, and reaffirmed your belief in a Divinity that can set things aright, all in one sentence."

I still have people come up to me and say they saw "that show when you didn't know the microphone was on and you cursed." We must have had the biggest television audience in history watching the show that day, and I think I've met them all.

Network television is an exciting ride; you never know what's around the next turn. And no road has had more turns than my route to the talk show circuit; it was strictly "back road." If you charted my course on a map, you'd be following along the "blue highways," color-coded to warn you they're mostly unpaved and potentially hazardous.

I didn't have an agent. In those days the only agents I knew worked for either insurance companies or the FBI. Besides, I figured a shepherd or a viking would have a better chance of getting on talk shows than a former third-string catcher.

All talk shows have talent coordinators (the entertainment equivalent of baseball scouts) who go out and find guests. Like scouts, they have bird dogs who give them leads or find people on their own.

Tom O'Malley, who was later an interviewer on "Candid Camera," was a talent coordinator for Jack Paar's "The

Tonight Show," THE talk show in 1957. I'd met Tom a few times, and we'd always talked baseball because he was a Cub fan. I mean a *real* Cub fan, the kind columnist George Will calls "99 percent scar tissue." Tom always told me someday I'd get on the show, but first he'd have to convince Jack because Jack didn't know anything about sports.

I was doing a lot of traveling on the banquet circuit then, and I'd recently taken some unexpected turns and found myself right out on the four-lane highways. From the Kiwanis and the Lions Club luncheons, I was beginning to move into the big banquets. At Pittsburgh's Dapper Dan banquet were people from the Hickok Belt Award dinner, who asked me if I'd appear at their banquet in Rochester. Mickey Mantle was the Hickok Belt winner that year, so all the New York sportswriters were covering the dinner. After hearing me speak, they asked me if I'd appear at the New York Writers' Dinner. Three in a row—I was starting to feel like DiMaggio on his hitting streak.

At the New York dinner, comedian George Gobel and I were supposed to provide the "light breaks" between the awards. I'm sure George wasn't worried, but for a guy who was used to sharing the podium with the president of the Optimist Club, sharing the dais with George Gobel was scary.

The dinner went fine, though, and it turned out to be the last stop on the highway before the talk shows, because in the audience that night was Jack Paar's neighbor. He must have said something to Jack about "this bald-headed ball-player you ought to have on the show," because now Jack was asking Tom O'Malley if I was the same guy he was always talking about. I was, and now I was on a network TV talk show.

The unwritten rule of hiring big-league managers also seems to apply to talk shows: work one and you work them all. A manager gets fired, goes through the revolving door, and comes out the manager of another team. Talk shows,

I'd discovered, are the same: after Paar there was Merv Griffin, Mike Douglas, Dick Cavett—and 30 years later I'm still doing "The Tonight Show."

Appearing on "The Tonight Show" is something special. It brings on a little more anxiety than usual, because you know no matter what you do, you're going to hear about it the next day from just about everybody you talk to.

"The Tonight Show" is Johnny Carson, the Babe Ruth of talk show hosts. Just like people always asked me "What's Barbara Walters like?" once I did "The Tonight Show," I'd always hear, "What's Johnny Carson really like?"

I know him only from the show. We've been in makeup at the same time, and we've talked after the show, but we've never gone out for a couple of beers or anything like that. Yet I feel if I called him and told him I was in trouble, he'd help me. Sitting on the couch talking with him, you always feel he's listening, not trying to think up a funny line and waiting to drop it in. He wants the show to look good. And don't let the cue cards fool you. Johnny Carson is a naturally funny man. He thinks funny but doesn't mind letting the other guy get the laugh. He loves to laugh and to make people laugh, and he has great timing. If I'd had his timing while using a bat, I'd still be playing. To be able to do what he does, you have to be a big talent.

Once I made it through the talk show and game show revolving door, I sort of became NBC's "designated celebrity." While I was doing "Today," I was also doing the daily radio show, so I was in the NBC Building every day. At that time, a number of shows were taped in the building, like Joan Rivers's talk show, as well as game shows like "What's My Line?," "To Tell the Truth," and "Match Game." During the winter, especially if we'd had a heavy snow and the streets were clogged, it wouldn't be unusual for me to get a frantic call saying "So-and-so hasn't gotten here yet. Can you come down?" One day I was asked to fill in for Ethel Merman, Eva Gabor, and Suzy Parker, all on different shows. Down to the studio I went, but they all made it just in time. I finally told Gil Fates of Goodson-Todman Productions that I wasn't going to agree to fill in again unless I could be Raquel Welch.

That "designated celebrity" role wasn't just for shows in the building, by the way. One day I got a call from the executive producer of the Miss America telecast for NBC. He wanted a "giant favor." The grand marshal of their parade in Atlantic City had just dropped out, and he wanted me to fill in.

I went, and it was a great learning experience. But if you're ever asked to be the grand marshal in a parade, I have one piece of advice: don't ride behind the horses. Not only is the view bad, but if the wind is blowing, I guarantee you'll get hit sometime before the parade ends. And don't wear a light-colored suit either, because it'll be a brown suit when the day is over.

Parades are great fun, though. Everybody has a lot of little girl or boy inside of them, and parades bring that out. I've been a part of the Macy's Thanksgiving Day Parade, and I've hosted the King Orange Jamboree Parade in Miami on New Year's Eve. The list of cohosts I've worked with reads like a "Who's Who" in *TV Guide*: Leslie Uggams, Shelley Long, Anita Bryant, Barbara Eden, Erin Gray, JoAnne Pflug, Rita Moreno, Toni Tennile, Sarah Purcell, and Marie Osmond. To be honest, that beats being in the team picture with Dee Fondy, Bobby Del Greco, and Carl Sawatski.

Televised parades are completely scripted for timing, but you still never know what might happen. I remember doing an interview with gymnast Cathy Rigby during the Macy's Parade and hearing the producer screaming to "get the wolfhounds in place." They were the next on-camera act, and nobody could find them. I could see them, but I was on the air, so I couldn't tell anybody that their trainer had them huddled in a corner, trying to keep them warm.

The world-famous Mummers were almost mangled one year at the Orange Bowl Parade. They were doing their best strutting down Biscayne Boulevard when one of them thought it would be funny to whack one of our technicians with the flat side of his sword while our guy was pushing a camera. Big Bob Ferrachio was well over 230 pounds, and he was getting ready to mum the Mummer when somebody stopped him.

Some of my most gratifying moments in television involve "The Baseball World of Joe Garagiola," a 15-minute pregame show for "NBC's Monday Night Baseball." Some of the memories are funny, some poignant, others exciting, and some nostalgic. The show was different, especially for a pregame show. In going beyond game recaps, injury reports, and reviews of the starting lineup, we got into all kinds of things. It wasn't a show about baseball, but a show about people, who happened to be involved in baseball in some way.

We laughed at one of the last of the baseball clowns, Max Patkin, and marveled at the youth and spirit of the players in Florida's Kids and Kubs League, where you have to be at least 75 years old to make the team. We went "inside," as pitcher Gaylord Perry showed us where he hid the ammunition for his spitball, and we learned how to catch foul balls from the "scientific approach" of a three-man team, who made their biggest guy block the aisle while the other two chased down the balls. We were touched by comedian Foster Brooks's dramatic presentation of his original poem "The Volunteer: Casey—Twenty Years Later," as he played all the parts, and we were amazed as minor-league manager Billy Scripture actually took a bite out of a baseball. We witnessed Yankee Stadium's face-lift and relived the feeling of tradition and friendliness of some of the other old ballparks, with visits to the sites of Pittsburgh's Forbes Field, New York's Polo Grounds, and Brooklyn's Ebbets Field, where they've removed everything but the memories.

In its first year, "Baseball World" was honored with a George Foster Peabody Award, dubbed the "Pulitzer Prize of broadcasting." And of all of my memories, which are my favorites?

Watching baseball greats Don Sutton and Johnny Bench compete in a bubble-gum-blowing contest. But Dodgers pitcher Andy Messersmith beat them all that year, and he told us about the stance, the strategy, and the discipline it took to be the best. Then he inspired the bubble-gum blowers of America with his words: "You have to have a lot of desire. It takes determination, perseverance, and practice. One must be able to take disappointment and try, try again." He also told us of the frustration of "having a good series, you're blowing well, then you go into a place like Candlestick Park, and the wind up there, it can really get to you mentally. You gotta watch out. . . ."

Then there was New York City Ballet dancer Edward Villella, showing us how he prepared for a performance, then giving his view of the "similar but different" aspects of baseball and ballet. He'd watch a film of a baseball play and duplicate it with the smooth moves of a dancer. I bet you never knew a batter in the box is really doing a plié or that the dancer's equivalent of circling under a fly ball is the pirouette. He showed us the dancer's way to "make a quick tag" and "get a good jump." He showed me what tough training really is and what great athletes ballet dancers are.

We gave American fans a look at baseball in Italy, starting with how they "talk some ball." Understanding a "lo strike out" is easy, but how about *il gioco forzato*, a force out? I hit into a lot of double plays, but I don't think it's quite as painful in Italy, where they call it *la doppia eliminazione*. Sounds like something the pope would give you.

The scoreboards in Italy use Roman numerals, and you haven't really enjoyed baseball until you've seen a team pull one out in the bottom of the IX.

And the Italian fans. The noise in the Minneapolis Metrodome sounds like a convent at vespers compared to the fans at Nettuno. They bring olive oil cans to the ballpark and for nine innings pound them flat. They hate the opposing team almost as much as they hate the umpires. They also bring mannequins to the ballpark, and when a guy gets a hit that hurts the home team, they tear the arms off and throw them on the field.

My favorite memory is of the courage of former Detroit Tigers player Gates Brown, who willingly took me and our cameras back to the Ohio State Reformatory in Mansfield where he spent almost two years of his life for breaking and entering. He wanted to show what prison was like, to get the message across to kids to do the right thing, to maybe keep somebody from going through what he did.

"When I walked through those doors," he said, as we passed through the entrance of the prison, "I thought it was the end of the world." But he made sure it wasn't, and he talked to several inmates while we were there to help them understand that. He'd come a long way since prison, and he wasn't afraid to expose this part of his past if it would help just one person. His example prompted one of the inmates to say, "It shows one man can open doors for all of us." I remember Gates telling them, "You were wrong and the man caught you. Keep your mouth shut and it's easy time. Keep making trouble and it's hard time."

"See you again," one of the inmates said, as we got ready to leave. "On the outside," Gates answered, and shook his hand.

One of my most "memorable" nights on television was when I was the "Man of the Hour" on one of Dean Martin's Celebrity Roasts. On the dais were such "comedians" as Mickey Mantle, Hank Aaron, Yogi Berra, Willie Mays, Maury Wills, and Charlie Finley. It was touching to see how much they all enjoyed the chance to send a few zingers my

way, as did the rest of the roasters, like Gabe Kaplan, Norm
Crosby, Jack Carter, and Pat Henry. On what Red Buttons
referred to as a "never-to-be-remembered evening," host
Dean Martin led off with this testimonial: "Joe Garagiola is
an inspiration to young athletes everywhere. I've never seen
this man with a drink, a cigarette, or a comb."

But the highlight of the night was Orson Welles. With his
deep, golden tones, and with the same dramatic intensity he
used in his famous "War of the Worlds" broadcast, he did
this version of "Casey at the Bat":

" 'Twas a gloomy situation
For the Cardinals from St. Loo,
With two outs in the ninth
The lads were trailing 5 to 2.

If they didn't win this game
The answer was quite clear,
For the good folks of St. Louie,
No championship this year.

But Kurowski slapped a single
With his mighty Polish stroke,
To show those guys who acted wise
He was no Polish joke.

Terry Moore then got a base on balls,
And Musial got one too,
And now a grand-slam homer
Would win it for St. Loo.

Then up came Joe—not DiMaggio
But Joe Garagiola,
A strikeout Joe, who didn't know
A base hit from Shineola.

"Let me get up to that plate!"
Joe cried, "for hitting I am ready!"
But the only plate where Joe was great
Was a plate filled with spaghetti.

Then the Cubs brought in a pitcher
Who really was a meanie,
With a wicked curve that seemed to swerve
Like a strand of wet linguine.

Contemptuously he looked at Joe,
And made some snide retorts,
Then blazed two fastballs past him
That burned his jockey shorts.

And now with but one last strike left,
Joe raised his eyes to pray,
And though he was Italian,
We heard him say "Oy Vay!"

The pitcher pitched, the batter swung,
And hit a lazy pop,
The outfielder sneered as if to say,
"This ball I'll never drop."

And that's when Joe pulled off his cap
And with it, his toupee,
His bald pate caught the bright red sun
And sent out a blinding ray.

The fielder tried to shield his eyes
From the flash from Joe's bald dome,
But as he did, he dropped the ball,
And four runs scampered home.

Oh, somewhere birds are singing,
And somewhere bands do play,

Somewhere fans are cheering,
And somewhere fans are gay.

Especially in St. Louie,
Where legend has it said,
The Cardinals won the pennant,
Because Joe used his head.

I can still hear the great Orson Welles, and I can still hear all the laughing. It was a great night, the kind that shows how unpredictable television can be. You never know what might be waiting down the road.

Broadcasting has taken me down many roads and to many places. Sportswriter Jimmy Cannon once called sports the "toy department of life"; I'd say the same thing about television. And I feel lucky that with baseball and television, I've been able to spend my whole life in the toy department.

"Pete Rose knows how to put everything in perspective: 'When you play this game 20 years, go to bat 10,000 times, and get 3,000 hits, you know what that means? You've gone 0-for-7,000.'"

○

11

Pages from My Notebook

THIS IS "MY Chapter."

In my neighborhood, on the playground, or in the street, choosing a team was fairly easy. It was choosing the positions that was tough. Some positions were easier than others. If you threw left-handed, you were the first baseman. If you weren't a very good player, but "one of the guys," you played right field. The real problem was that everybody wanted to be the pitcher.

But that problem was usually solved very easily, and I've never forgotten the logic involved. Not only did it solve the problem; it solved it with the same authority as a Supreme Court decision: that's it, no more arguing, the end, let's get on with the game.

The scene and the dialogue were always the same:

"I'm gonna pitch."

"You can't pitch. You don't throw hard enough."

"If I can't pitch, there's no game. It's my ball and you can't use it." Good logic that everybody understood. He pitched.

Over the years I've made all kinds of notes of things I've seen and heard. I've read plenty of newspapers, magazines, and team publicity releases, and I've heard a lot of things on airplanes or in "bull sessions." And I'm putting it all in this chapter, "My Chapter." Why?

Because it's my book.

You Sound Taller on the Radio

Television lets you make friends with lots of people you've never met. Sounds strange, but it's true. Now, when these "friends" see me somewhere, they want to be friendly, but sometimes it's tough to come up with a response to what they say. To this day I've never been able to figure out a response to this one: "I see you so much on TV you ought to know me." Or how about these:

○ "You don't look any better in person than you do on TV."

○ "You're one of my biggest fans."

○ "Aren't you who you are? If you ain't, then I won't be wrong."

○ "You look much better in person than you do in real life."

○ "You sound taller on the radio."

○ "Remember me? I was in the army with you." (I hear this one a lot around the All-Star game and the World Series. I'm convinced that the only two men I *was* in the army with who didn't call were Eisenhower and MacArthur.)

O "Didn't you used to do something?"

O "I remember you with Dizzy Dean, Pepper Martin,
and the Gashouse Gang." (Honest, I was a boy
once, and it was during those days.)

O "Hey, Joe, remember that time as kids when I
struck you out?" (I'm still waiting for the guy
who'll give me even a broken-bat single. So far I'm
0 for 40 years.)

O "You look just like you are."

O "You're ah . . . you're . . ." I say, "Joe Garagiola," and they say, "No, you're not, I know who
you are."

I can count on the fingers of a catcher's mitt the number of
times this one *hasn't* happened, and it always makes me
laugh. Like most airline passengers, the first place I usually
head for when I get off the plane is the men's room. I'm
standing there doing my thing when the guy next to me
turns and says, "Are you Joe?"

I answer, "Yep, that's me," and he says, "What are *you*
doing here?" Looking down, confused, I usually answer,
"I'm water skiing."

I never know how to answer certain questions. I usually rely
on one of three replies I've heard other people use. It's a
game I call "What to Say When You Hear . . .":

Q: "Remember me?"
A: "Should I?" (Jim Farley)
Q: "Your face looks familiar. Haven't I seen it some-
where else?"
A: "No, it's always been right where it is now." (George
Gobel)

Q: "Bet you don't remember me."
A: "I'll take half your bet." (Bob Feller)

Great Answers to Not-So-Great Questions

Hugh Downs always said there are no bad questions, just bad answers. That's usually true, but I think we've all heard the exceptions; that is, the bad question and the great answer.

Q: (To utility man Danny Heep): "What do you have to do to play regular?"
A: "Have the team bus go off the road."

Q: (To Charlie Eckman, career basketball man): "What's the greatest play you ever saw?"
A: "There's only two great plays. A basket to win the game and *South Pacific*."

Q: (To Yogi, in a word association game about some of the greats he's played with): "I'll mention a name, and you say the first thing that comes to your mind."
Yogi: "Okay."
Q: "Joe DiMaggio."
Yogi: "What about him?"

Q: (To Gordie Howe): "Did you ever break your nose playing hockey?"
A: "No, but 11 other guys did."

Q: (To Mike Schmidt): "What will you miss most about baseball when you retire?"
A: "Room service french fries."

Q: (To Jesse Barfield, during the 1987 pennant race between Detroit and Toronto, after Toronto lost 3–2 in the

13th inning): "Do you think the Blue Jays have as good a chemistry as the Tigers?"

A: "I don't know anything about chemistry. I flunked that in high school."

This overworked question to women sportswriters reminds me of a great answer from the late Selma Diamond, who was asked a similar question about being one of television's first female comedy writers.

Q: "How do the players and the male writers take to you?"

A: "I'm like Red China. I'm there, but they don't recognize me."

I Wish I'd Done That

I'm often asked, "Do you miss playing?" That's certainly a kind, charitable question, but it immediately tells me the person asking never saw me play. Looking back, though, there *are* a couple of things I wish I'd been able to do; I just wasn't a big enough star to try them. But how I wish I had.

Just once, in a crucial spot, I wanted to throw the ball *not* to the guaranteed-out base, but to the most unlikely base. For example, with the bases loaded and nobody out, the ball is hit back to the pitcher. He throws to the catcher, me, and everybody expects me to throw it to first base for the double play. I'd throw it to third.

The other thing I always wanted to do related to hitting. When you bat eighth, you think about a lot of things—like I hope he doesn't pinch-hit for me until at least the fifth inning. With the pitcher batting behind me, I'd often draw an intentional walk, especially with two outs. I'd always imagine waiting until ball two, calling time, and heading back to the dugout for a new bat.

Baseball Is *Still* a Funny Game

Dick Radatz, a 6′6″, 230-pound pitcher, came up with the quickest ad lib ever heard in a baseball fight. When the benches cleared and the free-for-all started, Radatz grabbed infielder Fred Patek, just 5′5″ and 148 pounds, and said, "I'll take you and a player to be named later."

Somebody asked Yogi Berra about the 1954 Cleveland Indians, who set an American League record by winning 111 games. "That was a good team," Yogi said. "Lemon, Garcia, Early Wynn, Al Rosen, and Bobby Avila—he had a great year. He got the MVP that year. I'm pretty sure he won it that year." Wrong. The MVP that year was Yogi Berra.

When one of the San Francisco Giants referred to St. Louis as a "cow town" during the 1987 National League Championship Series, Red Schoendienst wasn't too surprised. "He's so dumb he thinks milk comes from ants," Red said.

Somebody asked Bill North if he'd slowed down a step or two, and he said, "Young horse runs fast, old horse knows the way."

When Harmon Killebrew was elected to the Hall of Fame in 1984, he said, "My father taught me and my brother to play ball in the front yard. One day my mother came out and told him we were ruining the lawn. My father told her, 'We're raising kids, not raising grass.' "

In a rare game for Bob Gibson, base hits were flying all over the place. Maybe manager Red Schoendienst just couldn't believe what was happening, because it was quite a while before he headed for the mound to make a pitching change. When he finally got there, Gibson looked at him and said, "Haven't you been watching the game? Where have you been?"

Toronto hit 10 home runs against Baltimore, and after a game like that, somebody usually suggests taking roll call. But Frank Robinson had a different idea. He walked into the clubhouse and said, "Okay, all outfielders into the trainer's room for a neck rub."

Pete Rose knows how to put everything into perspective: "When you play this game 20 years, go to bat 10,000 times, and get 3,000 hits, you know what that means? You've gone 0 for 7,000."

Fan Mail: Kids Write the Best Letters

For a second-grade class project, the kids were asked to explain baseball. Their answers aren't exactly what you'd find in the rule book.

○ "This is the way you play it. First you shall have three bases. Then your bat is in your hand. Then you're supposed to throw the ball."

○ "The first batter will try to hit the ball, and they will run to first base, or second, or third, or fourth, or fifth."

○ "Three men stay at first base and two men stay at all five bases. And all two men run at the same time."

○ "Run the bases. And hit the ball. And stay in line."

○ "One person has the bat and one person has the ball and you throw, then you hit it with the bat, and don't hit anybody in the head with it."

○ "The game I like best is boys chase the girls. That is the way to play it. Just boys chase the girls."

○ "You hit the ball and you run to first base. If you get out, your friend will hit you."

Best Baseball Question:

"Why aren't there any umpires in baseball cards?"

Best Requests:

"On Wednesday I betted that the "Little House on the Prairie" would be on but your people blowing bubble gum had to come on and I lost 80¢ that night and please send me 80¢ because I'm poor. And it was your fault that my show didn't come on."

"You are one of my biggest fans in baseball, and I was wondering if you would send me an autograph?"

Worst Spelling but Great-Hitting Team:

"I nock a home run tonite and we wind 31–24. Do you ever nock won home run? Rite to me soon to send me yore pitcher of you. I give you won stamp you rite wit." (The stamp was glued to the letter.)

I'm Taking A Survey . . .

Some of the hardest letters to answer are the questionnaires. Why? Well, here's a sample of the questions—see if you can give your answers in 25 words or less.

"I'm doing a report on you in my Social Studies class. I would like it very much if you could write about a few times in your career that something important or funny happened, and if you could send along some other information too.
P.S. Send as soon as possible, please."

"For an English paper on sports announcing, would you please answer these questions?" There were a dozen, including: "What did you do, if anything, before you were an announcer?"

From a writer doing a survey of major-league baseball announcers for a magazine article came 14 questions, including "How did you get into broadcasting?; sum up your career, listing highlights. Feel free to expand on any point that I failed to cover. I know it's short notice, but I have a two-week deadline."

I Think "Garagiola" Is Easy to Spell

But I guess I'm the only one who does. I've seen hundreds of spellings of my name on letters I've received over the years, but my favorite is the postcard addressed to "Rocky Gatrizonia":

"Dear Rocky, Enjoy your TV work so much. Would you honor me with a photo?"

Most Confused "Today" Show Viewer:

Addressed a Christmas card to Joe Garjiola, and also wished Dave Downs and Barbara Walker a Merry Christmas too.

Honorable Mentions:

Digargiolla, I Give Up, Grazzalo, Joe Gar, Joe Today Show, Gagliorda, Garciola, Garugiziola, Demaigo, Garagida, Gargighate, George Gargiola, Gargarizola, Arasienie, DeRogiola, Fred Garaguila, DiMagio, Garrity, Joe the Catcher, Gargrola, Ghiregiolle, Joe D? G?, Gigriologa, Deogearola, Gradigolla, Greaheola, Joe Baby, G@*&%$#"a, Joe Go, Joe G———, Jgeoolo, Joe Gee-Gee, (from a guy with a Greek name 24 letters long).

Some of the spellings actually created new words out of *Garagiola* and made me ask myself, "What would I own if my name were . . . ?"

○ Garganzola: cheese shop

○ Gogagola: soft-drink-bottling company

○ Gaseola: service station

○ Grocioseola: supermarket

○ Grinola: health food store

○ Gargiogala: catering company

- ○ Gargello: gelatin factory

- ○ Gargalileo: observatory

- ○ Giradeli: chocolate shop

- ○ Grasarolle: landscape business

- ○ Graglioleum: carpet store

All of these names were actually written on letters sent to me, and it's a real tribute to the U.S. Postal Service that they were delivered. Check some of those spellings. A letter to "Joe Jgeoolo" looks like something you'd read to get your driver's license.

Actually, a viewer from Los Angeles showed me an easy way to remember how to spell *Garagiola*. Spell *garage,* minus the *e,* add 10, then add L-A. Garag-10-LA. Easy.

Overheard At Old-Timers Games

I always look forward to Old-Timers Games, because there's so much to talk about. For one thing, all ballplayers have a little bench jockey in them, and when they get together, the zingers really fly. And just like the players, some of the same zingers show up every year.

If the target's overweight, whether he's a player, a vendor, or a fan, you always hear something like "He's getting too much meal money" or "Throw a salad in there once in a while." Then some thin guy walks by, and Jimmy the Greek will give you five-to-one odds that you'll hear "He has a real athletic body—he's built like a hockey stick."

So while the "old-timer" has maybe lost a step or two, or

a little off his fastball, his sense of humor is as sharp as ever. Sandy Koufax, who certainly wasn't known for his hitting and doesn't mind admitting it, came up with this one. After barely hitting the ball during batting practice at an Old-Timers Game, he walked out of the batting cage and said, "The layoff didn't hurt. I haven't lost a thing."

Former Oriole slugger Boog Powell, on the state of his hitting: "When I swing, that bat really jumps off the ball."

Ralph Kiner saw Catfish Metkovich and said, "The last time I saw a pair of legs like that there was a message tied to them."

Lou Brock, analyzing teammates Billy Williams, Ernie Banks, and Willie McCovey, said, "Our black players are so old they don't even know how to high five."

Lou later added, about eternal optimist Ernie Banks, "Ernie's the only player I know who lives in Mister Rogers' Neighborhood."

In my only at-bat in the 1987 Old-Timers Classic in Washington, D.C., I hit a weak ground ball to the first baseman. Former big league catcher Ed Bailey said, "That's the first time I've ever seen somebody jammed by a 54 mile-an-hour fastball." Bailey almost had the guys contributing to help rebuild the zoo in his hometown of Strawberry Plains, Tennessee, after its terrible tragedy.

"We had to close the zoo," Bailey told us.

"What happened?" I asked.

"Our duck died."

Did I Hear That Right?

Have you ever heard somebody say something that sounds okay until you think about it? I've actually heard somebody say every one of these, and I'm still wondering if maybe I just wasn't listening right:

○ "We never went there in a long time."

○ "If you wake up alive, it's a great day."

○ "As soon as our difficulties are restored, we'll continue the game."

○ "After 10 innings the Cardinals lead the Cubs 3–3."

○ "He's got a great reputation, but nobody knows anything about him."

○ "If he were alive and heard what you just said, he'd die."

○ "So-and-so was buried yesterday." "Oh, my, did he die?"

○ "Those are false lies."

○ "It's a forgotten memory."

○ Upon receiving the award, a beautiful Grecian urn, the recipient said, "I'd like to thank all of you for this beautiful Greek urine I just received."

○ "At my church they have girl altar boys."

○ "You've gotta be born to be a hitter."

○ Reading the church announcements, the priest said, "Next Tuesday is the First Friday of the month."

○ "We'll have the questions to those answers in just a minute."

○ "Honey, if one of us died, I think I'd move back to St. Louis."

○ "All standing-room-only seats have been sold."

○ "He was feeling okay when he went to bed, but he woke up dead."

○ "The 8:45 train has been canceled. The 9:03 is the next train." It was 9:20 when the announcement was made.

○ "There's a good chance you'll make your connections, but this plane will be late even if it's on time."

○ "Welcome aboard Delta flight 1708, nonstop from Fairbanks to Los Angeles, with intermediate stops in Juneau and Seattle."

Take This Advice

Everyone has their own philosophy or some piece of advice they like to pass on. Here are a few of my favorites.

○ Lindsey Nelson:

1. Never play poker with anybody named Ace.

2. Never eat at a place called Mom's.

3. Never invest in anything that eats or needs painting.

○ Here's a travel tip from Birdie Tebbetts, who's traveled all his life and learned this one the hard way.
After being mugged in a hotel he said, "Don't yell
help, yell fire. Yell help and you hear doors locking;
yell fire and the hallway is full of people."

○ The Milwaukee Brewers' Paul Molitor, on what to
do during a slump: "Hope for luck and pray for
patience."

○ Tom Lasorda: "Never argue with people who buy
ink by the gallon."

That's Not Fair!

At 20 years old, I was catching for the St. Louis
Cardinals in the 1946 World Series against the Boston Red
Sox. I got four hits in the fourth game, in Boston, on
October 10th (I remember the date of every game in which
I got four hits). Anyway, you can imagine how excited I
was waiting for the newspapers that night. And do you
know what the headline read? "WILLIAMS BUNTS." I
was really upset, and I think I had a right to be, because it
just wasn't objective reporting. I mean, I got four hits in a
game as often as Ted Williams bunted.

Some of Baseball's Odd but True

The Detroit Tigers' Hank Greenberg had 100 RBIs before
the All-Star break in 1935, but he didn't even make the
All-Star team. Lou Gehrig and Jimmie Foxx were named
ahead of him. Greenberg finished the season with 170
RBIs.

A baseball travels approximately 40,885 feet, or 8 miles, during an average game.

Philadelphia Phillies left-hander Don Carman threw 40 pitches in the first inning of a game against the Pirates, including 18 to Andy Van Slyke, but didn't allow a run. "I had to ask what inning it was when I got back to the bench," Carman said. "They told me it was October 4 and the Cardinals had won the pennant."

Don Mattingly says he averages between 50 and 60 games with one bat.

And how about this fact, guaranteed to liven up your next cocktail party conversation: The spider, *Mastophora dizzydeani*, named for former pitcher Dizzy Dean, captures its prey by throwing a sticky globule at it and then reeling it in.

That's Great, But What Does It Have to Do with Baseball?

Whether it's in the clubhouse, on the bench before a game, or around the batting cage, when certain players' names come up, the conversation always centers around something special about their careers. Mention Joe DiMaggio, and you hear about his 56-game hitting streak. Say Johnny Vander Meer's name, and his back-to-back no-hitters come to mind. With Reggie Jackson, it's either his home run that hit the transformer at the All-Star game in Detroit or the three home runs he hit in a World Series game. Some names, though, while they always remind guys of specific stories, make you want to ask, "But what does it have to do with baseball?" Like:

Former White Sox catcher Moe Berg spoke seven languages.

Baltimore Oriole Dave Nicholson was so strong that once when he turned off the showers, nobody could turn them back on without a wrench.

Mention the name Jackie Brandt, a free spirit who played with the Cardinals, Giants, and Orioles and became an electrician after he left baseball, and you always hear the same thing: "Yeah, in the first house he wired, when somebody rang the doorbell, all the toilets flushed and the garage door went up."

A few theories from well-known baseball men also make me wonder what they have to do with baseball, but I like them:

Casey Stengel had a theory about everything. "It's a good idea for players to go out on the town in pairs after games rather than large groups. Eight guys go out and they all buy a round and you got eight drunks. Two guys go out and each buys a round and they come home sober."

St. Louis Browns pitcher Ned Garver's theory on nerve-calming went like this: "When things got tough and the pressure was really bad, I'd pick out some fan in the stands and ask myself questions about him. Where did he come from? How did he get to the game today? Things like that. It got my mind off what I had to do and relaxed me for the moment, and that's what I needed most."

When "Mr. Cub," Ernie Banks, was playing, he had a different technique. When he was hitting with the tying run on third and the winning run on second, what did he think about? "Lola Falana," Ernie said. "That relaxes me."

Baseball Is Stranger Than Fiction

And not just major-league baseball. These first two plays happened on college fields, but I'd have paid major-league prices to see them.

Florida Technological University was leading the University of Miami 1–0 late in the game when Miami sent in one of its good base stealers to pinch run at first. While Miami was making the change, a Tech player suggested that now would be a good time for The Play.

On the next pitch, as the runner broke for second, someone in the Tech dugout whacked two aluminum bats together, making it sound to the runner like the bat hitting the ball. Meanwhile, the catcher, who caught the pitched ball, threw a high pop-up to the shortstop, who began yelling, "I got it, I got it, I got it."

The runner, who had stolen second easily, heard the shortstop hollering, looked up, saw him catch the phony pop fly, and made a U-turn back to first. The shortstop's throw got him easily. The crowd thought it was the greatest play they'd ever seen, and the umpires, like the baserunner, were left wondering what had happened.

So practice paid off for Florida Tech, but they must have held their workouts at the theatre.

And how would you like to have been the catcher in this game between Pennsylvania's Indiana State University and St. Francis College, who made all three putouts in a triple play *and* made an error too?

With runners on first and third, the St. Francis batter struck out on a hit-and-run play for the first out. The catcher then fired the ball to the second baseman, who fired right back to the plate in time to get the runner, who broke off third for the second out.

Now the runner on first, who broke on the hit-and-run play, was headed for third. The catcher threw over the third baseman's head into left field for an error, but the left-fielder, who was backing up the play, threw to the catcher to get the runner for the third out. That catcher must have felt like he was playing one-wall handball; every time he threw the ball, it came right back to him.

In the big leagues, I was involved in a *very* unusual triple play when I was with St. Louis. I don't know why, but every time I see the Three Stooges' video "The Curly Shuffle," I think of this play.

The Phillies' Eddie Waitkus was the batter, with Richie Ashburn on second and Granny Hamner on first. Waitkus took a third strike, and that's when our Curly Shuffle began.

Ashburn took off, and my throw to third baseman Tommy Glaviano trapped him between second and third. Glaviano finally tossed to shortstop Marty Marion, who tagged Ashburn for the second out. Hamner was standing between first and second watching what was going on, so Marion's quick throw to Stan Musial caught him in a rundown. Hamner was finally tagged for the third out.

So it took a third strike, two rundowns in the infield, and about 15 people going in different directions to execute a triple play—and nobody ever hit the ball.

Frankie Frisch also holds a unique distinction. He says he's the only switch-hitter ever to take three pitches from each side of the plate during the same at-bat.

"I had a 3-and-0 count one day against the Dodgers when they brought in Watson Clark. I turned around, and damn it, Watty threw three slop nickel curves and I took 'em all—strike one, strike two, and strike three."

Best Excuse for Not Reporting to the Minor Leagues

Billy Gardner sent a player down to the minors who said he couldn't leave for two days because he had a second-floor apartment and a waterbed that would take two days to drain.

Words to Live By

"I went over there that night," Gardner said, "and sure enough, there was a hose coming from his bedroom window and water spilling all over the place."

The big star's cry is "Play me or trade me." The bench warmer has his mottoes too:

○ Play me or keep me.

○ Play me or bench me.

When you lose 104 games like the 1985 Pirates did, there's bound to be a lot of moaning players talking about quitting unless they're traded, and making all kinds of threats. So General Manager Syd Thrift decided to give his team a pep talk.

"I told them about a little starling that was flying south for the winter," Thrift says. "It was raining as the bird passed through Delaware, and as a cold front developed, the rain turned to sleet. Ice formed on the little bird's wings, and they got so heavy he couldn't fly, so he fell into a pile of fresh manure in a barnyard in Maryland.

"In the warm, dark pile, the bird thawed out, and he felt so good he began chirping away. Soon the barnyard cat heard his singing, found him in the pile, scooped him out, and ate him.

"The moral of the story: if you're warm and even if you're covered with manure, keep your mouth shut."

A Kid's First Ball

We put black tape around our first real hardball. I remember you couldn't play with it on the street or you'd wear it out.

With our first good baseball, we just played catch, and we had to be on the grass when we did it, too. Maybe we didn't treat it as well as my mother treated her statues, the ones she put the votive candles in front of, but we never let it get wet, either. Some nights it even had a bed to sleep in. That baseball meant a lot to us, and when I read this story sent by a fan, Charles O'Connor, I thought, "That really says it all for me." I think you'll say the same.

Question: What is the meanest, most demanding, exacting, unforgiving thing around that doesn't rattle his tail?

Answer: A Little League baseball.

The thing is as hard as Superman's underwear, round as the Jupiter Three, as slippery as a quarter at a dime carnival, elusive as a "C" in Geography, and doesn't care at all about big, brown eyes or sleeping under a pillow.

It will hit him, hurt him, shame him, maim him, tire him to exhaustion, bring silent tears to his eyes, and roll farther and faster when hit by the *other* side. It doesn't care about blue eyes either.

It refuses to travel in a straight line, can travel through a solid bat without a scratch, avoid his glove like he does a bath, always hit his sorest spot, and can find a hole in the fence like radar. It feels the same way about green eyes.

It likes the coach the best, his worst enemy second best, his girlfriend's boyfriend third best, and him least of all.

When hit in the air by the other side, it heads directly for the sun, and when hit on the ground, it heads like a magnet for the nearest rock. If he needs it at home it's at school. And if he needs it at school, it's always someplace where he has to walk by the teacher. Tears won't tame it, hope won't perfect it, kicking it won't hurt it, but practice will make it behave.

It lives fast but dies young, usually within a few short months, and asks for as little mercy as it has shown. Its value? Well, it cost new a yard mowing, two trips to the garbage can, and an hour and a half with the little monster. Surprisingly, it doesn't depreciate.

I personally don't know where you could find a used one, but you might try driving around until you spot an old rusty bike. Then walk to the door, knock, and ask the man with the gray temples how much he wants for his boy's first Little League ball.

"Ask yourself. If you're not happy with what you're doing, then you're not in your right place. There's a right place for everyone, and sometimes you have to take a risk to discover it."

○

12

You Start With a Dream

UNLESS YOU START, you will never arrive. When I first saw that line on a bumper sticker, I didn't think I'd remember it, but it's still with me, branded in my mind. My start was with guys named Lawdie, River, Ghosti, Pucci, NaNa, and Smokey. Hardly names that'll kick start your life down Easy Street.

Wouldn't it be great if you could just pick out a role model, connect jumper cables from his body to yours, and be on your way? But it's not that easy. You start with only a dream and absolutely no idea where you'll end up.

I believe God gives all of us two gift certificates when we're born. One is for a dream. All of us can dream, free of charge; there's no age limit, no entrance exam, no waiting list. We're all given a chance, a gift certificate, and it's up to us to cash it in. Poet Langston Hughes writes:

Hold fast to dreams
For when dreams die
Life is a broken-winged bird

That cannot fly.
Hold fast to dreams
For when dreams go,
Life is a barren field
Frozen with snow.

Just about the time you get comfortable with your dream, and you think you know where the road is taking you, the road divides, and you have to make a decision. Which way do you go? One path is well lit and continues in the comfort zone. The other one is dark, filled with doubts. Do you take a chance?

Ask yourself. If you're not happy with what you're doing, then you're not in your right place. There's a right place for everyone, and sometimes you have to take a risk to discover it. You have to risk the potholes, the bad road, whatever it takes to find the place you want to be. Take the chance—just be prepared to also take the consequences. You've probably heard "You can't steal second with one foot on first," and it's true.

You can't be afraid to fail either. You're going to get thrown out at second once in a while, but you have to keep coming back, keep trying. If you never get thrown out, you'll never learn. There's nothing wrong with being wrong. Experience is just mistakes you won't make again. Just dream your dream and do everything you can to live it. Do it and don't care what anyone else thinks.

If you are lucky enough to live your dream, it becomes a favorite memory. My dream was to be a major-league baseball player. I was lucky; I made it to the big leagues with my hometown team, the St. Louis Cardinals. About rookies, sportswriter Jimmy Cannon wrote: "You breathed the air that shaped your boyhood dreams because you lived between the foul lines with the chosen few." I sure knew what he meant. I'll never forget the feeling of being on the same field with the guys I had on the bubble-gum cards, guys like Joe Medwick and Pepper Martin.

Yet it takes more than dreams and risks to get you to your goal. You need to cash in that second gift certificate you were given at birth, this one for ignorance. A good kind of ignorance, the kind that lets you go ahead and do something before you have a chance to talk yourself out of it, before you can convince yourself you really can't do it. After it's done, somebody will come up to you and say, "How did you do that? You aren't supposed to be able to do that." By the time you realize you probably shouldn't have been able to do it, you've already done it.

It's like what track star Glenn Cunningham said when he was named the outstanding track performer in the 100-year history of Madison Square Garden: "I've never looked upon myself as someone special. Maybe it's because ignorance was always my greatest asset. I never knew I couldn't do certain things."

When somebody says you can't do something, just go ahead and do it. Just because they say you can't doesn't mean you can't. You have the right to fail, so go ahead and try.

Hold on to that dream or that goal. Don't give it up. The famous philosophers might have a better way of saying it, but I learned this lesson from one of my favorite philosophers, Tarzan.

Actor Johnny Weissmuller, the best-known Tarzan, was speaking to a group of aspiring actors, all hoping for their big break. When one of them asked him "What's the best advice you can give us?" Tarzan simply said, "Don't let go of the vine."

New York Times bestsellers— _Books at their best!_

4